...THAN LIVING ON MY KNEES

PART I

The Creation of a Cleansing System

HARALD ZIEGER

ISBN 979-8-88945-196-9 (softcover)
ISBN 979-8-88945-197-6 (ebook)

Printed in the United States of America.

Brilliant Books Literary
137 Forest Park Lane Thomasville
North Carolina 27360 USA

If you can't tolerate evil,
you have to walk the road to the end

—Harald Zieger

CONTENTS

PROLOG

The story is fictional. The persons are fictional. But not everything described in the story is fictional. It is based on the historical events which led to the collapse of the communist regime in the part of Germany which evolved out of the Soviet occupation zone at the end of World War 2 and became known as East Germany, the German Democratic Republic, or GDR for short. Although, it wasn't East Germany, and it wasn't a republic either. It was Middle Germany. East German territory was, and still is, occupied partly by Russia (today Oblast Kaliningrad) and Poland. And it was only a republic on paper, in which the power rested in the hands of a few communist oligarchs, dictators.

With the change of governmental attitudes in the Soviet Union, known widely as Perestroika, the people in East Germany and all the other nations of the communist bloc smelled the 'wind of Change' and started to throw away the cloak of fear and began to resist the demands of the oppressive system of misery and shortages. The growing amount of those who no longer backed down but instead stood up and marched around the churches in their towns every Monday increased dramatically. The communist leaders of the SUP (Socialist United Party) were old. They had no intention yet of giving up their powerful positions, allowing them to live luxurious lives compared to the masses' lives.

At the culmination of the growing resistance against the absolute despotic leadership of the communist party, a group of younger, not less power-hungry leaders took over to calm the storm and rescue the system from total collapse. That did not work. The people did not stop protesting because they saw through the smoke screens. Confronted with the decision to use brutal force to stop the - publicly called Counter-Revolution – or to back down, open the borders for all people and allow unrestricted, secret, and international monitored elections, they decided to back down. Not because they wanted but because the armed forces ordered to suppress the demonstrations with lethal force refused to follow those orders. Non of the officers wanted to have the blood of peaceful demonstrating civilians on their hands. The rest is history.

With the first free elections in 'East Germany' after 40 years of oppression, the communist party lost its majority dramatically. Within the year, Germany was united as the German Federal Republic, as it is known today.

BUT!

It could have come differently. It could have been that the officers were as fanatic as the new Secretary General was. In the summer of 1989, he heralded the Chinese Communist Party for their 'decisive dealing.' Crashing the counterrevolution on Tiananmen Square in Peking, he congratulated the leaders for defending communism with all available forces.

This book tries to outline the potential development of such a situation and the outcome of the application of lethal forces against the oppressed people of East Germany.

THE SITUATION

Three opposing forces are at work in the republic, which never was one. The republic was a dictatorship from the first day of her existence, and none of the leaders made a secret of it. Now she was on the verge of collapse. The nation was in disarray in any measure, economically, financially, and morally. And each of the three forces had different ideas of the outcome of the necessary restoration of law and order.

At first, there is the party in power, the communistic SUP, the Socialistic United Party. A new team of leaders, formed from the second line in command, has taken over the leading role. They had sent the Old Guard into more or less involuntary early retirement. They had reduced the number of decision-makers and are about to re-establish the structure that worked well over 40 years for their predecessors. They are willing to use any tool they have to make it work so that they can live the Old Guard's life. They certainly deserved a life of prestige and luxury; at least, they thought.

Second, an increasing number of people believe that the corruption within the leading communist party is the reason for their misery. They believe that they have to make the leadership of the SUP aware of the corruption happening daily at any level of the nation's close controlled and centrally organized command structure. The objective was to force the leadership to reform the SUP, allow free elections and have the people participate in decisions about the nation's future. The winged word was, 'If only the Leader would know that.' Their slogan "We Are The People," was attractive enough to draw an increasing crowd to their demonstrations, creating the most significant concerns for the people in power.

And there was a third force. Small yet unnoticed by the masses but exceptionally well organized and operating in secret. Small groups of genuine believers in freedom, despising the fantasy of the public protesters who thought that in the shad of the Lutheran Church, they were secure from the oppressive regime's possible reactions. The underground groups, operating in a loose bond of single people connections, believed that there was only one way to freedom: to eliminate the oppressive regime under the leadership of the SUP. They declined any idea of a reform of the current system. They saw the only solution as unifying the separated nation under a free elected government and a 'Free Enterprise' system. Those who were members of these groups had long ago recognized the system-immanent failure of communism and learned the hard way that even the Lutheran Church wasn't trustworthy.

CHAPTER 1

THEY DID IT.

The new leader gained a majority of the members in the Central Committee and used it to replace several of the procrastinators of the Old Guard. All were eager to clean the mess created by the indecisiveness of the 'Old Men.' Unanimous, they voted now their favored general of the political secret police into the leadership position, which had been vacant for several days when the former Secretary of internal security resigned angrily because of the removal of the old guard.

They also appointed a new Army General, Commander in Chief for all armed forces, excluding the State Security Police, which was an army in itself considering their vast number of heavily armed members. They had now their first meeting without the 'Old Guard,' and considering the country's explosive situation, it promised to be a turbulent and decisive meeting.

'Comrades, please let's begin, we have a long list on our agenda and no time to waste,' was the loud and clear voice of Werner Tauscher, the new Secretary General, to hear over the murmur of voices. Within a few seconds, the murmur died away, and the room fell silent.

Being sure that he had everybody's attention, he continued: 'We have several critical and drastic decisions to make tonight, comrades, and you all know that we have only two different ways to go,' he began his opening monologue. 'The current situation in our country is all, but rosy, and we all agree that we have to stop the downturn of the people's discipline and reestablish law and order.' 'Comrade Juergen will explain the explosive situation later, and we have to debate several suggestions and vote on them.'

'Comrades, we all know how it came to the current situation, and you're all here because you disagreed with how the 'Old Guard' handled the out-of-control situation. You all know how much I love them and admire their work of building this tremendous socialist nation, but every day they would have been longer in power would have brought us closer to the total collapse of law and order.

'Comrades, we have only two ways to handle this situation. As I said at the beginning, we all know what those are. Either respond to the requirements of the counter-revolutionists to agree to negotiations, or we have the understanding of our revolutionary brothers of the early years of the great Bolshevik revolution and destroy these vipers with root and branch. And as you all know me, I'm in favor of the latter.'

His words were followed by applause from all the members, and when he looked around the table, he saw confirmation in everyone's eyes of the nine members of the new inner circle of power. The most important point he had insisted on when he formed his new coalition, which helped him to send the Old Guard into retirement, was that the new Central Committee, the absolute power in the country, needed to be small. It needed to be able to decide quick and without concerns about collateral damage when it was necessary. Based on that, they had agreed to keep the number to 12 members and to install an additional institution called the extended advisory board.

'We have to make clear to our people, who are not in favor of the destruction of law and order, that the leadership of the party of the worker's class can analyze the current situation expertly. That the new leadership can handle the situation and hold those causing the turmoil responsible,' he said further, filling his statement with socialistic party rhetoric all of them knew very well. Actually, even if they once were aware of the platitude, of usage for many years in their daily conversations, working up through the ranks, they were not in a stage of deception where they believed every word.

'The people will soon understand that any action we take to get this situation under control was necessary to secure their way of life in a safe and socialistic environment.' He looked around again and was satisfied with the confirming nodding of their heads. 'We need to decide today which direction we want to go and what are the next necessary steps.' To have you all on the same page, I asked Comrade Juergen to give us a brief outline of the situation, and then we will start the discussion.

'Comrade Juergen, please.'

'Comrades, you all have watched the news on the TV reporting about the increasing number of people hiding behind religious freedom, which we gladly grand those backward living, mentally crippled people who believe that there is a GOD.' All at the table nodding their heads, acknowledging the increasing number of people, and the idiocy, in their opinion, to believe that there is a GOD.

He continued: 'Yet almost 90% of those participating at the so-called Monday Demonstrations aren't religious, more so, have nothing in mind with church or religion. All they want is to create a situation to undermine the leading role of the Socialistic United Party as the guarantee of the power of the working class and the achievements of our years of organization of the socialist society.'

Then he presented some numbers that in nearly every state capitol were very active groups organizing those demonstrations. The motto *We are the People* was only a camouflage for the real reason because this slogan allowed hiding their real objectives. According to the reports from the undercover agents placed within that movement, almost every single group had a core of hart-bidden enemies of the SUP and the nation's leaders.'

'We know that many of those hart core counterrevolutionaries are in direct contact with the imperialistic class enemy, but we do have not enough evidence yet to arrest them.' Then he went on to explain that there is a restructuration of the leadership within the Security Police necessary and that it would take a couple of weeks to remove the unreliable officers and replace them with those who are obedient to the chain of command. With a short side look to the newly elected Army General, he added that reports showed increasing sympathy with the growing counterrevolutionary movement, primarily among the leading officers within the armed forces. 'Comrade Frank, you have a large job to do, and we, the comrades of the SSP, will support you as much as possible.

He went on, 'We have to acknowledge that, over the last several years, the SSP has allowed the virus of imperialistic counterrevolution to infect almost all levels of our socialist society.'

Then he presented some numbers which should scare each of them and inspire them to begin the cleansing immediately. In nearly every town with a population above 5000 exist a group of people that is hostile towards the leadership of the SUP. More than 30% of all officers in the armed forces, including the police, are not 100% loyal to their superiors.

If not knowing it already, everybody in the room became clear about the situation and that they needed to draw a line in the sand if they wanted to stay in power. And the bad news was coming and coming from their point of view. There was nothing to color it over.

When the head of the SSP was finished presenting his devastating numbers, the General Secretary started the discussion, which became fierce at several points, and comrade Werner needed to calm them down from time to time. Finally, everybody had said what he had to say and blackmailed the predecessors.

'Comrades,' the voice of the Secretary-General drowned the ongoing disputes among the members, 'we have to set a list of necessary actions until our next meeting. During my meeting with Comrade Juergen this morning, we created an action list, and I want you to take your required actions seriously. We will meet here one week from now. I request a plan from everybody on the team on how he will fulfill those action points on the list. We have then, and I mean it, to decide whether we're willing to go the new road or to give up. It might be tough for everyone since we know that several of our relatives won't be able to follow those new rules, but we have to look at the greater good of the collective of our people and the revolution.

CHAPTER 2

NEWS FOR THE FRUSTRATED BASE

Bodo was furious. Even though the cold rain lashed his body, the raincoat did not help much to stop the water from getting on to his skin, and the high speed he was throwing his motorcycle through the curves of the dark and empty road wasn't a help either, he felt the heat rising inside of him.

His blood boiled while thinking back on the last two hours of the district SUP leadership meeting. Waiting, stay low, and keep watching! These softies totally misjudged the situation the party and the nation were in.

There was growing discontent with the way the SUP leadership handled the situation. Do they even know what was going on throughout the nation? As the Secretary of Agitation and Propaganda (AP), he had his finger on the pulse of the people. At least three, sometimes four out of five days and often enough on weekends, he was out of his office with the workers at the manufacturing plants and the Agricultural Cooperatives and talked to the voluntary leaders of the party on the front line. Many comrades were furious, as he was, to see that the achievements of 45 years of work for a better Germany went down the tube because of the inactivity of the SUP leadership and the apparent corruption within the party.

And every day, the audaciousness of the counterrevolutionary forces seemed to increase as long he thought about it, and he became more convinced that the critics were right. The leadership had lost every sense of reality. And that was true from the bottom up to the highest level.

From the corner of his eye, he recognized light and focused on the street only to be able to avoid a collision with an oncoming car with the left side headlights dark. You have to stay focused on your driving, he admonished himself, or you won't get home to your family.

With that, he moved all his anger to the back of his mind and concentrated on his driving. Although the streets were wet and an ugly cross-wind was gusting from his left side, he increased his speed. When he focused on driving and knew every meter of the road driving twice daily, he could easily handle these weather conditions.

When he arrived 20 minutes later at the farm house he had bought just a few months ago, he switched-off the ignition, rested the machine on the kickstand, and opened the barn door. Then he moved the motorcycle into the barn and grabbed a piece of cloth to wipe most of the water off the bike.

The door light over the house entrance came on, and his wife Sarina opened the door calling through the rain and the still gushing wind, now much closer to the cliff line, was strong enough to blow away her words. He walked back to the barn door and said loud enough that she could hear him: 'I'm just wiping off the dirty water from the machine and will be with you in a minute, dear.' He finished the wiping, and with the anger again rising inside of him, he threw the piece of cloth through the length of the barn, walked out, and ensured that the lock of the barn door was securely locked. Too many of the widely scattered houses in his neighborhood had been burglarized over the last couple of months, which was actually the reason that he was even able to buy this property.

Because when he was asked by the First Secretary of the district to show the care of the local SUP leadership for the people here, he found that this property was unoccupied. These burglaries were another issue he was sure wouldn't have happened just a few years ago.

When he entered the house, he was immediately enveloped by the warmth and began to sweat. He removed the rain-overall he wore riding his bike. After carefully hanging it over the hanger especially built for it to dry, he walked into the kitchen, where he kissed his wife, hugged his son, and fell on one of the chairs on the kitchen table.

The supper was on the table within minutes, and after she had filled the plates, they began to eat. For several minutes only the clacking noise of the silverware interrupted the silence. Sarina noticed that Bodo was nowhere near this home with his thoughts, and with a low voice, she said: 'Bodo, please shut the work off, at least until after supper. You won't change anything tonight.' He looked up at her, then at his son, and answered: 'Yea, you're right. It's just so sad that nobody is listening to me.'

At which point, his son Nick said: 'Dad, I'm listening, do I not?' Bodo couldn't do else but smile and say: 'Yes, you do, son, but that's not what I meant, I mean, our leadership is not paying attention to what's going on, and I'm concerned about how long that might go on.'

Nick answered: 'Our class teacher today said something like that and pointed out that the counterrevolutionaries are becoming bolder by the day.' Asking his dad, 'Why isn't the party doing anything against the increasing boldness of the enemy?' Because, at the center of power in the district, his dad knew more than all of his friend's dads in his class about politics and the party.

At this point, Sarina cut in and reminded Nick that it was time for him to get ready for bed. With an intelligible murmur, Nick stood and left the kitchen.

Bodo finished his meal and helped Sarina clean the dishes by drying them and putting them back into the cabinet. While doing so, he was absorbed in his thoughts again. Remembering a propaganda movie he had seen the day before, which showed how the women in the imperialistic part of Germany were forced to stay home and be nothing else but sex- and house slaves of the men.

But that wasn't really what flashed through his mind at that moment. It was more than one picture he could clearly see before his eyes which showed a machine where this woman in the movie placed all the dishes in, closed the door, turned a switch, and the dishes got cleaned and dried without being touched again.

Why don't we have something like that? Would it be much easier for our women to handle both work and household? But he chased off that thought immediately as irrelevant. They would have such things, too, when socialism was fully established, and they had time and recourse for that. When the dishes were done, he moved to the living room to turn on the TV because it was almost 7:30 PM, and the main news broadcast would begin any moment.

He did not pay attention to the newspaper at the side table. It was the official issue of the SUP and the primary news source in the nation since he had already read it because he had to as part of his work. This one at home was there because Sarina worked only part-time at the mayor's office, and when she came home, she needed a newspaper to stay informed.

Then the signature tune of the broadcast, 'Current Camera,' came on, and he focused on the TV. The first he noticed was a new anchor. He had never seen that man at the news broadcast or in any other broadcast at all. So he called out for his wife: 'Sarina, come in, let the stuff as it is! Something is going on in Berlin!' Sarina entered the living room and sat down just as the anchor began announcing the unbelievable news. He read the words from the paper in front of him in a professional and perfectly neutral voice.

'The Central Committee of the Socialist United Party, announces the following changes in the leadership of the Socialist Unified Party of the Republic.'

1. The SUP's central committee accepted the previous Central Committee's motion to be released from its duties and elected a new Central Committee who will lead the party through the current difficulties.

2. The previous Secretary General requested his release from his positions as the Chairman of the Privy Council and the position as the Chairman of the National Defense Council. His request was accepted.

3. The member number of the new Central Committee has been limited to nine to increase the decisiveness of the leading board.

4. The Central Committee dissolved all other leading organizations of the SUP by unanimous decision and published a decree for all affected organizations

5. Therefore, the Central Committee is the only decision-making organ in between party congresses. The Central Committee is working on scheduling the next and extraordinary party congress as soon as possible

6. The Central Committee unanimously elected comrade Werner Tauscher as the new Secretary-General and Comrade Juergen Pieker as his deputy. Further are comrade Alexander Dietz, Secretary for Economy and Development, comrade Gerd Hollorek, Secretary of Justice, comrade Karl Babel as Secretary of Education, and comrade Kurt Kreuger as Secretary for Information and Media appointed as members of the new Central Committee.

7. At its first meeting this afternoon, the Central Committee appointed General and comrade Frank Bode as the new Commander in Chief of the armed forces and member of the new Central Committee and comrades Walter Reichmann as the Secretary for Finance and comrade Bruno Tecker as Secretary of the Internal Control Commission ICC. Further was General comrade Juergen Pieker, as head of the State Security Police, appointed and as a new member of the Central Committee confirmed.

All members of the new Central Committee are sworn in on the republic's constitution. In a first statement, Secretary-General Tauscher addressed the current situation and promised that the time of indecisiveness would be over. He announced that the new leadership would present a comprehensive plan within a couple of weeks to resolve the problems some of the regions throughout the republic faced currently and appealed to the people to be active in discussions within their collectives and organizations to suggest improvements where necessary. All leaders at every party level have been instructed to openly welcome ideas and suggestions to improve people's lives. The central committee has scheduled an extraordinary party convention.

Then the anchor moved on to report about some demonstrations which had no large attendance, all in smaller district cities, and condemned the continuous slander of the republic by the imperialistic mass media.

More news about the outstanding achievements of the one or other collective at the socialistic production facilities followed, but Bodo and Sarina did not pay much attention anymore.

Too much surprised and excited as well as fearful of what these changes might ignite turmoil within the party, Bodo was torn about it and wondering what would happen next morning at the district party headquarter. Sarina looked at him since he was now silent for several minutes. Seeing that he was in deep thought, she asked: 'what do you think might happen there? They removed the whole Central Committee! That has never happened before.' Bodo looked back at her and said: 'That is the result of a long-expected cleansing of the top party leadership. Somehow comrade Tauscher must have gotten a two-thirds majority at the central committee to release the complete Central Committee. I wonder who else has been voted in. And only nine members, which is the biggest surprise.' The last sentence was more said to himself because he was already in deep thought again. It looks almost like a coup, an internal leadership coup. Considering the current situation could mean good or bad for this nation's future.

'Let's go to bed. I have to go up early tomorrow because I'd like to talk to Reiner and Peter before the hectic meetings begin, and the phone will surely ring off the hook.' With that, he went to the bathroom to get ready for bed.

CHAPTER 3

LOST TRACE

At the same time as Bodo was riding his bike through the night, in another district town, buckets were also raining, and the sparingly lit street was deserted. The few streetlights dangling on their poles, throwing the light cone back and forth, moved by the gusty wind. Ralf pulled the strings of his hood closer to keep the rain from running under his parka. Suddenly there was a noise behind him. He was unsure if he heard correctly because the rain and gushy wind might have created something out of the usual, but he was cautious.

Not giving away that he suspected to be followed, he accelerated his steps and knew that whosoever followed needed to do the same or risk losing contact. He accelerated once more and reached the next small side street corner at a safe distance as he had hoped. But nothing happened.

He knew this area of the city very well. Some years ago, he lived here for almost two years as a sublease with an old widow. Nearly all of the old buildings in the area have deteriorated over the years. Nobody had lived in any of these houses for years. The roofs were partly broken down, whole stories were inaccessible, and most of the entrance doors were blocked with plywood to prevent children from entering dangerous and close to collapsed buildings. This kind of deteriorated buildings often extended over large areas in nearly all nation's cities.

Within a few more steps, he reached the entrance of one of those buildings, of which he knew the plywood was manipulated so that it could be moved to gain entrance quickly without creating a lot of noise. He moved the plywood aside, stepped into the dark behind it, and closed the opening immediately without the slightest noise.

Even though it was pitch dark, he knew his steps inside the broken down building, and with that, he moved several steps to the side where he could see through the cracked cover of the broken window almost all the way down the small street towards the corner with the main street.

He had to wait just a few seconds to get the confirmation that his felt suspicion was correct. A man, clothed in a long black raincoat, reaching down to his ankles, his head covered with a dark hat, ran around the corner and stopped.

Slowly and carefully examining the wall of the old and deteriorated buildings, he walked down the small street, getting closer and closer to that window where Ralf was standing behind the plywood that covered the broken glass. Then he stood still. His gaze seemed intensively concentrated on that piece of plywood in front of Ralf, and his blood curdled. It felt as if this guy could see him through the plywood in the dark behind it, and he was almost about to make a mistake and step back. But he immediately envisioned the heaps of trash and broken glass right behind him since he knew there was just that small path he had cleaned up several weeks ago when he was investigating several escape routes. Holding his breath, he wished he could just become invisible. After a few more seconds, which seemed to be hours in Ralf's mind, the man turned away from the building, looking towards the main street, and pulled something out from under his raincoat.

Although Ralf could not see what it was, he immediately recognized that it must be the microphone of a walkie-talkie when he heard the man say with a low voice, 'alpha one for alpha three – over!' The static noise was clear to hear, and the answer was 'alpha one – go ahead, alpha three.' The man answered: 'contact lost'! There was a long pause with only the static crackle, then: 'alpha three, report back to base!' came out of the speaker, and it was clear that the man called alpha one wasn't pleased with the outcome.

The man in front of the building cursed to himself and murmured something Ralf couldn't understand. He began walking further down the small side street with a quick pace and when Ralf was about to move towards the plywood to get out of the building and move on to his destination, the man suddenly stopped, turned around, and returned.

Ralf froze and almost lost his balance as the man passed the building and disappeared around the corner after less than a minute.

Now, more careful than before, Ralf waited in the dark for another 5 minutes since he was already late to the meeting. When he felt secure that he could leave his hideout without being seen, he moved the plywood aside, stepped out through the opening, and made sure it was closed again.

Walking faster now and carefully watching his surroundings, Ralf arrived unchallenged at the meeting place. It was another one of those deteriorated buildings just on the opposite end of that area of the city where he could shake off the SSP man about 10 minutes ago.

Again with great care, he approached the entrance to the meeting place. He stepped into a closed house entrance and pressed his body into the dark of the cover. There he stood for several seconds, looking down the small side street in both directions. Only after he was sure that there was no traffic at all he crossed the distance to the other side with five quick steps. He moved directly into the gateway of a former coal delivery company, of which only the front wall with the gateway remained intact. About ten steps into the crashed building, he stopped and said with a low voice: 'Wer wagt es?' and another low voice answered: 'Rittersmann oder Knapp?' whereon the security guard this night it was Wilhelm with the nickname Willi, stepped out of his cover to greet him. 'What took you so long? Did you have a shadow too? Billy came a few minutes before you and said it took him three different route cuts to shake off his shadow.' Everybody is already down there. Go and see that you guys can speed up because it's ugly up here. But I think it will take time because we have a visitor.' Ralf thought about that for a moment and asked, 'Who brought him, and do you know him?' Willi answered: 'I don't know him, and he came with Leo.' Did they put on their masks before Leo brought him in?' was Ralf's immediate response.

As the security officer of their small but very skilled group, it was his responsibility to watch that the rules had been applied too. And it made him angry that he was late and more so that Leo did not obey the rule that no newcomer would be brought into the meeting point of the leadership team without a background check.

He walked out into the dark, overgrown former garden of the property, sneaked throw several abounded brushes, and through a hole in the surrounding wall. Right there behind that wall were the stairs down into the basement of a wholly collapsed house. Tentative touching the wall with his right hand, he walked the short way through the cellar, and when the wall on his right-hand side ended, he turned right and stepped down another seven stairs. Five more steps, and to his left side, he could now see the small lighted slit underneath the door teo their hidden meeting place. He pulled his mask, a piece of white linen painted with a Mick mouse face, out of his pocket and pulled it over his face, knocked on the door with the sign for that day opened, and entered the room.

Billy, Leo, and Dieter answered his short hello with a nod of the heads. Ralf was somewhat relieved. All but Leo had their masks on and turned to the guest, who was approximately his age and size. The guest stood to shake hands and said his name was Fritz. Everybody knew this wasn't his real name, but that was OK and security required that they keep it this way. For the same reason, they would use only numbers when they were not alone.

Billy was #1, Ralf #2, Willi, who stood watch today, was #3, and Leo was #4. Ralf looked at Billy and said: 'I heard you had trouble getting rid of the shadow too?' I had it relatively easy after recognizing the guy, but I almost missed him.' Billy answered: 'Man, that guy was good. I had to take three different routes through the ruins to be sure I lost him.' Ralf answered: 'I heard my guy talking through the radio with his boss, and that's when I understood they had three surveillants tonight. I wonder who the third one was after.' He said this and looked at Leo. 'Leo, why don't you explain briefly why you broke the rules and what is it our guest is offering us?' It was tangible that Leo wasn't happy about being criticized in front of a foreigner, but everybody knew what a risky step it was to have a meeting with an unchecked person. And they all knew that Ralf took security very, very seriously for good reasons.

Leo began to explain that during his last visit to his hometown, he was invited to the birthday party of one of his former classmates from high school. Since it had been several years since they hadn't seen each other, he thought it would be a good idea to go.

When he arrived, there were many people there whom he did not know. After the dinner, the guests split into several different groups, and the real party began with music and alcohol. Leo said he moved around from group to group, saying hello to several he knew but hadn't seen for a long time.

One of the groups caught his attention because they were intensively debating the current political situation. One of the guys disagreed with what the others had to say: peaceful overturn of the power and democratic elections and then building real democratic socialism in Germany. This guy questioned their common sense, saying that democratic socialism is an oxymoron.

The alternative could only be a free society where everybody is responsible for himself, and only those who, for mental or physical affliction, cannot help themselves should be supported. Only if human nature is free from restrictions can it develop its full potential and create wealth. Leo said further: 'I was astounded to hear that from this guy because I remember that he once was a very devout communist and youth leader in our city.

I remembered that he later fell from favor, and when he married – a Christian girl, after all – the communists repudiated him, and he disappeared from the scene. Now he was there, arguing that a peaceful revolution was a dream mostly drowned in the blood of the peaceful marchers.

'I decided to spend a few hours watching him, and during the next three days, I was hanging on his heels,' Leo explained further.

'The second night, I was almost ending my surveillance on him when I saw him leaving his home and moving in a way that made it perfectly clear to me that he was trying to cover his tracks. I followed and had to be extremely careful, but we had good training here, so I did not lose contact.

Finally, he went into a restaurant and disappeared into a back room. I chose a table in the corner where I could watch the door and waited. After 2 hours, five men left that room, all separated by 5 to 6 minutes, and he was the last one. That was when I decided to talk to him. I stood up from the table, moved towards the exit as I would leave the restaurant, and arranged to collide with Fritz. When I turned and apologized, he recognized me and said: 'Aren't you one of the guests at Gunter's birthday party the other day?' I answered that this was true and asked him if he always argued so freely against the government and the politics of the party in power. And I told him that I recognized him from the time when he was the top shot at the communist youth organization in town.

CHAPTER 4

A COMMUNIST BECOMES A CHRISTIAN

Now Fritz jumped in and began explaining that he had tried to follow his goal to achieve what he called the 'Change from Within' for a long time during high school and his first years at college. He really believed that the party was to be able to be reformed and to grant the people they claimed to lead the freedom they deserved. After all, he said, he believed that those who are definitely not proponents of the socialistic society should be let go.

Going on, he said, 'I argued with the leading comrades that the opponents are only a load to the system and the party was better off focusing on those who appreciated the accomplishments of the socialistic revolution in their part of Germany.'

'It was considered destructive and anti-revolutionary. You probably remember the effort to improve productivity by creating those specific workers' collectives where every single activity, personal or at work, even your thoughts, were evaluated to determine whether or not you were a productive and developing collective member. And the level of that evaluation determines your payment. I began to undermine the attempt to use personal relationships to evaluate the work ethic of leaders of the so-called youth brigades. I fiercely opposed these installations and torpedoed them wherever I could. I even did call it once the safest step back into a slaveholder society. That was the end of my carrier. I was removed from my positions and expelled from the party leadership team.

When I met my wife, who happens to be a Christian, I found my way to Christ and finally declared my resignation. Since then, I have changed a lot. I became active in our church and tried to increase the awareness of the church leaders about the increasing enslavement of the people. I rebuked their acceptance of the hostility of the SUP against Christians at work, in schools, and even in their spare time. But all I found was ignorance, ivory-tower thinking, and corruption. Yes, corruption is up to the level of bishops and above. And actually, no wonder.

After the agreement of the Lutheran Church leadership with the SUP to keep their mouth shut about politics and the SUP would leave them alone within their churches. They were able to negotiate the tolerance of money transfers for pastors from their partner churches in West Germany. The Lutheran Church authorized the bishops to monthly pay the pastors 500, West Mark, for those with a bachelor's degree and 1000, West Mark, for those with a Graduate Degree. That fact ensured devotion, and most of them obeyed the orders. I wasn't welcome because, at the Base, the Christians considered me suspect. A former communist can't be trusted. But our small church with just a few old ladies was happy to have somebody who could be sent to the meetings of the synod.

That was the point where I soon collided with the church's power. After a lot of anger and vain endeavor, I decided to go my own way and founded a group of active resistance,

We were four at first, but now, after almost a year, we have people in almost every village on the Island. The core group is limited to five, and we take security as serious as you. Only one member of the core group knows one member of another group. And they have it the same way. If one group's cover is blown, they won't find more than one other guy, and the chain breaks. Nobody in our core group knows anybody from, let's say, Lohme.

That has disadvantages because information travels slowly, but security is much more important to me than anything else. But I'm ....

Ralf interrupted him to point out that it was the same with them. He looked at Leo and said that it was a definite breach of rules. Security was more important than connections.

Fritz nodded and explained, 'I begged Leo to bring me in tonight because we have a huge problem. We've been hiding two refugees from the Soviet troops stationed in Sassnitz for over three weeks.

These are members of the Speznas who have been in Afghanistan, and they couldn't take it any longer. They tried to get through the border to West Germany, but they had no idea how quickly the exit from the Island was closed. They turned around and hid in our large forests, but after a week, they could not feed themselves, and one of them got sick.

When they tried to break into a barn, the farmer caught them, but he is one of our supporters. Now we move them around, but it's challenging because everybody knows each other in those small towns. We need to get them off the Island into a large city where they can at least sometimes feel like human beings.'

Fritz ended his long monolog with a deep-drawn sigh. There was silence in the basement, and only the sizzling noise of the candles burning to give light was heard. Then Billy said: 'First of all, many thanks for your detailed presentation of yourself because we're taking our security as serious as you do. Our #2, as our security officer, is right to criticize Leo. We want to know with whom we go in touch before a meeting.

We can only hope and pray that all that you told us here is true, and since you're here and know that Leo is part of our group, we're all in your hand if you're not who you said you're.' 'Leo,': he said further: 'Do you see a chance to get those two Russians from the island on one of your coming trips with your truck?'

Leo thought for a moment and answered: 'I've been thinking about that for several days. The difficulty is knowing whether the Workers Fighting Brigades are much longer used to check everybody leaving the Island.' Fritz said: 'Our group should be able to get detailed intelligence on the whereabouts of the WFB and their timetables. We might even have someone among them. I need some days to find that out.'

Then Billy closed the meeting by saying: 'Leo, guide Fritz back out and ensure you are secure when you remove his head cover.' Also, watch out for the SSP guys. They may still try to find out where we disappeared.'

Then Billy led them in prayer, saying: 'Let's bow our heads to thank the Lord. Dear GOD, heavenly Father, we thank you from the bottom of our hearts for guiding us into the next phase of our fight for freedom in this nation. We thank you for our brothers in Christ on the Island who finely could connect with our group, and we praise you and thank you for the further guidance in connecting to like-minded groups throughout the country. We thank you for your protection and the direction we receive from you through the Holy Spirit, and we pray all of this in the name of your son, our Lord and Savior, Jesus Christ. Amen!'

Everybody said a slight bye to Fritz, and Leo and Fritz left the cellar. After a few minutes, Ralf followed them to ensure everything was all right. Carefully avoiding any noise, knowing where to place his next step, he moved toward the security guard's place, and even after his eyes had adapted to the dark, he could barely see Willi.

The rain had stopped, but thick drops were still coming down from the half-collapsed roof at the door entrance. Ralf used the end of his knife handle to tick it in a certain rhythm against the wall and got the immediate attention of Willi. He was always very alert when he stood security, and all knew that.

Ralf closed in on Willi, and Willi reported: 'They just left the street. I ensured that nobody was at the corner with the main street, but beyond that, it's their deal.' 'That's OK,' answered Ralf. 'I just don't have a good feeling with those shadowing tonight. Something must have alarmed the SSP that they get out in this weather.' 'We will see,' answered Willi. And questioned Ralf how much longer it would take them into finishing. He was definitely chilled through. 'Couple of minutes,' answered Ralf, 'We will wrap up the meeting and be done. I'll walk with you home and tell you what happened.'

Ralf returned to the cellar room where Billy had already extinguished most of the candles, and they talked over what they had heard so far. Billy said, 'After all, we have probably gained a connection to the Island we have been looking for a while. And we can only hope that this guy is for real.' With a; 'Let's go home and see what comes out,' they left the cellar and moved as carefully as always out into the doorway. Again giving the signal to let Willi know that they were on their way, they met Willi and Billy moved on out onto the small side street after Willi ensured it was safe.

Ralf and Willi waited another five minutes before they made their way out of the area. When they finally reached the area where the buildings were still used and people were on the street, they began to feel more secure, yet did not forget to change direction suddenly, and twice they walked into one of the cheap beer bars on the street to see if someone would follow them. But it seemed that the SSP was done for today. When they closed in on Willi's apartment, Ralf had completed his report, and Willi was on the same page as everyone in the core group. Willi could enter and leave his Apartment from three different directions, making it much easier for him to do so unnoticed. Ralf said bye and moved on to get home himself. Although he was now pretty sure that he did not have any shadow, his attention did not reduce at all.

CHAPTER 5

PREPARATION IS HALF THE VICTORY

Bruno Tecker, comrade Bruno as his comrades usually called him, was on his way to the building of the central committee of the SUP and was deep in thought. He had the privilege of having a huge corner office with a view of the Spree River, with many secretaries and assistants. After the meeting last evening, he had a brief meeting with comrade Kurt who the Secretary-General asked to have a media release ready for the main TV news broadcast this night.

There wasn't much to do for Bruno because Kurt was the most experienced man in the world in creating a severe yet optimistic-sounding release. But since they were almost friends, he sat with Kurt, fine-tuning the few bullet points the media would even get. His idea was to call on the people to participate actively with suggestions through their collectives and organization. Kurt really appreciated it because he hadn't considered this kind of encouragement.

Meanwhile, Bruno thought already on his agenda points, which mainly focused on a plan to reconstruct the party organization. It was necessary to eliminate all the tokenistic members who used the party only for their own benefit and often did not even pretend to be one of them.

The car stopped in front of the back gate, which two SSP soldiers guarded, and one of them walked to the back of the car to check the person in the seat. He recognized the Secretary and greeted him with a friendly green, which wasn't even recognized. He waved to the other post to open the gate. The car stopped at the rear entrance, and Bruno told the driver to get breakfast at the cantina and be around since anything was possible these days.

In his office, he opened the safe and took out the agenda of last night's meeting. Then he hit the command intercom button for his Senior Secretary twice. Within seconds she opened the door, balancing the tablet with breakfast in one hand and the notebook under her arm. He took a sip of coffee and a bite from the deli roll, and still chewing, he said: 'Karin, I need all regional Assistants in my office as soon as I'm through with the breakfast. That means, in about ten minutes.' Seeing the look on her face, he adds: 'OK, make it 15 minutes.' While eating his breakfast, he was flying over the headline of the main newspaper, the party-owned 'New Germany,' which used the press release as the front-page story filled up with the background information about the new members of the central committee.

The comments about him were short and precise. That's what he really liked about the writers at the state-controlled media; they knew who was in control.

His position was often misunderstood, and the position's power and influence were underestimated. And those who did that had to pay a harsh price if they forgot to apologize. The journalists knew that since they went through a 5-year education of total submission to the party. They wouldn't have been accepted in the first place without the correct and blameless personal reports.

The intercom sounded, opening a connection to his senior Secretary, who let him know that the regional Assistants were all assembled and ready to come in. He put the newspaper aside, walked over to his desk, and pressed the answer button. He said: 'Send them in.'

The door opened, and a stream of men walked into his office, crossing the fairly large room over to the conference table. He grabbed his notebook to join them at the table where he took place at the head. While moving his chair to the right position, he saw his senior Secretary entering the room, carefully closing the door behind her. She walked over to a small side desk where she would take notes of the meeting, which would later become the minute of this meeting.

Bruno knew that she could stenograph every word even when the debate was agitated and chaotic. She was even able to make some very important notes about the gestures and behavior during those debates, which made her reports even more valuable. He loved it to re-assess them in his mind, sometimes for hours, supported by her additional notes to the minutes, and only he got his hands on.

He was really impressed by the straightforward and decisive leadership Werner showed. Although the situation throughout the country was critical, he knew that the party still held all the power since they had a very powerful instrument to control any opposition, the State Security Police. The SSP was the party's guarantee to stay in power no matter what, and the decisions made during the last two weeks would ensure that it did not change.

With a nod of his head, almost as a self-confirmation top his thoughts, he looked around and into the asking faces of his assistants. All were carefully chosen and often monitored for several years after they caught the attention of a local party leader. They would then go through the party's own schools and universities and then try in low-level positions whether or not they could submit to the party's authority. After several years in jobs with increasing responsibility, they would finally be promoted to a position as deputy secretary of a district. And after some years in that position, carefully monitored, they would finally be called to become a regional Assistant of the Secretary of ICC.

He focused his attention back on the room, and after an additional look around, he asked for a short situation briefing from each of them. Everyone had used the early morning to get a first reaction report from their direct subordinates, the district Secretary of ICC. The general tenor was positive. The message from all district party offices, at least for the Secretaries of ICC, was a joyful appreciation of the change in leadership. Although the drastic reduction in the number of members of the Central Committee aroused some concerns, the overall message was supportive.

After the last assistant had finished his report, Bruno gave a short briefing about the enthusiastic atmosphere within the central committee. He explained that every member was fully aware of the situation and the necessity to create an immediate action plan to stabilize the situation, end the counterrevolutionary effort of the class enemy and formulate a long-term strategy to avoid similar situations in the future.

He began the discussion of possible steps, saying: 'Comrades, you're the most important pieces in this puzzle to secure the power of the party, to get the people back to focus on improvement of productivity, and to get the local party organizations back in order.' I'd like to hear your ideas on how we can do that according to the central committee's instructions for an action plan.

After almost two hours of sometimes agitated disputes, they finally had a list of bullet-points to create the action plan. Bruno was holding himself back as always, following the back and forth of the reasoning and carefully watching each of his assistants, especially those three he considered potential successors for the time he would retire.

They finalized an eight-point action plan under his leadership, none bothering with writing down anything. First, they knew that Karin would have it down better than they could, and secondly, Comrade Bruno wanted them to focus on the debate and not be consumed with writing down words.

Since one of the points was an immediate face-to-face meeting with their district secretaries, with the instruction to report back the next day with the results, Bruno ended the meeting not only to instruct them all again to absolute secrecy about the action plan. Although all knew that everything said in Bruno's office was an absolute secret, he knew that one or the other had a close friendship with comrades within their district and thought it necessary to the point that out again.

The regional Assistants moved out without standing around and talking among them as they usually did because they were in a hurry to get to their offices and arrange everything for their immediate travels to the district capitals. Since the country's capital was almost in the center of the country, it wasn't really challenging to have their meetings with the district secretaries of ICC early afternoon.

CHAPTER 6

TO FIGHT A BATTLE, YOU NEED TO FIND THE RIGHT FIGHTER

Karl, the regional Assistant of the Secretary of ICC of the United Socialist Party for the northern region, including the three northern districts, was in a hurry. Although the telephone system was 25 years behind modern technology, Party phone connections were always prioritized over any other phone activity nationwide. It was the only stable, secure connection. Yet, it took almost 20 minutes to get the district secretary on the phone because his Secretary did not dare to call him out of the meeting with the First District Secretary. Finally, when he had him on the phone, it needed only a few words to make it clear that he should be better prepared to answer all Karl's questions when he arrived right after lunch.

Now on the road, Karl was somewhat released that he had been lucky to get one of the most experienced drivers of the carpool. This one was perfect, and he immediately understood the urgency when Karl told him he needed him to give it all. Since their car had a specific license plates, no policemen would dare to stop them for speeding. That was another nice privilege Karl enjoyed. With that, it was just a few minutes after noon when they arrived at the office building of the district secretariat of the SUP.

He told the driver to get something to eat and to rest because they would get back no matter how late.

The front desk officer had already called the district secretary, who had instructed him to call as soon as the assistant arrived. The district secretary appeared even before Karl had finished instructing the driver. They shook hands and walked upstairs to the small office the district secretary of ICC called his own.

For a moment, Karl felt the old feeling coming back when he was sitting behind the desk with the cabinets too close behind so that he couldn't move much around. But he loved it. He could read the reports and study the detailed reviews of the activities of comrades who had forgotten what it meant to be a member of the USP. It was his place where he could think through his steps to find the hook to hang the traitors.

Something had changed during the last three years since he was called to the capitol, and this guy was promoted to replace him. It wasn't his office anymore, and it did not look like it had ever been. The trash from several days was oozing out of the trash can. Large piles of paper, probably unread reports and files about problematic comrades, were piling up and filling the desk so that it was almost impossible to work on that desk. He looked again around, and at that second, it darned him that this comrade was not up to the job.

Why didn't he see this before? What had clogged his eyes so that he did not realize it earlier? Pushing his thoughts aside, he focused on the nervous explanation his district secretary gave about the different counties of the district from the perspective of the function as the Secretary of ICC. He almost fell back into his thoughts about the past because it was nothing but a bunch o excuses for why things were as bad as they were ever reported before.

Karl had to admit that he had made several mistakes in the past, and the largest was that he did not realize much earlier that this comrade was absolutely out of place. He interrupted his seemingly endless tirade about the untouchable First County Secretaries (FCS) because they were friends with the powerful First District Secretaries (FDS), and asked him about their files.

At least they were in order. Karl said: 'I would like to get the ten best and the ten worst comrades at each county office, and I need a place where I can work without interruption. Then I want you to call everyone to tell them to stay at the office no matter what until I call them and tell them to go home. I want them to prepare a brief report they can give me over the phone. I'll go to get something to eat, and when I'm back, I want to start working immediately. Comrade, it appears that you're struggling with some issues that hinder you from doing your job in the way it needs to be done.' Karl paused for a moment, looking him directly in the eye, and said, 'Comrade, we're in a challenging situation, and we need comrades in leading positions like yours who are up to the job. And not just that, but to give 120%, ready to give more than requested. Before I leave tonight, I have your complete report in hand. Did I make myself clear enough?' The district secretary was now not only nervous, but he was also almost breaking down. Thick drops of sweat appeared on his face, and he virtually fell into his chair.

Karl almost followed a small impulse inside of him to tap the guy's shoulder to encourage him, but he did not. No mercy, he thought and felt at the exact moment that this was a great opening line for his report to the Secretary of ICC. Now was not the time for sympathy. Hard and draconic decisions needed to be made, and the only way to get the situation handled was to have people in place who could clean the party's leadership positions with an iron brush.

He walked out to the front desk, and, changing his mind about going out for some lunch, he asked for a room where he could work and would have a phone ready. The woman at the front desk completely understood his position and was competent and helpful. She led him into the office of the first district secretary because he was at a meeting with the city SUP secretary at the capitol.

After he had settled in, avoiding sitting at the chair behind the desk and just starting to read the first file, there was a knock on the door, and he called, 'Come in!' The door opened, and the woman from the front desk appeared with a can of coffee and a plate with several sandwiches. With a hesitating smile, she said, 'Sorry for interrupting you, but I thought you might be hungry.' Almost overwhelmed by her obvious care for him, he suppressed that feeling immediately. One of the basic rules in his life was to always be at a distanced seriousness, especially with subordinates. 'Thank you for your care, and yes, I'm starving,' was his answer with a voice with almost zero emotional components. 'And please, can you make sure that nobody interrupts me.' If somebody asks for me, please come through the intercom.'

She left the room, and he went back to reading. He had started with the ten files of those who were the worse county ICC and was immediately pulled into a net of intrigue and gossip reports from people, party members who not only had no business to report to the district secretary about them. What he read confirmed again his impression he had since several years that the SUP had evolved into an organization of brown-noses and bootlickers. Careerists use the friendship formed at universities, and they push and promote each other into positions where they had no business to be. He decided to skip the phone calls, which would only add to the useless complaints, wasting his short time and focusing on reading instead.

He was aware of his boss Bruno's frustration in his heart for a long time, and he knew that the party's new leadership would listen to him. As more, he felt obligated to present the best plan for his district.

After reading several personnel files, he recognized that he had begun just to scan them since they appeared almost identical when something caught his attention. This one was different. These reports were not only about the Secretary of ICC in that county. They included the Secretary for agitation and propaganda. They blamed both for being close friends and complaining about the Secretary's intense relationship with the Secretary for agitation and propaganda with uncountable people throughout the county, even though many of them were not party members. The report further complained that all efforts to get the county's Secretary of the ICC to reprimand him failed because of the relationship and corruption.

The exact second he thought this could be the man he needed, he hit the intercom button and asked for a secure phone line to the Island county office. Just a few seconds later, the phone rang, and he answered. The woman at the county office was probably instructed with whom she was talking and was cooperative. He heard three ring tones and an excellent and friendly voice: 'comrade Reiner speaking, who is there'?

Karl introduced himself and asked him if he was alone in his office and could speak freely. Reiner answered: 'yes,' with a slightly questioning tone. Karl then explained: 'I'm here at the district office going through some reports and came across several reports about you and comrade Bodo. He seems to be a good friend of yours. That leads some of our comrades to believe you're shielding him from disciplinary consequences for wrongdoing?'

'Comrade Karl, I don't know what kind of reports you're reading right now, but I can ensure you that if we would have just a few more comrades in our party as Bodo is, and many, many less of those who are only complaining, our party wouldn't be in the situation it is.' And going on, he said further: 'If you jump into your car and drive through our county, you will probably find more people in every single village, town, collective, and factory who know and appreciate Bodo personally much better than the name of our new Secretary-General. He has a knowledge of our doctrine and Marx, Engels, Lenin, and many written books from our leaders that is second to none. I can't tell you whether or not he graduated from the party academy, but I can assure you he is better than many of the professors I had there.'

For a moment was silence on the phone. Neither Reiner nor Karl said a word. Both were hanging on some thoughts till Karl said: 'Why is he still in that position at the county level when he is that good? Someone must have recognized his potential and promoted him.'

'You are asking me, comrade Karl?' was the immediate answer, 'Or are you thinking loud? I believe you have his report files in front of you and try to fish for my opinion.'

'No, comrade Reiner, that's not the case. The truth is, I had no clue who this comrade was before I actually looked at your report file. And I'm really impressed with what I see. Actually, that's not true. I should say what I don't see.'

'What do you mean by that, comrade Karl?' asked Reiner.

'Comrade Reiner, I've been in this for almost ten years now. The party is my life. I spend every minute discovering what I can do to improve the purity of the doctrine and the unity of the party behind these doctrines. Unfortunately, until a few days ago, we at the central secretariat were as powerless as many other great comrades throughout the nation.' That has changed; he did not say but thought this last sentence.

Then he went on: 'Comrade Reiner, how long would it take to drive from here to your office?' The answer came immediately, 'Depends on how fast you can drive without trouble with the police. And Reiner added, probably two hours and 40 minutes. Give or take ten minutes for traffic.'

Karl thought for a moment that the idea he had developed while driving up to the north, which had formed a much clearer picture since he started talking to comrade Reiner, was too bold and courageous. But then he remembered the instructions he got from his mentor, somebody he suspected this comrade Bodo did not have. His mentor, now the Secretary of ICC at the Central Committee, said once: 'The best ideas are those which always appear to be inexecutable. Never forget that!'

With that, Karl said into the phone, already reaching for the intercom, 'Comrade Reiner, please make sure that comrade Bodo is available in about two hours. And be there yourself, ready to meet with me. I may need your help, and I have to be back at the capitol tomorrow at 10 AM.' Receiving an astonished, 'Yes, I'll be here and get Bodo ready,' he threw the handset onto the phone and called the front desk woman to find his driver and to send the district secretary of ICC to him. The district secretary appeared within a few minutes, followed by his driver. Karl instructed the driver to be ready to go within the next five minutes, and when the door closed behind him, he focused his attention on the district secretary. In a brief outline, he mentioned all the facts about the party's current situation and, therefore, the nation. He pointed out that the main reason was a party apparatus that had grown over the years into a self-serving bureaucracy of complacent wannabe imperators. That was over now. The establishment of the new Central Committee, with a limited number of very decisive secretaries, was the ground for the renewal of the nation and the re-establishing of the organization's leadership.

He paused for a moment and asked then, 'Comrade, it is up to you whether or not you will be a part of that renewal movement or you're ending at the dung heap of history of our party.' Your performance in this crucial position is miserable, and I have neither the time nor the will to tolerate failure for another day.' He went on, 'You were chosen as my successor because of the references given to the secretary, and it seems that either those references were false or something devastating happened in your life.'

The district secretary explained that he discovered his wife had an affair since about seven months. But he did not want to lose her, and therefore he pretended to know nothing about it. About two months ago, she told him to his face that she would get divorced and take the children. All of that had thrown him out of order.' He finished his story, changing from self-pity to bravery in his tone, 'But I can push that aside and come back to my former performance. I can do that; just give me some days, comrade Karl.'

'You better look for another job. You should find at least one of those you have shielded from justice.' Karl looking him directly in the eye, already standing up, said, 'Sorry, comrade, you've had your chance.'

Pointing to the files on the conference table, he said, 'It might take some days, but those are numbered. Make sure those situation reports ready for transfer as soon as possible.' And with that, Karl was out of the door on his way to his car. Passing by the front desk, he placed his business card, a luxury only a member of the central secretariat had, in front of the woman, 'Thanks for the sandwiches. Those were really appreciated. Call this number if you ever need to talk to me about something significant.'

In the car, he instructed his driver, 'You know that I have a meeting with the Secretary at 10 AM tomorrow morning. It is up to you how much rest you get. We have to be in Bergen a.s.a.p. I need to stay there as long as necessary. We will drive to Berlin from there direct.' All the driver said was, 'Comrade Reiner, consider it done.' With that, he started the car and then hit the road to the Island.

CHAPTER 7

FINDING THE FIGHTER
IS ONLY A FIRST STEP

W as that just real? The thought went through Reiner's mind as he slowly recaptured the last few minutes and was totally consumed by the just-finished phone call with one of the most powerful men he had ever talked to. It took him several seconds to realize that this man was really on his way to their office, not to have a secret meeting with the first county secretary but with him. And Bodo, of course. But why Bodo? He wasn't even in his department. He wasn't his supervisor, besides, if there was misconduct and violations of party rules. As the county secretary of the Internal Control Commission (ICC), he was responsible for not breaking those rules. What a joke. For several years, he had tried to rain in the county's party leadership, including the county's first secretary, but in vain. He was blocked and ridiculed, and when he tried to get the district ICC involved in solving the issues, the reaction was silence. Now, out of the blue, the assistant to the central secretary ICC was on his way to meet him. That was so unreal that it took him several minutes to sort out the thoughts flying through his mind until he remembered to call Bodo to let him know that his day would change.

He dialed Bodo's number, and when Bodo picked up the phone, he said only, 'Come over now.' Just a few minutes later, the door opened, and Bodo, remaining at the door, asked, 'What is it that you need to see me; you know that I'm on my way to the fisher cooperative to explain the changing at the leadership. They aren't all together daily, and I have to use that chance.'

'I know, but I have a surprise for you. Come in and sit down because I don't want to pick you up from the floor.' Bodo stepped into the room, closed the door, and sat at the visitors' chair in front of Reiner's desk. The small office was the same as Bodo's and stuffed with the same standard furniture as all party offices at that level.

'OK, I'm sitting. What is so incredibly important that it could slam me to the floor?' Reiner answered with a bright green on his face, 'You're about to become a celebrity. Do you know to whom I talked about you for almost 20 minutes? You have no idea, haven't you?' Bodo looked at him as if he had just missed a truck by an inch, shocking his head, 'You're right. I have no idea to whom you talked because I do not listen to your phone conversations. Shall I go across the hallway and ask Georg?' Reiner burst out laughing, saying, 'Not necessary. I'll tell you because I have to ensure you're not leaving town. My big boss is coming hither and wants to talk to you.'

Now it was on Bodo to laugh out loud, saying, 'Your boss, that wimpy of a useless chair filler in the wrong place? And you believe I'll cancel an important presentation of the challenges, changes, and opportunities the new leadership gives us because that useless piece of crap wants to talk to me?'

With that, Bodo was almost out of the chair and at the door when Reiner stopped him with a loud voice, almost yelling at him, 'Stop, Bodo, let me finish!' Bodo stopped moving towards the door, turned around, and said, 'What?' 'It is not my boss, I mean not my direct boss but my boss,' Rainer answered, and now it was on Bodo to laugh. 'What is that supposed to mean? That makes no sense at all.'

Reiner began to tell him about the phone call he received and briefly what they had talked about, leaving out the part about Bodo's qualifications and history since Reiner not precisely knew what happened to Bodo that he ended up at this deserted place. He finished giving Bodo a brief report on who this comrade Karl was. Karl was a legend among the ICC people. He had discovered more corruption and brought more corrupt party leaders to justice than anybody else.

Bodo understood the party structure much better than it appeared and maybe even better as Reiner did, and with that, it was immediately clear to him that one of the most powerful men in this struggling nation was on his way to meet with him. Something extraordinary must have caught the attention of that comrade that he was taking the burden onto himself to drive to the Island. Startling out of his thoughts, he tapped Reiner on the shoulder and walked out the door to his office.

He closed the door behind him and grabbed the phone to call his wife.

'I'm awaiting a high-ranking visitor and have no idea when I'll be home. No, I have no idea what this comrade really is up to, and I do not want to speculate.'

With that, he was back in his thoughts. And immediately, he felt anger rising inside of him about the betrayal of his brother Fritz. He was the coming star within the local organization. Well educated knew to argue, and always had the right answers ready before the questions even were asked. He was on top of the youth organization in the city from the first day at college and had enjoyed several special promotions never seen before for comrades at his age.

He was his idol, and in his shade, Bodo could climb up the ladder right behind him. Whenever he was asked about his name and if he was related to Fritz, he was proud to confirm and most of the time got recognized even more for his work. Bodo really had that dream that they could both make the ascent into the highest possible positions in the party and accomplish everything for socialism in their country.

Then, suddenly, Fritz threw everything away. And for what? Individualism for the benefit of the people and not the party ideology! The greatest enemy of a socialist nation on its way to communism. Lenin made it very clear throughout his books; there is no room, absolutely no room, for any fulfillment of individual rights or ideas in a socialistic society. Everything needed to be subordinate to the collective and the party's rules. Everything had to serve the unchallenged leadership of the party. You can't have the victory of socialism and the transition to communism when you have to secure the destructive personal behavior of the individual from the collective.

And then it became even worse. After the party tempered justice with mercy and approved his application to the university to get his graduate engineering degree, he thanked her with a slap in the face.

Suddenly he declared he now believed in GOD, und this Christ, ha, what stupidity. After studying all the scientific confirmations as part of the graduation, how could he even think this stuff had any value? But somehow, it was predictable after he married that Christian girl. She wasn't bad, and Bodo always thought it would come the other way around; she would find her way into reality and join the party.

And this was the last nail in the coffin for Bodo. His brother openly declared a break with the party, which was the leading force of the worker's class towards a communistic paradise for all working people. This was where Bodo's carrier suddenly stopped. He had the delegation to start his study at the party's own university in his pocket, just throwing in some more journeys on the fishing cutter to safe a little more money.

One morning when he was on his way to his cutter, the party secretary of the company caught him and asked him into his office. There he told him he was very sorry, but the comrades at the party's ICC decided he could not move up to higher levels in the party hierarchy with a traitor as a brother. And to Bodo's surprise, he understood the reasoning immediately. He did not blame his comrades for the decision to end his carrier. He agreed with their decision and found it wise. But all the more, he began to hate his brother Fritz. It came to the point that Bodo could not cover his hatred even at his mother's home. Whenever Fritz appeared there, Bodo left home. They did not exchange one single word. Especially after Bodo a few weeks after the bad news told Fritz that he, Bodo would make sure that, if it came to the point that the party needed to use deadly force to secure socialism for this country, Fritz would be one of the first to be rounded up and shot.

A knock on the door startled him out of his thoughts. He answered, 'Come in!' The door opened, and the man entering the room was unknown to him, although he thought he might have seen him several years ago but could not remember where and on what occasion. Karl entered the room and closed the door behind him. The handshake was firm and confirming, and Karl looked Bodo direct in the eye.

After a short moment, he looked around the office. Nothing shocking, the standard furniture as in all party offices at that level.

'Comrade Bodo, I'm happy you could make it possible to wait for me and arrange some time for us to talk.' Bodo couldn't hold back to answer ironically,' How could I deny a meeting request from one of the most powerful men in our beloved party?'

Karl, unsure how to take that statement, hesitated for several seconds before answering, 'That power is at first owned by the party and secondly at the brink of collapse.' He went on, 'I actually like that strait to the point attitude because my time is limited, and I have to be at a meeting at the central office at 10 AM tomorrow. So let's talk about the party, the situation, how you see it, and what you think is necessary.'

Bodo, leaning back in his chair, did not hesitate to show his surprise, 'You asking me? Me, the brother of a traitor. The once greatest hope in our district to become a leader with the right heart for the party? You really want to know what I think should be done after I was denied to begin my study at the party university?'

Bending himself forward over his desk so he was very close to the face of Karl, Bodo said, 'The short answer is taking the ten worst and most corrupt party leaders of al 10 districts, have a public litigation and shoot them in public.'

His voice was like ice, and Karl could virtually hear every single world falling like ice to the desk and brake with a clink.

With a green on his face, Bodo leaned back again and said, 'But the party doesn't has the guts for that anymore. We have lost our excitement for the cause. So, while I'm doing my best at the base, you guys in Berlin are sitting on your hands and letting the counter-revolutionaries take over.'

Karl looked at him and couldn't avoid inwardly greening because he loved what he heard. While Bodo continued to explain his point of view on what went wrong over the last fifteen to twenty years, Karl analyzed every sentence Bodo said and compared it with his own opinion and how this comrade would fit into his plan. This comrade clearly had the potential to become the SUP's Feliks Dzierżyński.

Finally, he interrupted Bodo's analysis of the failing party policies, pointing to the time, and said: 'Comrade Bodo, I'm nearly hundred percent in agreement with you. The only difference is that all those who are now in a position to change things did not have that ability before. Since a few weeks, we have had a different situation in the party's leadership, and I can assure you that we will clean the party from top to bottom without mercy and an iron brush.'

Looking straight at Bodo, he continued with a tone of expectation in his voice, 'But that needs comrades who are clean, not tinted with anything that even slightly smells after corruption. And that needs comrades willing to stick with nothing and to be as unknown as possible to the public. Comrades who are willing to do even the most horrible things to get the truth out of the traitors don't hesitate in their work.' He lowered his voice so that he almost whispered, 'Comrade Bodo, are you willing to be one of those? Are you willing to give it all? Are you willing to do whatever it takes to get the party back to its roots, even if it requires unconventional means? Are you willing to go this way even when our comrades in USSR disagree and try to stop us?'

USSR was a catchword for Bodo, who was so astonished that he barely found his voice, 'Those comrades are far away from the doctrines of Lenin and Marx as the Earth from the Sun. Their critic could only mean we do it right. I always go with the Thaelman sentence, *'You did something very wrong when your enemies applaud you.'*

Karl could barely fight to laugh, 'You really have the right attitude, comrade Bodo. But I need a definite answer to all the requirements. Are you willing to take it on and walk it through? If you can give me a clear yes now, I'll leave it by that, and you'll hear from me within three days.'

Bodo looked back at him, turning his face away from the window, and with almost the same ice in his voice as at the beginning of their meeting, 'You give me the gun and the ammunition, and I will eliminate all betrayers. And I mean that not only figuratively. I'm just not sure that the leadership has the guts to stand by it.'

Now it was on Karl to smile. He had found the individual he needed to make his idea work. He could now drive back to Berlin and present his idea tomorrow, knowing that he could answer the most important question he would be asked, 'Who do you think would be able to do such a job?'

'Actually, I dislike buying a pick in a poke. And I haven't heard anything about the conditions or the chain of command.' said Bodo with a thoughtful tone, 'But I understand what you would want me to do and that the end justifies the means. That is enough for me to say yes, under one condition, I get a written piece of paper, signed by the Secretary-General, that it means exactly that, THE END JUSTIFIES THE MEANS! And I chose the people who work for me.'

'Comrade Bodo, as I said before, I need some days to get everything set up so we can establish this position in a sting operational environment.' Getting out of the chair, he stretched his hand over the desk so fast that Bodo was almost still sitting when he grabbed it. With a firm handshake, holding Bodo's hand a second longer than usual, Karl said, 'Comrade Bodo, I'm glad I did drive out here to meet you. Because I strongly believe that you're the comrade who can cleanse our party from those who walked away from the irrevocable doctrine of the leading role of the worker's class and their only legitimate representative, the communist party.' With that, he walked to the door, turned once more, and said, 'You don't need to show me out. I know the way,' and was through the door.

With a deep breath, Bodo fell back into his chair behind the desk and said, 'Did this happen? Or was that a dream?' He jumped out of his chair and went to the restroom. Holding both hands to fill them with water, he put his face down to refresh himself, and when he looked up and saw his face in the mirror, he couldn't avoid smirking. Looking at his watch, he cast the thoughts about a new future away and went back into his office. It was long after office hours, and he hurried to get out and on his way home.

All day was fantastic weather, even though he did not get much of it sitting in the office instead of being out at the fishery collective, where he would have been had this mysterious comrade Karl not killed his schedule. Although he was again deep in his thoughts, he actually enjoyed thinking about extreme problems when riding his motorbike. He could enjoy the nice weather, the fresh, slightly cold air filled with the the smell of the first wild spring flower along the street he drove home.

What would that mean, being the cleansing iron brush throughout the party? Would they really give him an absolutely free hand? Would he be able to work with, without, or even against the SSP? Knowing that the former, now in the doghouse, Minister for state security and commanding general of the SSP, had tried several times to recruit comrades inside the party organizations to report about their comrades and bosses. Bodo himself had to reject two or three times the proposal that the SSP would find a way to get him into the Party University if he reported on comrades they would bring him together with. At the first of those meetings, he looked at that SSP officer in plain clothing, asked him if he had lost his mind, and walked away. The second time was at the SSP building on their specific invitation, officially based on questions about his brother. He told the two officers that if they would ever again contact him with such a treasonous approach, he would write a letter direct to the Secretary of the Central Control Commission. They never approached him again. But he was sure they found some corrupt comrade who knew nothing about the doctrine of the communist party power system, willing to report for a slight advantage. And he and his friend Reiner were almost sure that George was one of the comrades doing that. Reaching his home today at daylight, he shook off his thoughts and said hello to his wife and son, who were sitting outside on the terrace waiting for him with supper. Because of the beautiful warm early spring day, Sarina had decided it would be great to sit outside, and Bodo was very thankful for that. During supper, they talked about Nick's day at school and Sarina's day at the major's office, and both spoke about the exciting discussions about the change in government and the news and all that stuff going on during the day, TV and radio. Bodo listened intently because both were secure sources about the reflections of the nation leader's politics among the people at the base government and the schools, which means youth and future of the country.

Than Sarina asked, 'How was your day? How did the meeting with the fishermen go?' Bodo thought for a moment whether or not he should at least give her a hint about the suggestion the surprising high-ranking visitor had made but threw that thought immediately away. It was neither the time nor the issue he would talk about freely before even the framework was set up, and for sure not in the presence of Nick.

With that in mind, he answered elusively, 'No, I couldn't make it. Something other important came up.' And recognizing her questioning sight and knowing that the next question wouldn't take long and get him in trouble, he said, 'Don't you think that our office was the same, maybe even more, chaotic, exciting situation all day long'?

With a smile, Sarina answered, 'I can only imagine.' But then she went on, 'Somehow it must have a huge effect on your work Bodo, with all those dramatic changes not only the party leadership in persons but all the changes in the leadership structure. Does it not?'

'Meetings occupied the whole morning, and the main focus was to define the exact agenda for every secretary and their team under consideration of the appeal of the new Secretary-General to all citizens to bring in ideas and suggestions for the restructuration of the nation. Since there are no instructions given by the district leadership yet, it was all more like brainstorming.'

'Why didn't you get instructions from the district party, dad?

'Oh Nick, come on, you know the answer yourself, do you?'

'Well, hmmm,' he thought for a moment, 'Because the comrades at the district were brainstorming too?'

'You see, Nick, when you spend a little time to ponder your thoughts before formulating a question, you may often find the answer already.' With a look at his watch, he said it was time for Nick to enter into the nightshift mode and that he would use the lovely evening to clean his bike since it had been affected by the bad weather over the last several days.

CHAPTER 8

THE PLAN – CLEANING NEED TOOLS

When Karl entered the car, he had only a few words to say to his driver, 'Get us home as soon as possible, but drive safe so that I can make some notes.' He knew that the ICC drivers were among the best to be found in the whole nation. His Boss, Bruno, was the most experienced man he had ever known when discerning men's characters. His investigative instinct was so highly developed that he often needed only a few minutes to determine the facts.

Karl had something similar, probably because Bruno had taken him under his wings and carefully coached him as his mentor. And Karl had the same feeling about Bodo. Bodo was well educated about the party's history, better than many graduates from the academy. He also could look through the curtains people tried to pull in front of their iniquities. And, what was the essential character to fill the position Karl was developing? He was merciless, absolutely merciless against the traitors, those corrupt members of the party, and others in leadership positions who participated and profited from the degeneration of the party as the leader of the worker's class. He began to write down the bullet points for the concept of a position, slowly taking on forms in his head since he had been chewing on it since the morning when he left office. It should be a position that would have to report only to the assembly of the Central Committee and would therefore be outside of the reach of a single and maybe selfish reacting member of the Central Committee. After he had several bullet points, he began to outline the description of each of them.

When he was at the point where he had to find a name for that new position, he found that was the most challenging issue of his whole effort. Finally, he decided to give it a preliminary title for the presentation and thought to use it as another highlight of his presentation to ask the team to finalize it. He thought a little longer about it because he knew he must have at least a suggestion in case nobody came up with a useable name. Suddenly he had the right idea and wrote it down immediately.

The new position would be Office of Investigation and Revision = OIR. He formulated the responsibilities of the head of the office and his sole power to choose his team members. The OIR would have offices in every district capital, and the only line of the report was to the head of the OIR. The Central Committee would have the right to refuse the suggested team member if the reasoning why the head chose them and their file was not conclusive enough. Because of the extreme secrecy this office would work in, any member had to write and sign a statement that he voluntarily committed suicide because of his break of the trust the party entrusted them with, in case he broke that trust in any form. That was the key for the Central Committee to agree to transfer almost unlimited power to this office. But Karl had that feeling in his gut that Bodo was somebody, no, that wasn't correct, the only one who could be trusted because he would never, under no circumstance, break that trust. And if he should come into a situation where he had to make an essential decision, Karl was sure he would choose the party above everything.

Those were the real comrades needed in situations like the country's current stage. This position had to run a cleansing operation throughout the nation. This operation would cleanse the leadership from the lowest to the highest level and through all the institutions. And with these thoughts in mind, he wrote a detailed plan for that operation. He developed the structure of the organization and the rules and regulations this organization would work under.

It was long after midnight when they arrived at his home. Although he was tired and knew he would not get much sleep, it wouldn't change much in the near future. But he felt good because he believed he could present a systematic solution to the problematic of corruption that had infected the party apparatus over the years of sloppy leadership of the past decade. With these thoughts in mind, he released the driver from duty, and within a few more minutes, he was in bed and sound asleep.

The following day he was up early enough to have a decent breakfast and reread his plan, rehearsing the presentation he would give during the meeting. After preparing for his day at the office, he knew he would be swamped and maybe controversial because he also knew that several of his comrades would reject his suggestion.

When he arrived at the office, he called his secretary, gave her his notes, and instructed her to write them and have copies ready for the meeting. Then he picked up the phone and asked his boss's secretary if there was a chance to meet before the 10 AM meeting. She asked him to wait and put him on hold. When she came back, she told him he could be there at 8:15 and would have 15 minutes. He thanked her and was glad to have the chance to present his idea to his boss before the official meeting since he was aware that it could be controversial because it was a ruthless approach to the problem. But his discussion with that comrade Bodo in that small office in the small town at the county on that island had made it clear to him – this was the only chance to save the Party from losing control of the nation.

After he had finished some phone calls, his secretary came through the intercom, telling him that she was done with the transcript of his notes. Carefully he read word for word to make sure it exactly was what he wanted to present, and when he was done, he gave it back to her so that she could make copies. When she was done with the copies, it was time for the meeting before the meeting.

Karin, the senior secretary, waved him through, so he went straight to the office door and entered comrade Bruno's office. His boss was still sitting in the comfortable sitting area at the corner with the large windows giving a great view of the great place in front of the central committee building and the wide four-lane road with very light traffic.

Bruno waved him to come over to the corner, sit with him on the sofa, and get himself a cup of coffee. Bruno was still reading the New Germany and having breakfast as always in the morning and would typically not have accepted any interruption. But with Karl, that was different. Out of his four district assistants, Karl was his most appreciated protégé. The coffee smell was different from the stuff Karl got in his office. However, all employees at the central committee, as most of the party's employees, had the privilege of buying goods and products unavailable to the average citizen. It was a kind of compensation for their hart work with often uncounted hours for the nation's benefit. At least, that was what most of them believed. But Bruno had even better sources. His was the real stuff. He got his coffee directly flown in from Ethiopia every other month because the ambassador in Ethiopia owed him his job, his freedom, and maybe even his life.

He handed one of the copies of his plan to Bruno. 'Comrade Secretary, please read this. I believe that could solve the problems we must deal with as the Internal Control Commission.' And while filling a cup with coffee for himself and topping it off with cream and cane sugar from Cuba, he thought about whether or not this privilege was corruption too. But that thought disappeared within a microsecond because they deserved these little extras. They, the top leadership of the party in power, had such an enormous responsibility for the welfare of the people they needed to get the best available.

It took Bruno only a few minutes to read the paper since it consisted of just a few pages. His first mentor, an old fighter who had worked with Thaelman underground and passed away some years ago, taught him that there were several rules for a good plan. It was one of the basic rules to keep a plan simple. The simplicity allowed less intelligent subordinates - and often enough supervisors - to follow and to agree. Bruno wasn't one of those, but it had become second nature to Karl to follow the KIS principle since Bruno loved it too.

When Bruno finished his first reading, he filled his cup with coffee, topped it with cream and sugar, and slightly turned the coffee with the teaspoon. Looking out of the window, he said, 'When did you put that together?' Then looking back to Karl, 'Do you know this guy? What was his name?' Thumping through the pages, 'Ah JA, Bodo?' And he reread the plan without waiting for an answer, this time with much more concentration than the first time. That was his style. He would throw out two or three questions and then go back to something else to give his assistants time to formulate their answers because he wanted answers to them without needing to ask again.

The first question was easy answered, 'Comrade Secretary, I put that together last night on my way home.' Bruno lifted his gaze from the paper and looked at him, saying, 'Bruno is OK when we're alone. I told you that a long time ago, Karl. You're like the son I don't have.' Karl said, 'I know, Bruno, it is just the situation, and I did not sleep much, and I'm still a little exhausted.' Bruno said, 'When we're done with our meeting, you go home, get some sleep and take the rest of the day off without looking up from the paper.' Karl was surprised by that offer since there was so much work to do, but he gladly accepted it. He knew that this was Bruno's way to compliment him and, most importantly, that he agreed with his plan. He answered, 'Yes, I'll do that, and I actually met this comrade. His name is Bodo. He is just one amazing, extremely well-educated, and energetic comrade.'

Bruno had finished his second time reading the plan and putting the pages on the table; he leaned back in his chair and looked direct at Karl. 'I knew there was something in you nobody else has seen; from the first moment our common friend introduced you to me. You have a certain and rare talent to find the right people for the job. But this is too big to let it pass just so. I have to meet this comrade, and I have to present your plan to the central committee. Since it is my department and my responsibility, I guess they will all agree. Here is what we're gone do. You present this plan at the meeting, and we will see who else comes up with an idea and what. I'll go with yours because I think it a brilliant and we can run it as a covert operation. Then I want you to arrange that this comrade gets brought to Berlin, and I want him to be here tomorrow. Then you can take off.'

With that, he gave Karl a signal to leave him alone, and when Karl left the office, another comrade from the information department was waiting to go in.

CHAPTER 9

A SECRET MEETING IN A PUBLIC PLACE

Thick wades of smoke hanging in the air, combined with the typical smell of low-quality beer, made the air at the railway station's restaurant almost too heavy to breathe. As always, being extremely careful when entering the immediate area of a conspiratorial meeting, Fritz had changed direction several times. He walked into three stores to buy some small stuff, and twice he stepped back into the shop he had just left to find out if somebody would make a suspicious movement.

All those safety percussions took time, but since he wasn't a beginner in covering his tracks, he was ahead of the meeting time. As the last step, he used the restroom, which had a second exit to the platform. With a few quick steps, he was through the door onto the platform and back at the concourse entrance to check the hall to see if there were any unusual movements. When he was sure there wasn't anything or anybody there that seemed out of the ordinary, he entered the restaurant.

Stepping through the door into the smoky room, he immediately moved several steps sideward out of the entrance area and out of the attention of a possible waiting SSP spy. Scanning the midsized room, which was occupied by approximately 30 people, mostly in groups of three up to 6, he was sure it was safe to enter.

The corner table, next to the bar, close to the second exit of the restaurant to the platform, was empty. Walking along the wall, he went to that table and sat down. With his back to the corner, he had the whole restaurant in front of him. The waitress came after several minutes, asking lethargic, 'What do you want?'

'I'll take soda.'

'Pfff, soda, who is drinking soda?' Shaking her head, she walked away to place the order. Fritz checked the time and saw Leo entering the restaurant when he looked up. In almost the same manner as Fritz some minutes before, he stepped aside and scanned the room, and even while their eyes met, he did not make known that he had recognized Fritz, what he immediately noted as very positive. After a few more seconds, Leo walked along the wall towards the table Fritz was sitting at and greeted Fritz with just a nod.

At that exact moment, the waitress appeared with the soda, which was placed in front of Fritz on an already somewhat soaked and several times dried-up beer coaster. She looked at Leo, and he said without waiting for her question, which probably would never have come, 'Same for me, please.'

'Ohh, it's soda day today.' She turned around to the bar to get another soda ordered. Fritz and Leo did not talk until the overloaded, and lustless waitress brought the soda for Leo. When she was gone, Leo began,

'I parked the truck at the fuel station at Dwasiden and walked through Garden Lane, which gave me plenty of opportunities to stop and talk to some of the people in their gardens. Nobody followed me. And I know that you take security very seriously, so I think we're safe now.' How is the situation with our two packets?'

'We really need to get them off the island. I was at their place two days ago, and although the one with the damage has gotten some maintenance, thanks to the Lord, we have a maintenance specialist in our group, but we need to get them out of the barn and into a normal home and care.'

'Fritz, we know and understand your problem, but you know that we have to be very careful. Yet I shall tell you from our #1 that we have contacted our friends at the lake, and they are willing and able to receive the two packets anytime. I asked for this meeting because I'm on my way to Dranske, where I have to load some interesting stuff. I have to pick up 100 small matrasses, and on my way back, I could take your two packets.'

'That sounds awesome. We need you to have a stop for a coffee break at the Sea Perl restaurant Glowe. What time will you be there on your way back?'

'Let's see, driving up there is about one hour, paper pusher work, loading another hour, and then forty minutes back to the restaurant. Takes about three hours from the moment I enter the truck. From here to the truck, add another thirty minutes, give or take.' But what is about the Workers Fighter Brigade units? As I could see coming over the R'damm, they're still stopping every single car and truck leaving the island.'

'That's the good news I have. The group on duty tonight is from Altefaehr, and the commander of this group is one of us. Although he is the only one in that group on duty tonight, at least as far as we know, he has started reducing the search's intensity. I don't know his name, and I don't know the chain of contact to me, but I can ensure that the group on duty tonight will not move a hundred matrasses on your truck.'

'That's excellent news. With that, I'm on my way.' Leo looked at his watch and then scanned the restaurant for the waitress, and when he made eye contact with her, he waved to her with a gesture to pay. Looking back at Fritz, 'I'm at the Sea Perl between 8 p.m. and 8:30 p.m. I'll stay in there getting something to eat for less than an hour, and I'll park the truck backing it to the bushes. I'll do an around check that looks like to make sure everything is okay when I come out. Tie a piece of red cord around the end of the security rope when the packets are loaded. If I see that, I'll turn the key and drive.' If not, I'll return to the restaurant and use the restroom. If I come out a second time, I won't check anything. I'll just leave.'

'Plenty of time for us to get everything set up. Please let your people know how thankful we're.'

'Thank the Lord because he made all of this possible to help those who need help.'

Finally, the waitress made it to their table, and both paid for their soda pop with the right amount of tip not to attract attention. Since Fritz did come in first, he said goodbye with a nod and moved through the nearby door to the platform. Leo waited for another couple minutes and walked through the main door crossing the concourse.

He walked fast toward the main exit to the concourse forecourt, stopped just at the large swing doors, turned, and walked to the restroom. When he was done, he walked through the door onto the platform, only to turn again and walk back into the restroom. After he could not notice any suspicious movement around him, he left the concourse and walked through Garden Lane back to his truck. Not without stopping to exchange words about the great-looking garden with some of the owners. When he arrived at his truck, he intended to check the tires and brakes, but actually, he checked for the several signs he had installed on his truck which would give him a signal that somebody had messed around with it. Everything was as it should be, so he jumped into his driver seat and was on his way.

CHAPTER 10

MOVING A LOAD OF SOMETHING ELSE THAN MATRAZZES

Fritz had left the concourse through a sideway. This exit was used mainly by insiders who used the small door next to the office building to shorten the way out of the station. Again, being very careful, he did as if he had forgotten something and walked towards the main entrance, only to stop half the way and turn down the street toward the town center. Everything was clear. He greeted several people he knew with a nod of his head and was relieved when he reached his car, parked in a small side street next to the large famous hotel, without anything unusual happens.

Driving out of the city, he carefully watched his speed, knowing that at this time, the people's police usually had established a speed trap along the exit road. Because the main street of his hometown was made of cobblestones from the beginning of the century, it was very poorly maintained, and one could only drive very slowly. The last mile was covered with asphalt, which tempted many to speed up too much. The police knew about that; although the people knew it, it was just too tempting.

Sorting out the following steps he had to take, he was planning to move their Russian guests to the backside of the parking lot of the Sea Perl restaurant. The funniest thing about that whole story was that the hideout for the refugees was right under the eyes of the most fanatic, bitter, and hate-filled man on the island, his brother. He had to focus on the necessary things to get the action done. With that, he moved the upcoming thoughts about the beginning of the enmity to the back of his mind.

He had chosen the long way to enter the village from the west side because the east route held a greater chance to be seen by his relatives since he had to pass through the whole village to reach the separate laying farmhouse of the member of his group who sheltered the Russians.

Although he would avoid crossing the whole village, he still had to pass the school and the enclosed sports field, where several students were still active. He thought for a second that he had seen his nephew. His nephew might have looked at the car, Fritz but immediately chased off the thought because he was far too fast to be recognized. Entering the driveway onto the farm house, he slowed down, do not miss the small side way which led direct to the large barn at the back of the farm yard. Slowly passing the side way, he backed into it and drove the curvy way, lined with brushes, backward for about 180 yards. There he stopped direct at the backdoor of the barn. He closed the car door as silently as possible and knocked at the barn door with a stone he had picked up from the way in a certain rhythm. He stepped five steps back from the door so that anybody in there, looking through the small hole, could see who he was, putting both hands in his pants pockets as an additional signal that everything was okay.

The door opened, and Nicolai, the senior of the Russian Speznas soldiers, jumped out in a forward roll, rolling the jump force damping over his left shoulder, and was up on his feet, all in just a few milliseconds, scanning the car and the brushes, a smile appeared on his face, and he looked at Fritz,

'Fritz, seeing you goott, coming into our house.' He said with his heavy Russian accent. Both walked through the door into the barn. The other soldier, some years younger, was lying behind a stack of machine parts on a heap of straw. His name was Olek, and although he was much better than some days ago, he still had difficulties breathing and moving around. Fritz walked over to him, greeted him, and talking to both now,

I have good news, brothers. We will get you off the island tonight. Oleg, are you feeling strong enough to travel?'

'Oleg, good. Many good and can have travel.' And with a look at Nicolai, 'Nicolai, much helping me travel.'

'Listen, my friends, we have a truck tonight, which has a load of mattresses and gives you enough cover to get off the island. There is another group that will take care of you, and I just hope and pray that you might be out of the country soon. I'll see the farmer let him know, and you get everything together and remove whatever could reveal that you were here. I'll be back.'

Fritz walked over to the main barn door and opened and closed it carefully to make no unnecessary noise. He crossed the front yard by calling the dog by its name, letting it know that he was a known, friendly person. With a short double knock on the door, he entered the house where the farmer was already waiting for him.

'I saw your car coming down from the road and thought you'll take a look at our friends. Oleg is doing much better but has a long way to go.'

'I'm actually here, picking them up. We can get them off the island and to their next step towards freedom.'

'That's great news, but.'

'But what? What's your concern?'

'As I said, Oleg is doing much better, but he isn't really fit for a long trip under these circumstances. Anyway, I know it's necessary, and we have to use any chance we have to get them out of here. Although having two Russian refugees, whom the whole Russian Army is looking for, including the WFF police, in a hideout not even a mile away from the greatest communist seen after Lenin himself, is somewhat encouraging, don't you think Fritz?'

'I thought about that several times when the news warned about these extremely dangerous criminals. Especially when my brother gave those interviews, how the island workers, farmers, and fishermen would support the official agencies' efforts to capture these murderous criminals, knowing that they were almost in his backyard, I could barely hold myself. But it's time to get them on the road, and I'm really thankful that we got the connection to the mainland to arrange their transfer.'

'Watch your back and let me know when you need anything I can help with.' They shook hands and embraced each other, and with a mutual 'GOD bless you,' Fritz walked out to the barn. Since it was not even mid-April, the twilight had already begun to shift towards darkness. When he entered the barn, he found Oleg and Nicolai ready to move on, each with a small bag over their shoulder with the few items they possessed.

'Oleg, did you take your medication on time? We may have no chance to get that done during travel.'

'Yes, yes, me did do that.'

'Okay, friends, let's move out. I need you to sit low in the care as long as we're near the village. We don't have to drive a long distance, though and I hope Oleg doesn't suffer too much.'

'Oleg, okay,' said Oleg with a smile on his childlike face, which was still a child's face. Just a little over 20 years, he looked much younger, but his face was marked with the scares of the horror he had experienced during his time in Afghanistan. Fritz had long felt deep hate for the Russian troops in Afghanistan and thought that every single one of them was just a feral killer. But when he listened to the story of Nicolai and Oleg, he understood that there was only one way for them not to be part of that war, to be dead. None of them had volunteered for the army or the special unit Speznas.

They were drafted, and when the physical verification weeks were over, they were selected for the most brutal, most feared special troops within the Russian army, the Spezas. After several months of bestial training in fighting techniques with and without all available weapons, the drill had made them fighting machines. Both had seen friends and comrades die during the training because everything happened with real bullets, real knives, and the standard folding spate, which was in their hands' the most dangerous weapon.

After both were securely hidden in the car, Fritz drove out of the small sideway with no lights and was very slow since it was nearly dark. The moon wasn't up yet, and with that, they would have almost total darkness when they entered the truck at the parking lot.

Soon after arriving at the main driveway, Fritz switched on the headlights. The main road was empty, and he could now accelerate to normal driving speed. After a short drive of about 35 minutes, he reached the outskirts of that village, where the truck would park in the parking lot accessible from the wooded area on the backside of the restaurant. He had to turn into a small, unpaved side street with only a few homes and after he had passed those homes, he turned left again. To get back behind the woods, they would have to cross.

He parked the car at the passage to a field beside the woods and sat still for several minutes after shutting off the engine and the lights. They all got out of the car and closed its doors slowly and with as little noise as possible.

Fritz, pointing to the woods, whispered,

'There are the woods we have to cross. On the other side is a parking lot, where a truck should show up in about ten to fifteen minutes. Let's go.' Looking at Oleg, 'Oleg, you're okay so far?' he whispered.

'All okay by my,' Oleg answered with a visible green, even in the dark.

'We won't have much time there on the other side of the forest, so I'll say good bye now. Let's pray' They joined hands, and Fritz began, 'Dear Lord, we are thankful for your protection of these two brothers in Christ. Who, by your grace, were not only able to see the light, recognizing Your Son Jesus as the Lord and Savior but also could escape the brutal life of a special army unit which's only objective is to destroy lives and souls. We thank you, Lord, for saving them and sending your angels to securely guide them out of this hostile nation to freedom where they will be witnesses for your Glory.' Amen came unison from all three. Both Russian soldiers gave Fritz a vast hug, and Nicolai had to turn away because he was too overwhelmed.

Fritz turned around and walked towards the woods, followed by Oleg and Nicolai at the end of the group. Although they walked slowly and tried carefully to avoid any loud noise, it happened that one or the other of the group would step on a dry branch. But the permanent blowing coastal breeze dampened that noise, and they crossed the wooded area without any trouble within ten minutes. When they arrived at the edge of the woods, all three went down into a prone position and began to scan the parking lot. The area where they hid at the wood's edge was almost pitch black and dark. Only a few cars parked at the lot, and all of them were directly in front of the restaurant within the reach of the few street lights sparingly lit the front.

Then it happened, a truck entered the parking lot and drove around the other parked cars under the reach of the street lights. It looked like it would park there, and the excitement that he transport unit had arrived cooled down. But then, as if the truck driver had thought differently, the back-up light came on, and the truck began to move backward in their direction. And as if the driver knew where they lay at the edge of the woods, the truck stopped right at their spot, about 3 yards away from the edge. The driver shut the engine, and in the silence following, they heard the door open and close and the steps of the driver walking to the restaurant.

They waited for another five minutes. Then Nicolai stood up and bent over with a few fast steps to the back of the truck and began to untie the rope holding the tarp. He climbed up and disappeared behind the tarp. Just to reappear within a second, holding the tarp open, he waved Oleg to follow. Oleg walked over to the truck, followed by Fritz, who helped him to climb up to the loading area. Without a word, they shook hands, and knowing that it would be a miracle to see each other again, Fritz closed the tarp and secured it with the rope while he could hear them moving through the matrasses to hide as well as possible. Knotting a red cord around the end of the rope, he placed the agreed sign for Leo that his guests were boarded and moved back through the forest to get to his car.

He drove back onto the main road and parked across from the restaurant. A stack of unused construction material, already completely overgrown with weed, gave him good cover to watch the restaurant's parking lot. After about twenty minutes, Leo came out and walked straight to the truck, walking around the truck, it appeared as if he would check the tires and the security rope on the tarp. He entered the cabin, started the engine, and hit the road. Fritz followed at a secure distance until the connection with the main highway, where Leos' truck turned right in the direction of the main land, and Fritz turned left to get home.

CHAPTER 11

AND I WILL OWN THIS ISLAND

It was approximately 10:30 the morning after the surprising and meaningful visit of that powerful assistant of the National Secretary ICC when Bodo and Peter were back at the office from that delayed meeting with the fishermen from the Fishing Cooperative. Bodo was very thankful for the help Peter had provided because, without his connections, none of the fishermen would have been there after they had lost the day's work when they all stayed on shore for the meeting, which was canceled suddenly.

Peter was the power at the party's county leadership office, close to retirement age, he had seen many come and go, and many of them were in influential positions much higher in the party's hierarchy. Yet, he never accepted the call for a higher position, which many wondered about, but only a few knew why. One of those few was Bodo. It was a long story that held the truth about the party's situation. Corruption at the highest levels of the party wasn't new. And although Bodo was relatively young compared to Peter and had experienced corruption in many different situations, Peter had seen more than a comrade could bear without to be compromised himself ore to turn insane.

'Thanks again, Peter, for your great help. I'd not have been able to pull that together. Although there was a lot of criticism, I believe we could convince most of them to give the new leadership a chance, do you think?'

'Bodo, I must tell you that a lot of work needs to be done. Cleansing work, I mean, within the Party and outside. And it needs to be made public. Otherwise, nobody will believe the news when a stiffened pupped is reading some lines from a piece of paper.' They reached the door of Bodo's office when they heard his phone ringing. 'You better go in there and take that call, see you at lunch,' Peter walked down the hallway to get upstairs to his office.

Bodo closed the door and reached for the phone since the office was small enough to grab it without many steps necessary.

'County Secretary AgitProp, comrade Bodo speaking, who's there?'

'Comrade Bodo, great that I finally get you on the phone. Comrade Karl is speaking, Assistant to the Secretary ICC. We had a little exchange of thoughts yesterday at your office.'

'No need to remind me. It's just a little less than a day since you were here. So you're calling to let me know I shall forget everything we discussed. You probably run into a wall of concrete with your plan?'

'Just to the contrary, comrade, just to the contrary. Listen, I need you to get home now, pack stuff you need for about a week, and do you have a car?'

'No, I have family and a bike. Why do you ask, and what shall I pack for?'

'Slow down, comrade Bodo, slow down. The Secretary wants to see you. He wants you to be in his office tomorrow at 9 AM.'

'I can be there. I have driven to Berlin several times with my bike, no problem.'

'No, not with your bike. I can't risk that you're exhausted or have an accident or so. You drive home as soon as we end this call, pack your stuff, Get some rest, and put some thoughts together about the issues we discussed yesterday if you need. I'll have a car at your place at around 3 p.m.'

Comrade Karl, I can't just drop everything I'm working on and run away. And what do I tell my boss here?'

'First, your boss up there is not your current concern; I'll call him right after we're done. And the work you do, as important as it is, we have a much more important work to do for which we need you up here, or did you change your mind about what we talked about yesterday?'

'No, comrade Karl, not a bit. Today I believe it is even more necessary to do it and to do it right then I thought yesterday, and it will be even more tomorrow.'

'Okay then, get ready, and I'll see you tonight. I really meant it when I said get some rest because I need to brief you when you arrive.'

'Comrade Karl?'

'Yea?'

'What about my family? Can I tell them that I'll start to work in a different position? Can I tell them we will move?'

'Yes, you can tell them, nothing specific as you understand yet, but yes, you can. See you tonight.'

With that, the phone went dead. Bodo stood in front of his desk with the handset still in his hand when the door opened and Reiner stuck his head through the opening.

'Bodo, are you coming?'

Startled out of his thoughts, Bodo placed the handset on the phone and said, 'No, I'm not coming. I need to go home.'

'It's the First Secretary meeting you won't miss, Bodo. That will create some trouble for you.'

'It doesn't matter. I'm gone anyway.'

Reiner's face showed total surprise about these words, and fearing that something had happened to his friend's family, he asked, 'Everything okay with you and your family?' Bodo smiled and said, 'Nothing that you think, I can't tell you now but be assured, if everything goes as I believe it will, you will hear from me within two or three days.'

'Alright, Bodo, it's your butt you put to the fire of the secretary. I'm going. See you,' and he was out.

Bodo retook the handset and dialed the number of the major's office in his hometown, where Sarina worked part-time as the secretary.

'Majors office Lohme, her voice came through some statics.'

'Hello dear, it's me. I'll tell you everything when I'm home; I'm leaving the office now.' I need you to get home and pack some stuff for me for about one week.'

'Something happened, Bodo?'

'Nothing bad, but I can't talk over the phone about it.'

He hung up and turned around, looking at the cabinet behind his desk, running everything through his mind that was in there. He knew nothing personal, and all that stuff was needed by the comrade who would replace him. Then he went to the cube at his desk and opened the file drawer, where he had several files about his ideas and concepts for a situation he had played out in his mind several times during the last three years. But in his wildest dreams, he would never have thought that the day would come to make it a reality. He grabbed all of those file folders and put them in his briefcase. Then he took a piece of paper form the note pad on his desk and wrote on it:

Called to Duty.

Back in some Days?

, and stuck it with a piece of tape to the cabinet door. Anybody entering the office would immediately see and could read the message. A few minutes later, he was on his bike and on his way home. Although the air had cooled down during the last days after the rain, it was still a lovely early spring day with a lot of sunshine. The trees with all kinds of greens of early popping leave buds, lining the street were flying by as he speeded up to get home to tell the great news about the fulfillment of his secret dreams.

Curving into the unpaved road leading to his home, the thought that he might have to leave his beloved bike at the barn for a long time brought some thoughts of melancholia. Still, he pushed that immediately aside in expectation of all the great things which would come with the new position. He wasn't even done with jacking up his bike when Sarina entered the barn.

'Bodo, what happened? I was so afraid when you called that you were coming home?'

'Calm down, Sarina, nothing to fear, just the opposite. All the hard work for the last several years will finally pay off.'

'What's that supposed to mean? Can't you just stop to talk in riddles?' she was almost angry, now nearly exploding in curiosity and not getting a straight answer.

'Not here where the trees have ears. Let's get in the house, and I'll tell you what I'm allowed to tell you.'

Together they walked over to the house and went into the kitchen were Sarina had already a fresh coffee brewed in a large jug. She filled a cup and put a piece of cake on a plate for each of them. But before Bodo even could take a bite, she was asking again, 'Will you tell me now or do you want me to die out of curiosity on a heart attack?'

Bodo had to put his coffee cup back on the table because he did not want to spill the coffee, laughing aloud,

'I'm not permitted to tell you details yet, but this is what I can let you know. Yesterday, when you asked me about the day, I did not tell you everything because I was asked not to. I had a surprising visitor from the party's headquarters in Berlin.

'Ohhh.' Was all Sarina got out, then clapping a hand over her mouth.'

'Yes, you're right to be in awe, and so was I. Who am I that these people would even know that I exist? That was my first thought when Reiner told me to cancel my meeting with the fishermen of the collective. Then this guy stood in my office—the Assistant to the Secretary of the ICC for the Northern Region. We talked for about two hours, and when he left, I thought it was the same old game they always play up there on the top. Only words, no actions, because when they start to think after they speak to people at the base, and they begin to realize what it would mean for them, their own comfort, they immediately get cold feet. Not this time, though. Right before I called you, this guy, this assistant, called me and said to go home. He said he would send me a car to pick me up and be ready to stay there for at least a week.

'Did you put some stuff for me together?'

'This is almost unbelievable. Do you think they will listen to you, to your plans and strategies? A yes, I got everything you would need into the suitcase. I had to take the big one though because I packet the two suits. I thought it might be good you have them since I did not know where you're going, but now it makes even more sense that you have them. Maybe you can get one or another new shirt in Berlin.'

'Sarina, come on, I'm not going to Berlin to search for shirts.'

'You're right, and they might be too expensive anyway.'

Now Bodo laughed again. 'You know what, if that is what I think will happen, happens, you won't find a shirt in the whole country we can't buy. Okay, I have a long and strange day in front of me, and I'd like to get some rest. I'll lie down and ask him to be quiet when Nick comes.'

'Go get some sleep; I'll take care of everything.'

Bodo walked into the living room, arranged some of the cushions on the large couch, and with a blanket over him, he was soon sound asleep.

When Sarina touched his shoulder to wake him up, he thought he had just dozed a few minutes, but the clock on the wall showed him that it was almost three o'clock.

'Bodo, your car has arrived. I gave the driver a cup of coffee, and there is one for you. Please come out.'

'Yea, let me refresh a little bit at the bathroom, and I'll be out in a minute.'

When he entered the kitchen, the driver stood up immediately,

'Comrade Zipper, I'm Dieter. I'm the driver of Secretary Tecker, and I have been ordered to be at your service. The main order is to get you to Berlin a.s.a.p. and safe.'

'Sit down, comrade Dieter; we have enough time to have a good cup of coffee before we take on the challenge to get to Berlin as fast as possible and safely too.' Sitting down, Bodo asked, 'Comrade, how long are you driving, comrade Tecker? Tell me a little bit about you.'

'I'm now with comrade Tecker for almost eleven years, and before that, I was the driver of General Miller at the 11th infantry division. I'm an auto mechanic by trade, and when I served my three years, I asked the General if he could help me find a professional driver job. He wrote a referral and sent me to the Party's Central Committee.

When I was standing at the front desk to get somebody to talk to, a comrade came down the stairs, looked at me, and asked me what I was doing. I said that I was a driver, and before I could even explain anything, he said, okay, that's what I need. I did not move, so he took my arm, pulled me over to the car pool, signed a paper, grabbed a set of keys, and threw them to me. Let's go. I need to be at the SSP headquarters in 10. We were there in eight minutes, and when we returned to the Central Committee, he said, for whomever you dove so far, you're my driver from now on.'

'That's very impressive. Would you please load my stuff? I'll be out in a minute.' Dieter left the house, and Bodo turned to his wife, hugged her, and with a kiss and a smile, said, 'I'll call you as soon as I can. I just don't have the faintest idea what the next couple of days will look like.'

'I know, Bodo, I know; I wish you all the best and that all that you dreamed of for the sake of our party might become a reality.'

With that, Bodo walked out and entered the car, which was, no wonder because of whom it belonged to, an imported Volvo. He entered the back seat and found his briefcase right next to him. The driver started the engine and turned the car. To Bodo's astonishment, the engine was almost not to hear. The cars he knew were as loud on the inside as outside since sound insulation was either unknown or even at the most expensive available cars, the Soviet license-manufactured Fiat, called Shiguli, ineffective. Using the opportunity to get more information about the lifestyle at the Central Committee, Bodo asked the driver, 'That's a very nice car, do all of the Secretaries have those?'

'Only the Central Committee members, and I believe they need them because they are on the road many hours and miles every month. This car is equipped with a short-wave radio; if necessary, we can call anyone with a phone connection. The call will be scrambled so nobody can understand what is said if we need and back there you have a full equipped office place. You can unfold a desk right out of the arm rest. And the engine, although it was potent originally, was powered up by Volvo before they shipped the car. With that, I'll get you safe and fast to Berlin.'

'I believe you comrade Dieter, but first, we must pass the bottleneck called the Ruegendamm.'

'Unfortunately, that's true, comrade Zipper.'

Driving through the village, which was now his home for about three years, he knew of the people. Right at the end of the village, where the houses stud more and more separately, for a second, he thought he had seen Fritz's care driving down the unpaved driveway to one of those detached farmhouses. But it might have been an illusion. When they passed by the school's sports field, he was tempted to ask the driver to turn into it to say good bye to his son Nick as he saw him playing soccer with his classmates. But he decided not to because they would lose time, and his son would be curious, asking all kinds of questions he could and would not answer. And it would pull a lot of attention towards him, which he wanted to avoid anyway.

After they reached the island's main highway, the driver hit the accelerator, and the car began flying down the road. Yet the engine sound was just like the purr of a cat. Bodo looked out of the front windshield from his back seat for a while and decided to read the New Germany newspaper he had entirely missed by the hustle and bustle during the day. There was a long article analyzing the forces behind those so-called peaceful protests emerging out of churches in more and more cities throughout the country. Most concerning was the increase of the counter-revolutionary movement with increased public demonstrations.

And then, back on page three, an even more interesting yet small and almost missed analysis of the corruption among party leaders in different regions. Although, as the writer stated, nothing was officially provable because nobody wanted to speak out against the often mighty men in their tiny kingdoms. Bodo took out one of his files and made a note about the reporter of this article. He thought talking to this man might be helpful in his new job. And I will own them all. I will own the Island and every taitor to the cause.

Several times he was startled out of his reading because the car made sudden movements when the driver had to pass slower cars and accelerated using all the power of that great engine, which Bodo had never experienced because the distance to the next curve wasn't really long. But he was good and did an excellent job in estimating the distance of the oncoming traffic, the speed of the cars to pass, and the ability of his own car to accelerate enough to pass and still have enough time to decrease the speed before the next curve.

He was again deeply occupied reading the newspaper when he realized that the car hadn't moved for a while. He looked up and, covering his eyes with his hand against the deep hanging sun, he looked forward through the windshield. A long line of cars and trucks was in front of them, moving a couple of yards now and then, only to come to hold again. It took him only a second to realize that they had arrived at the checkpoint at the Ruegendamm. A platoon of the WFF brigade of the Peoples Shipyard Stralsund manned the checkpoint.

'Comrade Zipper, I believe we're at a point where we either stay several hours in line or we're going to use the credentials I have as the driver of comrade Teller.'

'Yea, comrade, this is the checkpoint because of the two criminal Russian soldiers who deserted from their unit a couple of weeks ago.'

'A couple of weeks and not caught yet, unbelievable.'

'That's what I say. They must have help because otherwise they would long have come out of their hidings and try to steel or rob something to eat.'

'We may lose at least an hour here, comrade Zipper.'

'Go ahead and see if you can get us around that line.'

Dieter left the car and walked along the highway to get to the check point. When he came closer to the WFF men, he was spotted by one of them and immediately asked to stop and raise his hands while the man pointed his AK 47 direct at his chest. Two others, also pointing their guns at him, moved from both sides, staying out of the fire line and very professional towards him. One stopped at about ten feed, and the other closed in, taking his AK over his shoulder and moving to his backside. He began to pat him down, 'Who are you, and why are you walking in the dark towards the checkpoint?'

'I'm the driver of the Secretary of the ICC. I was sent to pick up one of the comrades from the county party leadership, comrade Zipper, to bring him to a meeting with Secretary Teller in Berlin. My credentials are in my left-side inner jacket pocket. Can I show it to you?'

'Yes, get it out but very slowly. We are all nervous here because these Russians are Speznaz, and we don't want to have a hand fight with them. We would rather shoot on sight, which we have approval for.'

Dieter slowly moved his hand into his inner pocket and grabbed his Central Committee Special Pass with his thumb and index finger. He pulled it out slowly and handed it over his head backwards to the WFF man. With his flashlight, the WFF man could immediately identify that he had the driver of one of the most powerful men in the nation in front of him.

'You can relax, comrade. I'm sorry, but these guys we're looking for are really dangerous, and we don't want to get caught off guard. Please come with me to the commander.'

Still, their weapon in a ready position, yet not pointed direct at him anymore, the WFF men closed in behind Dieter and the man who seemed to have a say in this group. When they reached the check points command stand, a small wooden cabin was at the side of the road. The group's leader handed the pass to the commander of the checkpoint,

'He is the driver of comrade Teller, Secretary of the ICC, and has comrade Zipper with him, whom he has to bring to Berlin.'

The commander, inspecting the driver pass carefully, took it out of the plastic cover to hold it against the intense light from the cabin's ceiling so that he could clearly see that the seal was embossed. Now sure that everything was right with this guy, he turned towards Dieter,

'Apologies, comrade, but we have to be sure.' And back to his men, 'Make sure the comrade can pass immediately and send one of our motorbikes in front of them over the bridge to get them through the main check point.'

The darkness covered the scene outside the pool of light since the sun had completely disappeared behind the horizon. Some commands and a motorbike appeared out of the darkness. Dieter jumped on the back seat, and the bike was within a few seconds next to his car. The street, closed for oncoming traffic, allowed Dieter to pull out of the line of cars and follow the bike with a flashing light on top of a pole mounted. With increasing speed, they were soon across the bridge and at the main check point where the bike stopped. The man at the checkpoint changed some words and waved him through. Several minutes later, they were out of the city of Stralsund and increasing his speed. Dieter was back in his element.

All that, including the investigation of him at the checkpoint, had taken approximately 15 minutes.

'Did you have difficulties convincing the comrades that we can't wait for several hours?'

'No, no difficulties, but I had to reveal my identity and yours. Otherwise, they would probably have shot me at the spot.' He laughed at his remark, but he was immediately corrected by Bodo, 'Nothing to laugh about, comrade. I hope these men don't talk around too much to make it public that I'm on my way to a meeting with comrade Teller.'

'I'm sorry, comrade Zipper, I did not think about that. Otherwise, I could have them committed to secrecy.'

'Which would have made it even worse because they would have something to speculate about. I'll see that I get a little nap, and you see that you get us to Berlin as best as you can.'

'Yes, comrade'

With that, Bodo tried to make himself as comfortable as possible to get some sleep, and within a few minutes of contemplating the fact that those Russian criminals were still on the run, he dozed away.

CHAPTER 12

NEVER UNDERESTIMATE THE DETERMINATION OF THE WORKERS FIGHTER FORCE

The driving on the island's main highway towards the Ruegendamm went uneventful until Leo reached the end of the colon of cars waiting to get checked by the WFF platoon in charge of that checkpoint before the bridge. There was a second one at the other side of the bridge, but since Leo was driving this route often, he knew those weren't intense in checking. It was mainly the second layer of security, just in case something went wrong.

It was already about ten PM when Leo began his stop-and-go movement towards the armed workers who took their job quite seriously, contrary to what Fritz had promised during the meeting. Every single car and truck was intensively searched with a high level of professionalism, so Leo almost doubted that this was regular WFF troops. All people in the car were forced out, had to have their hands behind the neck folded, and stand in line at the side of the street facing the fields, guarded by two members of the group pointing their AK47 direct at their backs. Two others were standing at the front and one at the back of the car, far enough off not to get attacked from inside the car suddenly. Two others would carefully investigate the inside of the car and the trunk. This procedure was repeated with slight changes depending on the car or truck type.

Then nothing happened for about 20 minutes at all. Leo wondered what was going on when he realized that the soldiers at the barricade got replaced. He understood that he had almost run into the wrong platoon because he was too early. He had approximately twelve to fifteen vehicles in front of him and could watch the change in the behavior of the WFF members. Those at the cars were still very careful not to be attacked by surprise, but the cars' investigation was much more cursory. And the guys at the barricade seemed to have a lot of fun and laughed a lot.

Then his truck was the one to be searched. Carefully obeying the commands, he slowly opened the door and stepped down to the ground. Then he folded his hands behind his neck and walked over to the field. The group leader took the motion task papers from his dashboard and came over to him to ask some standard questions,

'You're coming from?'

'Dranske'

'The truck belongs to?'

'Peoples Shipyard Stralsund'

'What's your payload?'

'Matrasses'

'Your license plate?'

'AH 89-54'

During all that time, two of the group were pointing their guns at his back and the other two at the truck while the other two were searching the cabin. Although he could not see anything, he knew the pattern. Then he heard the security rope of the tart being loosened and the part being lifted. He was confident that none of these guys would bother to move 100 mattresses to investigate if the Russians were hidden under them. Yet his heart rate increased, and a cold sweat began to cover his body.

Tapp! The steel-nailed boots of the WFF man hitting the asphalt with a loud noise jumping down from the truck, 'Nothing here,' came the call from the back of the truck, and Leo nearly let out a sigh of relief and could just hold his breath. The group leader tapped his shoulder with the motion task paper, 'Here is your motion task. You're free to go.'

'Thanks,' Leo was almost at the truck's door when the group leader called after him, 'Wait, one more question.' Leo's blood curled, 'Yea?'

'Did you see anything suspicious on your way up to Dranske and back?' Hesitating for a moment and slowly shaking his head, Leo answered, 'No, nothing out of the ordinary.'

'OK, get out here and see that you get home.'

With a deep feeling of relief, Leo entered the cabin, closed the door, and started the engine. Slowly steering the truck around the barricade of the checkpoint, he accelerated to the standard speed limit and was soon at the second checkpoint, where he was just waved through. Following the main highway for several miles out of the city, he finally reached the side street where he turned right and then again a right turn and another mile, and he arrived at his grandparents' farm.

He drove past the main yard door, stopped, and backed towards the large two-winged door. He jumped out of the cabin and unlocked a small door that was built into one of the two large door wings. He went through it, turned a large square-shaped timber from horizontal into a vertical position, rotated it out of the two heavy steel locks on each door wing, and opened both wings. He walked back to the truck whose engine was still running, climbed into the cabin, and backed the truck very professionally, even in pitch-black darkness, right through the open doors of the huge barn at the end of the yard. He shut down the engine and let out a deep, drawn sight.

Jumping out of the truck, he closed the yard door and walked back to the cargo area. In a low voice but clearly hearable without the engine noise, he called the Russian refugees,

'Brothers, you can come out now. You're safe for the time being.' Some noise from the back of the cargo area and movement of the tarp where pushed mattresses hit it indicated that they had heard him, and a few moments later, the older one, Nicolai, put his head forward.

'Brother, you sure? Commen out herr?'

'Yea, come out. Both we need to get in the house.'

Nicolai jumped down from the cargo bed, and Oleg followed. Since he was still somewhat weak, Nicolai supported him, and they walked the short way from the barn to the house together. Leo opened the door and called, 'I'm back, grandma, and I have visitors with me.'

A small woman with short-cut gray hears and a friendly smile under her glasses came around the corner into the hallway.

'Leo, could you not tell me before you left that you'd bring your friends? I'd have made something to eat. Now I'm not ready to put something on the table.' Leo embraced his grandma and then turned around and introduced the Russian soldiers to her,

'Grandma, this is Nicolai, and this is Oleg. Both are those allegedly incredibly dangerous criminal soldiers who dared to flee from the Soviet base last month. Thanks to like-minded Christian freedom fighters on the island, they could be hidden and get medical treatment at least. Oleg had flu and is still weak. Both are brothers in Christ and need our help.'

What are you keeping them here in the hallway? Do you want them to die?'

'Come in, brothers,' she now talking to the Russians, 'Come in, I'll get you something warm to eat, and then I'll go and prepare two guest rooms' Oh Lord, what is it in this world that they can't let these young man be home with their families' she murmured before herself, and everybody followed her into the kitchen. She was immediately busy fanning the flames in the huge coal-burning stove, checking the water basin at the side of the stove, and when she discovered that it wasn't completely filled, she asked Leo to get some fresh water from the pump in the yard. Within a few minutes, Leo was back with two buckets of water which he used to fill that water basin at the edge of the stove. The fire was now up and burning, and grandma was moving pots and pans around, creating a hot meal from the leftovers of the dinner she had prepared for her and Leo, but he did not show up as it happened often.

In the meantime, Leo put plates and silverware on the table and filled glasses with fresh water he had filled from the second bucket into a pitcher.

'Don't be shy. Drink, and your food will be ready in a minute,' encouraged the Russians to relax and make themselves comfortable. Hesitating, yet with visible joy, both seem to realize, for the first time in many years, that they were safe and did not have to be afraid that the door could fly open at any given moment. That an officer would beat the soul out of them to get his will done faster than he even knew himself what that will was.

Both emptied their glass in one big gulp, and Leo realized that they might have had nothing to eat or drink for several hours. Especially for Oleg, that must be feeling horrible. He filled the glasses again and said,

'You can drink as much as you want, just take it whenever you need, and when grandma is done with the meal, you can eat as much as you get swallowed down. Don't be shy. Feel home, please.'

They both smiled again, 'Brother, we goott for thankink you and friend from island. With no help, we dead already. And we shot; we be beaten dead. Have seen many times in Afghanistan. Lost many comrades because not fight dirty war for officer wanted tried to flee. Dying hanging on ankles with head inches over the nest of wasps which had the nest in earth hole,' Nicolai let only a small piece of the horrible experience they had gone through out in these few words, but it was enough to make Leo's blood curl and grandma, putting a vast pan sizzling hot, with meat and potatoes and red cabbage wonderfully fragrant, on the table,

'Why don't we thank and ask the Lord to be with us while we get you filled a little bit so that you can sleep well?' Leo and all bowed their heads, and Leo prayed, 'Dear Lord, we thank you for your protection for our Russian brothers and for the guidance we had. We thank you for being here with us as the scripture says, and for the food, we can provide, in Jesus's name.' And all said, 'Amen'

'I'll go upstairs and prepare the rooms for our guests,' grandma said and was on her way out, only to be stopped by Nicolai, 'Grandma, I call you allow that? Please Oleg and I one room? Please he ill and I want watch for Oleg?'

'No problem, Nicolai, it might not be as comfortable for tonight, but tomorrow we will see what we can do.' Turned around and walked to the stairs.

'Ok, friends, I need to give you some instructions. We are living in a so-called square-yard farmhouse. The street front is built by the house and the huge two-winged door. It is closed on the south side with that big barn where I parked the truck. The east and west side is close with some additional barns. You can walk around inside the yard any time you want, but let grandma know at any time where you are. People from the village come during the day and usually ring the bell one can hear everywhere throughout the yard. Please don't move the curtains during the day in your room or switch on the light when dark, because this room is on the street and you can be seen. We will have a doc here tomorrow or the day after, and he will check Oleg. You need to get some rest, and in the meantime, we will prepare your transfer to the next step towards the border.

Nicolai and Oleg grinned from one ear to the other. 'We sleep in a real bed, you said, walking on sunny day in yard' Oleg asked with unbelief that he would be able to walk in the fresh air in daylight after so many weeks of hiding and only coming out of it in nights.

'Yes, you can walk outside in daylight and enjoy the sun if it shines. But please be careful, we're somewhat separate from the village, but people come by during the day. It is a normal street in front of the house.'

'How many time we stay?' Nicolai asked to get a more practical sense back into the discussion.

'I don't know, Nicolai, I really don't know. We have to establish contacts with groups we're not connected to yet, which takes time because we have to be very careful. It is not only about you; we have built connections with other groups and hope we get you transferred through those groups toward the border. The most difficult part is to get through the borderline. We cannot help you with that; we can only bring you undetected as close as possible. The breakthrough is up to you.'

'No worry, Leo, we soldiers have special training. We get through borderline. Need in good shape and healthy,' he said with a sidelong glance at Oleg.'

'We will get you there, Nicolai, I promise. But as I said, we must be very careful, which means sticking with the rules and having patience.'

Grandma appeared at the kitchen door and told them the room was ready for them.

Leo walked with them upstairs and showed them the guest bathroom and bedroom which was separated by a wall with a door from his area since it was many years ago the living space of his parent before his dad became a military-bonze and, with that, his apartment at the garrison city. Since he knew that grandma had everything prepared, he did not bother to check for towels and pajamas, wished them a good night, and remembered the rules again. He left them alone.

When he entered the kitchen, grandma was already done with the dishes and sitting on the kitchen table reading her bible as she always did at the end of the day. She looked up at Leo,

'You could have told me you are about bringing guests, especially those special guests.'

'I'd have granny, you know. But I did not know I'd bring them myself until this afternoon when I met our contact in Sassnitz.'

'I see. Was it difficult to get through the checkpoints at the dam?'

'Not more than I thought it would be. I almost blew it because I was too early. But that was because of the group that garrison the checkpoint when I was about to be checked. Just two cars in front of me changed the troops. Those guys who were released were awful thoroughly.'

'Praise the Lord that you did not get caught. I'm going now. Do you need anything?'

'No, granny, I'm fine. I'll just read a bit and go to bed too. It was a long day. I have to be at the shipyard at 6 AM. Good night' He hugged grandma, and she went back to the section of the house where the bedroom on the first floor was.

Leo shut off the light and walked upstairs to his area. After he was done in the bathroom, he sat down in his room, which was large enough to have a bed, a seating area with a couch ad chairs, and a working area with a large desk. The desk actually belonged to his granddad, but grandma gave it to him. Sitting down in one of the chairs with his bible in his hands, Leo looked at the desk, and his thoughts began to wander to the events of the day at first, but then farther back into the past, a past which wasn't really long ago, but as more horrible, as he could bear anytime he thought about it.

CHAPTER 13

YOU CAN BLOW A MILITARY CAREER EVEN WITH A GENERAL AS FATHER

Leo's grandpa was a renowned and widely accepted leader of the agricultural collective. His father, at least that was what was planned, should follow grandpa's steps and study agricultural science at the university. But during his last year in high school, he suddenly decided to become an army officer. Since he was a parachutist with the Association for Sports and Technique for many years, he had no problems getting promised to become a paratrooper. This was very special; you usually needed connections to the top of the Army to get that arranged. Grandpa wasn't really happy and expressed that at any appropriate or inappropriate opportunity. That led to a lot of trouble between them, and grandma had to smooth the waves.

Right after finishing high school, Leo's dad went to the Army Academy and excelled in all subjects. When he was done after for years, he was immediately sent to special training to become an officer at the paratrooper. He finished on top of his class and was commanded to the island. Leading a platoon of paratroopers that included two very experienced NCOs was a great advantage for his further career. He learned a lot of things during the daily practice which wasn't taught at the academy.

When he met his wife, he was already on a steep path to a top position within this elite troop of the nation's military. Leo had a very great childhood. Since his mother's grandparents owned a large house in Sassnitz, he had the chance to grow up among other children whose parents were not with the military. He admired his father, who was sent to the Soviet military academy, which was usually necessary to go through if you wanted to get promoted above the rank of captain. And because of his excellent results, he was granted an additional one-year training with the Soviet's special troops 'Spetznaz.' When they had military parades on the national holiday, he walked proudly at his dad's hand with his uniform filled with medals.

And with that, it was no wonder that Leo applied for membership at the AST to begin his training as a parachutist. Over a few years, he was one of the best and the leader of the competitive team of their hometown organization. But the school did not go as well as his parents would like. His mother's parents died when he was 6 in a car accident, and his mother had a tough time and was hospitalized for depression treatment for several months. And died a few years after the death of her parents.

With the irregularity of his father's service at the garrison, he was often at his father's parents for many months, and he loved them dearly. One reason was grandma, a good soul, and another was the tractors and machines at grandpa's barns. He spent many hours with grandpa repairing machines, taking engines apart, replacing parts, and putting them together. And it was always a great moment when grandpa told him to turn the key to start an engine they had just finished repairing.

When the time came to decide about his future career, he was not willing to go to college. He decided to go through special education to become a diesel engine mechanic at the local people-owned Fishery Corporation. He had a two-year education and graduated as the best of three classes. Yet he had not neglected his hobby at the AST. On the contrary, since several military training weeks were mandatory during school, he improved his military and parachuting skills. When the drafting officer saw his records from the AST, he offered him to be drafted to the paratroopers. Although the officer did not know that Leo's father was actually an officer at that regiment, he knew from his file that his father was an officer with the army. Since paratroopers had to serve at least three years, Leo had to sign for that period, but that wasn't really a problem since he was a perfect product of the nation's education system, which meant he knew his obligations.

He went through the boot camp without any trouble or difficulties since he had always been active. He actually graduated from boot camp as the second best. Upon arrival at the operative troops of the paratrooper regiment, he was immediately recognized as the son of the regiment's commander. At the specific request of his father, he became a member of the second battalion. And for whatever reasons he never really could find out, his platoon leader seemed to have a specific interest in him. Leo was chosen to fulfill every single of the lowest possible jobs the platoon leader could find. And he was never fast enough through the obstacle course or the swimming exercises. But he enjoyed being part of the country's most secret and famous military unit and the hard training, including tactic, shooting, and hand-to-hand combat, which totaled almost 1200 hours every year. He loved all the challenges so much that he thought about extending his service with the military to a ten-year obligation, considering a military career as a high-ranking NCO.

Then all changed, and his fun, playing Special Forces soldier of the worker's paradise army became a burden.

Grandpa got sick. Very sick. He had a severe heart condition, and the doctors were very concerned because his health decreased rapidly. It took them several weeks to discover that a specific virus was reducing the heart muscle strength, and all they could do was reduce the progress. There was a solution; the doctors knew about that, but it wasn't available in the overachieving country of the Worker's paradise. Although he has been brainwashed all his life that the rotten capitalistic system was on the edge of collapse, it appeared to have everything that made life easier or even saved lives when necessary. At least not for the average citizen. Suppose grandpa was allowed to visit his brother, who was living in the other part of the separated German nation, that detested rotten capitalistic Germany. That enemy of the worker's paradise was about to attack the peace-loving communistic part of Germany at any moment. If he could just visit his brother, he would have a chance of complete healing within a few weeks. But, there was that huge but. That but was his son, Leo's father.

Since he had just been promoted to Lieutenant General and was at the top command of the country's army's most secret Special Forces unit, grandpa needed a special travel allowance to leave the country. Even though he had the age at which people usually would not be denied to travel to the workers' class enemy's territory, he needed a particular signature. When Leo was home on one of the rear weekend leave of absence, he considered his grandparent's house more home than his father's house, and suddenly his father arrived. Since Leo wasn't under his direct command, his father did not know that Leo was home, and Leo had no intention of meeting with him. One reason was that he knew about the struggle of grandpa to get his travel allowance to his brother in the West. He knew his father had refused to do anything to help him so far, yet to the contrary, he hadn't even answered grandpa's multiple attempts to reach out to him for help, not once.

Since the door to his room was open, Leo could hear his father and his grandpa's reasoning about the quality of the nation's healthcare system and how great it was that everybody had healthcare for free. Suddenly, the voice level increased, turning into an argument.

'What does a free health care system mean to those fighting a fatal disease curable in the rotten capitalistic world with a handful of pills the highly praised free health care system can't provide?' Grandpa was getting cynical now.

'You should hear yourself praising the enemy of a nation you fought all your life to build as a stepping stone into a better world.' His father answered, 'You have no right to destroy my career only because you believe that the physicians are not able to get you the best possible treatment. We have the best in the world. They know who you are and how hard you worked building the socialistic agricultural victory in our nation. They appreciate all your fight for socialism here. They know they could study and become the best doctors because of people like you.'

'Son, now you should hear yourself. Are you telling me that these doctors will heal me by reading from Marx's Capital or Lenins' State and Revolution' grandpa was bouncing out the words now, and it was clear to Leo that he was agitated and barely he got enough breath to speak.

'I can't listen to this defeatist talk. You can't blame our socialistic fatherland for your illness. Where is your pride as a comrade? Will you throw the cause of the liberation of the workers of all nations out because you got sick?'

Obviously, This was too much for grandpa to take, and Leo was surprised to hear words like that spoken by someone who fought his whole life at the front row of the SUP as the well-known leader in the area and most highly appreciated by many, even non-comrades. Rising his voice with, even upstairs, sensible struggle to breathe since his heart was almost too weak to pump the blood through his body in the time necessary,

'I spend my life fighting for the cause, but all I see what we accomplished is degeneration. Only idiots can still believe the heroic and pathetic smearing in the papers. While we get told day-by-day lies after lies about the victorious socialistic achievements, the reality shows a different image. The centers of the cities with hundreds of years of history are falling apart. The work ethic, once envied by the world, is devastated. Our productivity is that of a third world nation and the products you can buy if they are even available, have no quality. And then you look over to the other side of that deathly fence where capitalism is slowly rotting, and you see just the opposite of what we have. And you tell me I shall die believing in these lies? All you need to do is to sign this piece of paper, and I'll get what I need to live some more years. Is that asked too much from a father to his son?'

The silence was defining, and Leo, although he could not see them, could feel the icy hatred crawling up the stairs.

Then his father, speaking with a voice he could barely identify as his, 'I'll never sign a letter like that. I swore an oath to the party and this nation. What you ask me to do is equal to breaking that oath.' He obviously jumped off his chair, because Leo could hear the noise of it flying through the kitchen, even though grandma was now yelling what he was thinking about talking to his father that way.

Now fearing that it may get violent, Leo was on his way downstairs when he heard his father, 'I do not have a father anymore. This is the home of a traitor, and I've nothing in common with those.' He slammed the door and was already in his car and out of the farmyard when Leo was down.

The agitation of the argument was too much for his grandpa. Even though the ambulance was there within 20 minutes, which was a miracle and it would be the only miracle, Leo's grandpa died three days later at the hospital. His heart just failed. His father did not attend the funeral, and Leo was so angry that the confrontation with him ended in him knocking his father out cold in his own office. He was court-martialed and was not sent to prison but dishonorably discharged because of his father's intervention and high reputation. This was the turning point in his life. Because of this, he could not get the seaman's book back to work at a fishing trawler and was ordered to work as a truck driver for the shipyard in his grandparents' town. He moved in with grandma, and she returned to her old, well-known optimism that the future could not be worse. The dishonorable discharge included expulsion from the party, which saved him a lot of additional trouble because he would have applied for that if it would not happen. It took him several months to open up to his grandma about the deep discouragement with where the country was going and that his father had put his career and position over the life of his own father. First it was somewhat strange to him, since he had been told all his life that believing in GOD was something only stupid or mentally ill people would do. And grandma led him to the bible.

Beginning reading the bible, he realized that some of it made more sense than the stuff he had learned in school. And mainly because grandma was just asking questions. It took almost three years, but finally, he could pray for forgiveness and took Jesus as his Lord and Savior. He found the connection to a group of people his age at the church in town and was really surprised when his former NCO appeared one day at one of the Wednesday night meetings. That was when all started, and finally, the group separated from the youth group at the church because they discovered that the group was infiltrated and one of the youth pastors was actually a spy for the SSP.

Shaking his head, he came out of his dream with open eyes, and when he looked at his bible in his lap, he was at

Jas 2:26: For as the body without the spirit is dead, faith without works is also dead. (KJV)

It was time to go to bed; the next day would be another hard one.

Leo was up earlier in the morning than usual because he wanted to be at the shipyard before the daily routine began. He wrote a short note for the Russians to stay away from the windows and to be careful when being outside to avoid discovery. After a cup of coffee and a slice of bread with some fresh cold cuts, he went out, opened the yard door, drove the truck out of the yard, and closed the huge two-winged door as quietly as possible not to wake up his new-found Russian brothers in Christ. Then he was on his way to the shipyard.

After about 25 minutes of an uneventful drive, he stopped at the shipyard checkpoint, and after the guard had a brief look at his travel orders and exchanged a few words about the men the Russians were still looking for, he was allowed to enter. Now, it never happened that the guards just waved him through. Although they had known him for almost two years now, and they knew the truck he was driving was owned by the shipyard, they would always check the driving orders. But since these two Russians deserted, they were even more careful, checked the loading area, and even looked into the cabin. But mostly when he was leaving and not this morning at that early time. The mattresses were soon unloaded, and the day's work had him immediately covered with all kinds of transportation requirements.

CHAPTER 14

EVEN COMMUNISTS LOVE LUXURIOUS ACCOMMODATIONS

T he car stopped in front of a huge door, and when Dieter pressed a button at the car console, it began to move upwards, giving way to the underground garage. But the way was blocked by a kind of steel gate, and only now Bodo realized that a small side door opened and a guard came out. Dieter showed his credentials, the guard gave a signal, and the steel gate disappeared into the street.

He drove down the ramp and parked the car right at the door. At the same moment, the door opened, and Karl came out with a big smile, and Bodo had to hurry to get out of the car to be ready to greet him. 'Comrade Bodo, I'm so glad you're here now, and I hope you had a safe and comfortable journey. Dieter sometimes takes fast a little too seriously, and since he is an excellent driver, you may get thrown around, even in a car like this.'

'Glad to see you too again, comrade Karl, and no, Dieter did not exaggerate the demonstration of his excellent driving skills.'

'Happy to hear that. Please stay ready, Dieter. You may wait at the guard area, where I can call you when I want to leave. Please, comrade Bodo follow me. We have arranged for your accommodation at the guest house of the Central Committee where you're currently, you may have noticed.'

Walking through the door into a hallway that led directly to a large lift, Bodo said, 'No, I did not notice because I thought we would be at the Central Committee Building direct. Mainly that is because I have never been here and secondly because of the tight security.'

While they waited for the lift, Karl explained, 'We have to have that here too, not only because of several international guests we accommodate here but also because of the increasing security concerns based on the current state of the country.'

'Did you actually have incidents with the criminal counter-revolutionists here, comrade Karl?'

'Not here and not directly targeted at one of the leaders, at least not in the immediate past, but there was an attempt some years ago when the motorcade of Secretary Bruno was attacked.'

The room was on the top floor, and when Bodo went through the door, he stopped in awe because it was not a room. It was a suite.

'We thought we would comfort you and put you on the top floor where nobody else usually stays. We know the next few days will be tough, and you might not have much time to sleep, but at least you will have a quiet place to rest and work.'

'Thank you so much, comrade Karl.' What is my schedule, and what is the agenda for the next days?'

'OK, first of all, we can skip the comrade since we both know we're comrades, and we're at the start of a complicated and hopefully successful reform process. So please call me Karl whenever we're not at an official meeting, and I'll just call you Bodo. Is that OK with you?'

'Sure comr…, uh, I mean Karl. Might take a while to get used to it.'

'Understood. Here is the rough schedule for you, which may change in one way or another depending on the actual situation during the coming days. Tomorrow at 8 AM. we will have a car at the garage, the same place where I picked you up. We will have a meeting with Secretary Bruno at 8:30 AM. In the afternoon, currently scheduled at 5 PM. you will be at the meeting of the new Central Committee to present yourself and answer questions about you, your career and work with the party. It is not required to present a plan or scenario of how you'd process the assignment. I have developed a framework for establishing a special agency inside the party. You would lead the agency to cleanse the party and the party-controlled organizations. Also, all corruption and filthiness grew throughout those over the last 30 years. Here is my three-page framework. I want you to go over it and develop your agency based on that framework because it has already been given the general approval by the members of the Central Committee.'

'When do I need to outline the structure and bullet points to present it?'

'I'm not sure yet. It depends foremost on the impression the Central Committee members get from you tomorrow. Suppose you can convince them that you're the right person. It might be required within three or four days.'

Wow, not much time, but since I have been thinking about what needs to be done to get this nation back on its track toward the great communistic nation we once dreamed about, as Marx and Lenin described it in their writings, I do not need much time. I want to get some organizational structure into place, though.'

'What do you think you'd need immediately?'

'Some kind of office structure, I mean secretary, phone, and so on?'

'Don't worry about that. We will get you a secretary working for you here at your office.'

'Do you mean this suite includes an office?'

'Oh, I'm sorry; I was so occupied with telling you what's ahead that I forgot to show you around. As you can see, we're in the living room currently. There, on the right-hand side, this French double door opens to a completely equipped office. Come, have a look.' They walked over to the door, and when Karl opened it, Bruno almost thought he was dreaming. The office was as large as the living room and had two desks. One was huge, really large, with a phone on top that he had never seen in his life. It was one of those mysterious touch-tone phones Bodo had heard about. And the other desk was a little smaller, almost enclosed by shelf and drawer cabinets, and had the same type of phone.'

'That's the place for your secretary, and she can enter the office through that separate door directly from the floor. We will have one for you starting tomorrow.' Turning around, Karl led Bodo across the living room to the other side, where an equal French door opened to the bedroom. On the right-hand side, right behind the huge bed, was the door to the bathroom, which was almost luxurious, equipped with a large bathtub, a shower, and a separate toilet. Again, Bodo was astounded by the size and the comfort that room promised.

'Now, did I promise too much, Bodo? See, it is not that we, the party's leadership, indulge ourselves in luxury while the workers have to fight with some inconveniences. Still, this building is for our international guests from brother parties worldwide, and we wanted to comfort them.'

'Oh, I completely understand that we have to differentiate between our guests and us, especially when they come from countries where they are oppressed and still have to fight for the freedom of the worker's class.'

'Now, you understand, I just wanted to make sure that you know it's for our special guests, and for some days, the central committee and I want you to feel like that. When everything is approved, your day will change in a few days, and you may think back on this nice place more often than not. I'll let you alone now, have a good night. See you tomorrow at the office.'

With that, Karl turned around and walked out of the suite.

CHAPTER 15

THE COMMUNIST LEADERSHIP HAD ENOUGH EVIDENCE TO SENT THE REBELL TO THE SHIPYARD

Early April weather in the coastal area was always very unpredictable and could change within minutes. On that day, arriving from another trip, Leo was at the material storage building early, and although the air was fresh from the light breeze coming in from southeast over the Sund, it promised to be a nice day with a lot of sunshine. He thought about the enormous transition the country had undergone during the last few days and wondered how they would absorb the increase of oppression as he walked over to Billy's office. He knocked on the door in a particular, unsuspicious rhythm and walked in, and almost fell down the two steps of stairs. Billy's office was lower than the ground level, and because he was so much caught by what he saw, he paid no attention. Fritz was sitting at the small meeting table with a bright green on his face, 'Leo, watch your steps. We need your ability to drive the truck to support the great socialist worker's efforts.'

'Fritz, great to see you here, but what happened? Shouldn't you come to this place without an official reason? You could endanger all of us. You know that.'

'Calm down, Leo. I was just about to tell Billy why I was here and how that happened. Now, since you're here, I have to tell it once less,' he said, smiling, embracing Leo, and all sitting down again.

'After we separated at the closing of our last meeting, carefully watching my back for trailers, I drove home since I had taken the day off because I did not know when you would be able to arrive. When I arrived home, my wife told me that my boss had sent somebody to tell me that I had to go to my company's headquarters in Rostock and be there in the morning. I had a very nice, unpleasant conversation with our HR manager and two SSP officers about the conspired connection to the class enemy for about an hour. I was questioned, and they told me that I'd lost my mind believing in GOD and how I could be so stupid to declare that publicly. To make the story short, I was punished with removal from my job at the naval base, had to report to the shipyard division of our company, and here I'm. I'm now forbidden to work on anything close to radio transceiver systems. Besides the problems I have now with going home every night, I had to rearrange the leadership team of our cell on the island. Since my number two was a great talented leader from the beginning, it wasn't a big deal with him. But convincing the other three guys on the leadership team was not easy. Now that's done, the cell works and is as solid as before, and I'm here and need work.' With a bright smile, he added, 'you know what work I mean, do you?'

'I can only guess, was Leo's answer,' greening back at Fritz. 'So your firm has you now doing what? Are you working for our board or at the shop?'

'I'm at the test and setup team for the winches and generators. I'm not allowed to touch any transceiver anymore. But I believe this took me out of the immediate focus of the SSP. With that, I may be even more valuable for the movement.'

'Do you have something specific in mind? Billy asked, 'not that I want to know too much, but if you want to join our group, we need to know what is going on.'

'Don't get me wrong, guys, but I'd rather start my little action and keep you out of that for security reasons. But I need your help from time to time, and you and the whole movement will benefit from it.'

Moving closer to Billy's desk, Fritz caught the attention of both and continued with his voice down to a whisper, 'I have almost finished the development of a microprocessor-based transceiver. Especially now since I can't get home during the week.'

'What can we do to get that done,' Billy asked. 'We are no electronic gurus like you may need, and none of us understands a bit of how these things work.'

'That's not the help I need. I want you to agree to a secret meeting at your place, and we can discuss my idea in a more secure area.'

Billy and Leo looked at each other, and then Billy said, 'I need to contact the others, and I will let you know. Leo is your contact. Stay safe.'

With that, Fritz said good buy and left the material manager's office.

Fritz, immediately after he broke off with the communist party, realized that there would be a need to have the possibility to exchange information with friends and like-minded people. His knowledge of the communist party's doctrine and their suppressing tool, the State Security Police, the result of years of training in the system, allowed him to see the writing on the wall. Analyzing the situation of the current state of the nation led to the conclusion that there were only two ways, either the total opening of the borders, which would end in the final unification of West and East Germany or the installation of a total authoritarian and open dictatorship, eliminating the fake parliament and all parties but the SUP.

With this early cognizance, he went to work. He spent almost every spar hour developing a solution for a communication system that would allow connecting all underground operating resistance groups by exchange of information. His connection with former classmates working in different electronic companies throughout East Germany gave him access to almost non-existent components. The two largest electronic component shops were located in Berlin. His friend and former classmate Reinhard Ponta was a tinkerer and worked on a device to record TV signals in digital form. He lived in Berlin and was always willing to spend his spare time on the hunt for components he and Fritz could potentially use.

Over the last two years, Fritz solved a lot of issues with getting designed the radio and creating a stable connection between the digital-to-analog converter and both the radio on the analog side and the microcomputer on the digital side. One of the toughest issues was the inability to know whether or not the microcomputer chips he received from another friend were functioning. He had no way to test them until they were integrated into the designed circuitry. And only after he was a hundred percent sure that his analog output circuitry and the digital input circuitry were functioning correctly could he know that the microcomputer was the reason for failure. He had finally finished the design, using a plug base for the microcomputer, which allowed him to run a basic test for flashing the program, program a few datasets, and transmit those datasets to a second unit via radio. A tremendous help was the literature he had collected at the stands during the Leipziger Exhibition. He received later even more application instructions from the West German and an Italian representative of the US company Texas Instruments. Although specific for their components, those application instructions were extremely helpful in calculating the oscillator circuits. It was just a shame that the SSP appeared two days after he got the big books from Italy and confiscated two because he had them open in his tinkering room where he was working. They seemed unaware of how many he had gotten and didn't even ask for the TI books from West Germany. That saved the whole project. And now he had a system that exactly worked how he had envisioned it.

The microcomputer and the radio were transmitting at 765.005 MHz and receiving at 765.500MHz. Thus he could use several parts of the radio for both functions, and the whole communicator fit in a small plastic box the size of a cigarette package. It was equipped with a reed contact that switched the communicator on and off with a magnet. The point for the magnet was marked with a small red dot, and the sequence was 3 seconds for on and 6 seconds for off.

To test the battery lifetime, Fritz had one of the first finished and functional communicators active for over two years, and the battery still sends a 65% charging level. The communicator was programmed to wait after the activation for 2 minutes to receive data or analysis requests and would go into sleep modus after that time. Then, it would wake up every 10 minutes and run on low power mode, which meant that only the receiver section was powered. It would shut down after 30 seconds with no signal received to a programmed sleep cycle running only the timer and the wake-up circuit. That guaranteed very long battery life.

The data were loaded with a handheld unit that looked very much like a calculator. A display with five lines of 25 characters and a standard calculator keyboard was all that was needed to program the data into the communicator

The system was based on groups of numbers with five characters in each group and four groups in a row. The number of rows of data programmed was only limited by the data memory size of 128kb.

For the last eight months, Fritz field-tested his communicator at two places. Both places were on the road to his workplace and pretty well hidden, in his opinion. One was in the socket of e sculpture for the men lost at sea. Some years ago, when he was still active in the communist youth organization, he had organized a clean-up of the area where that memorial was. While doing so, he discovered, by chance, that the memorial was set on the socket but not fixed. It was kept in place by its weight, and when he accidentally stumbled and hit the memorial with his body, he realized that an empty space was under the partly lifted memorial. The second unit was in the soffit area of a small shop that sold handmade soaps. The owner had asked him several years ago to mount a light over the shop door, and when he had the unit ready to be field-tested, he told her he needed to check the wires to ensure there was no short circuit because mice could have chewed the insolation.

On his way home from work, he would find a reason to sit down in a nearby small coffee shop or place flowers at the memorial. Since he was known as a former electrical engineer on a fishing trawler, it wasn't unusual to do that.

He would need a few minutes to wait, having his 'calculator' in activation mode. When the communicator woke up, the calculator would connect, receive the data stored on the unit and send a new data set. The calculator's buttons for [M+] and [M−] would initiate the functions. The transmission power was very low, on purpose, because he wanted to avoid detection of the signal by chance, and the battery life was directly related to the power used when transmitting. The signal was at the minimum level when he was inside the small cafe across the street from the device. He had to sit at the windows and direct the antenna of the calculator device optimal for the receiving unit to initiate the exchange. Even at very low temperatures during the winter months, he could get good connectivity and read and transmit signals without issues.

It was time to get them out in the country and connect the different resistance groups. He had 21 units ready and had enough material to build 10 more. Fritz was already in contact with his sources to arrange for the purchase of another ten microcomputers. He wanted to always have a reserve in case a unit failed and needed to be replaced. He needed the Stralsund underground resistance group to spread the communicators throughout the country and hoped they could. Although several of his former classmates were politically in agreement with Fritz and despised the communist system that hindered them from making the most of their education and ambitions to invent and develop new ideas, they were not at a point to actively work with the resistance. He knew Reinhard and Bernd but none of the others. Maybe Bernd and Reinhard had contacts in other regions of the country who were willing to risk all to destroy the communist system. But first, he would talk to the SUR (Stralsund Underground Resistance).

CHAPTER 16

NO RAIN DOES NOT MEAN A SECURE WALK TO THE SECRET PLACE

Even though the day had been slightly warmer and it had not rained, April on the Baltic Sea coast could still be fresh and, after sunset, really chilly.

Fritz was on his way to the secret meeting place, and although he was relatively sure that the SSP did not consider him a current person of interest, he used all the skills developed over the last two years to ensure he wasn't followed. The city of Stralsund offers many more opportunities to check if he has a tail, even when there are two or three who substitute each other to make it more challenging to be detected. One of his best tools to detect the SSP guys was to walk to the bus station close to his apartment, where he stayed during the week since it was too far to go home every night. It wasn't the distance, but much more the time it took with the most unreliable public transportation system. You never knew when the train would be on time. And although some workers at the shipyard used the train to travel every day, none of them traveled farther than to the main city of the Island, Bergen.

At the bus station, he jumped into the first bus arriving, no matter what line it was and where it went. He always planned enough time to get to places when he had to ensure to arrive without a tail. The easiest detection was when someone suddenly ran from a corner or an entrance across the street to catch the bus. He walked to the back of the bus and watched if there was a car suddenly leaving its parking place and followed the bus since nobody jumped in the bus before it left the bus stop. That was not the case; with that, he was already pretty sure he wasn't under observation. But to be on the safe side, he left the bus at the second stop, crossed the Frankenstreet, and entered the small Jacobiturmstreet that led between the destroyed Jacobi Church and some broken down houses to Langenstreet. He turned right and, after a few hundred yards, left into Jacobichorstreet.

This was a very small street, actually more like a walkway with completely uninhabitable houses on both sides. Windows and doorways boarded up. While the inner cities of many towns fall apart, the outskirts of them grow by the hundreds of apartments every year using cheap pre-cast concrete blocks to stack story onto story without any comfort. These houses demonstrated the whole misery of the communist system within less than a mile. He had to cross Papenstreet to get to the ruin where the entrance to the secret meeting place was. But he still had time and wanted a last check to be sure. He entered a small shop on Papenstreet where an older lady sold useless stuff for tourists who had not yet arrived since it was just the beginning of April. Looking at some of the figures formed out of the so-called firestones, he used the possibility to watch what was going on o the street, especially the small Jacobichorstreet, which he could see for almost the whole length.

In the meantime, the sun was completely set, and the few streetlights in Papenstreet, of which one was right at the crossing with Jacobichorstreet, weren't able to really light up anything.

He excused himself and left the shop, disappearing in the dark, crossing Papenstreet outside of the range of the street lights. He walked close to the wall as he entered Jacobichorstreet. He stopped two houses before the entrance to the secret meeting location and stepped into the doorway, which was boarded up but still gave room to hide.

After a short waiting, he crossed the small Jacobichorstreet and walked to the entrance, which was the remains of a completely broken down doorway of a no longer existing house, and with a low voice, uttered the challenge for the day, 'Zu Dionise dem Tyrannen.' A few seconds later, he heard the answer, 'Schlich Moeros den Dolch im Gewande.'

He walked through the opening and greeted Willy. 'You are the last one. Let's go in. I am freezing.' With that, Willi turned, and Fritz followed into the basement of the no longer existing house after carefully crossing the overgrown former garden.

After everyone was settled in the small basement room, lit by some candlelight, Billy opened the meeting with a short prayer. He turned to Fritz.

He started, 'Fitz has been moved to work at the People's Shipyard because his mother-in-law received too much support from her relatives in West Germany. As painful as it might be for Fritz, it is almost impossible to drive home during the week, as great as it might be for our movement.

'Let me briefly explain what I understood from the extended meeting I had with Fritz in my '2nd office' the other day. And Fritz can then add everything or correct what I missed or did not repeat here correctly. Fritz had started investigating the ability to create a secure way of communication by exchanging messages. We all know spies exchange important messages using a 'Drop Box.' We all have seen it many times in movies. Somewhere on the way to work is a specific light pole, tree, or traffic sign on which the party who has the message indicated with a before agreed to sign that there is a message in the drop-box. The drop-box is emptied and the sign erased, which often is the way information is exchanged without personal contact. But we also learn from those movies that if there is a suspicion, the person is under investigation, it will be discovered, and the information falls into the wrong hands. Our telephone system is of the technology of Emperor Wilhelm II., and even if we could use it, the SSP would listen to every word.

'Am I understood so far?' Multiple murmurs, such as nothing new on that; everyone knows this, what's the news in that?

'OK, I get it, friends. I am closing my monolog to the wise men with this. For many months, we have tried to get in touch with like-minded people in other towns all over the country. We mostly failed because we could not communicate and securely exchange critical information.

Fritz has a fantastic Idea, and he asked me to get this meeting to discuss it and how we can help him and us with this idea. Fritz, the floor is yours.'

Fritz looked around and, with a green, started, 'I know, everyone is asking what I could do that the most affluent spy agencies in the world couldn't do. And honestly, I don't know why no one else in the spy world has thought about that yet. Maybe they have but considered it too complicated to set in motion. Most of the time, a bureaucrat decides where the money is wasted. We always need to remind ourselves that the enemy is not necessarily more competent than we are. They just have more resources they can throw at us.'

With a deep breath, he continued, 'Based on my study, I am familiar with microelectronics, microprocessor technology, and all that is connected and available in our country. Unfortunately, as with many other technologies, we are far behind the international corporations and what in the West is available. But I have a handful of friends I can trust with my life from my time at the University, and one of them has access to electronic items I can use to realize a secure communication system. All of those connections can source everything I need to build the system. Over the last two years, I have developed and, in the meantime, 21 systems manufactured. I brought one with me, and I will take the time to explain how it would be used.'

Fritz looked around and saw that everyone was hanging on his lips. 'The system is based on a microcomputer, and as you can see, about the size of a cigarette package.' With these words, Fritz pulled a small plastic box out of his pocket and placed it on the table. In addition, he pulled another item that looked like a calculator from his other pocket and placed it next to the box.

'The Black-box is the communication system, and that thing that looks like a calculator is the programming device. The communicator is powered by a 9V battery and has 64kb of storage for programming and 128kb for data storage. That might tell you not much, but it is necessary to remember. At least for the second number. This number tells you that the communicator stores roughly 128 thousand characters, a little less, but that's not so important. And I believe it is more than we will ever need. The programmer has a display with five lines and twenty-five characters each. The communicator is activated with a small magnet because it has an internal Reed-Switch. The unit is on by holding the magnet on the small side with the red dot for 3 seconds. The unit switches off when you hold the magnet for about six seconds.

'Wait for a second,' interrupted Willi, 'there is no indication whether the communicator is on or off.'

Fritz smiled and answered, 'Great observation Willi, and thank you for bringing that up. Honestly, I was already tempted to ask if you are still awake and have not fallen asleep. Let me demonstrate how that works because we are at the point where I will show how to enter messages into the unit.

Fritz took out his small pocket bible and explained that this was the best book to code a message for the beginning. Later it would be necessary to agree with all further connected groups to establish a common list of books and give it a five-number code. Here in the example, we use the bible, and I will give it the code 5 1 0 0. Let's say a second book is Schiller's 'Don Carlos,' and we would give it the code 5 2 0 0. In our example here, my first five-number group would be 5 1 0 0. That tells the receiver of the message that he needs to take his bible to decipher the message. Since there are several different translations, we must ensure everyone uses the 1916 translation from Martin Luther. Fritz looked around again to see if he was still followed and saw all of his friends looking at him with great interest. He continued, 'I will now make a complete transmission of a message and then show you how to read that message out.

First, we have established the source for the code:

5 1 0 00

Now we have to tell what book or chapter in the Bible, or when it is just a book, it is only the chapter. Since we are working with five-number groups, we have four groups in a line and as many rows as we need. Let's say we chose the 2nd Kings, book number 12 in the Bible; our first group would look like this. To get all the characters we need, we chose chapter 4, verse 16. And the second group would look like this.

5 1 0 0 12   0 4 0 0 16.

Now the message text itself. We want to let the message receiver know we want to organize a meeting of all #1 officers at the Designer Outlet Berlin Mc Donald. We would shorten the sentence to: 'meeting at mac d berlin design center d1204 t1500 L1' To make it easier for us to code the text, here is an example of how you could do it.

And he aid, About this season,
1 2 3 4 5 6 7 8 9 10 11 12 13 14 15 16 17 18 19 20 21 22 23 24

According to the time of life, thou shalt
25 26 27 28 29 30 3 32 33   34 35   36 37 38 39 40 41 42   43 44 45 46 47 48   49 50 51 52

embrace a son. And she said, Nay, my lord, *thou* man of God, do not lie unto thine handmaid.

Fritz numbered the characters of the text until 52 and said, 'That should do it. I don't think we need more. If we need more, we can go and number more characters. One of the rules for good coding is to use different numbers for the same character if available within the text you have chosen. It makes it more difficult to break the code. And we won't use the same verse again. The Bible has 66 books, so there is no need to stick with one. The more you variate, the more complicated it is for the SSP to break the code.'

And after a second of thinking, he added, 'They shouldn't ever been able to get their hands on the message if you play it safe.

We would code it like this:

5 1 0 0 12	0 4 0 0 16	41 42 5 15 17	32 33 10 39 41
21 26 9 11 20	29 45 8 24 3	38 19 8 33 24	27 5 24 14 5
29 0 0 0 0	3 12 04 0 0	15 0 0 0 0	45 1 0 0 0

We must also remember that the last three of the five-number groups we program are first: the date, second: the time, and third: the addressee, either L1 for the number one or L2 for security or even ALL, which means the message must be transferred to the next known communicator.

We have an 8-bit data bus, so we need to tell the unit when a number is complete and when a group is complete. The programmer always shows the last four rows of data. The unit automatically recognizes when a fourth group is complete and switches to the next row.

Fritz continued with the demonstration and said, 'We have the message now coded, and now we need it to be written into the memory of the communicator. We can't know the status of the communicator because there is no indication. You remember, I activated the communicator several minutes ago when I kept the magnet at the red dot for about

3 seconds. Since then, the communicator has been in receiving mode for 60 seconds and went to sleep mode for 10 minutes. And that is on purpose.'

'But our programmer, 'calculator,' can stay on for much longer. We will now write our code to the programmer's memory. It has the same memory size as the communicator. To tell the programmer the completion of the number, we use the commata key [,], and for the end of a group, we use the dot key [.]. With an equals key [=], we signal the end of the message. When we have written all the five-number groups into the programmer's memory, we hit the [M+], which is the command to transmit the message to the communicator. It is necessary to tell the communicator that the transmission is complete, and the communicator can go back into sleep mode. If the communicator is awake and in receiving mode, the transmission starts, and you can see on the programmer's display, line by line, disappearing. With the transmission complete, the communicator sends the number **10** back to the programmer, which stands for A and means acknowledged.'

Fritz hit the [M+] key, and everyone leaned over to see the display of the programmer. Line after line disappeared, and the number 10 appeared on display within less than a second. Billy was just amazed, and all he could say was, 'Wow!' Ralf, though, with at least some understanding of the functionality, although his primary studies at college were high voltage and energy, said, 'That solves one of the most significant problems underground organizations have, secure communications. Most organizations get destroyed because of tracking their exchange of messages. It is just fantastic, Fritz. But how do I get a message out of this thing, ah communicator?'

'That is really easy, Ralf,' Fritz answered. 'The programmer has a [M-] key. Let's say this communicator is hidden in a tree hole somewhere at an Autobahn Raststaette. And all you know, it is near the parking area's center. You drive to that parking lot and find a spot close to the center. You take your programmer, switch it on, and hit the [M-] key. Then you get out of your car, lock it, and go to the restroom, restaurant, kiosk, or whatever is there to spend 10+ minutes. Remember the 10-minute interval of check mode of the communicator. When you come back, you check the programmer, and when you see the message in the display, you can scroll up and down with the [+] key and [-] key and drive off. Nobody, even the most suspicious SSP officer on your heels, will have the slightest idea that you just received a secret message.'

Ok, Fritz said, here is the message we just transmitted to the communicator a few minutes ago. Saying that, Fritz hit the **[M-]** key, and nothing happened. 'Remember the sleep mode cycle,' Fritz repeated.

Every eye was on the display of the calculator-like-looking programmer, and it was total silence in the room. The only noise was the sizzling of the candlelights burning on the table. Then, after about a minute and a half, suddenly, numbers appeared on display, and line by line, the message was transmitted to the programmer.

```
5 1 0 0 12     0 4 0 0 16     41 42 5 15 17   32 33 10 39 41
21 26 9 11 20  29 45 8 24 3   38 19 8 33 24   27 5 24 14 5
29 0 0 0 0     3 12 04 0 0    15 0 0 0 0      45 1 0 0 0
```

They all talked at the same time, 'Awesome!' 'Almost a miracle.' And Leo, with an astonished voice, 'It works!'

After the excitement had settled, Ralf had to remind them several times to reduce the volume, and everyone calmed down again; Billy asked, 'What do you think would be the next step?' 'Do you have more than one of these things, ah, I mean communicators?'

'I currently have 21 tested and functional communicators and about 40 programmers. I can put together another ten communicators within the next two months if I get the parts in time. Those are already ordered, but you never know.'

'That would mean we could install 21 communication hotspots, and we could create a secure communication system with 21 underground groups throughout East Germany,' Ralf thought out loud.

'Do you know of 21 underground groups in our country?' Fritz asked.

'No, that would be fantastic. Although I believe there are probably more than 21 groups, I am not sure they are as organized as we are. We have contact with some. Ralf knows more about that since he is our security officer. Ralf, what do you think is possible?'

Ralf thought for a moment how to answer, and, finally, with a deep-drawn sigh, he said, 'I am not sure we can just run around and hand this tool to the groups we are in touch with currently. There is that group in the Schwerin area, which is pretty well organized and seems to be safe. And then I feel very good with the guys in the Neubrandenburg area. Billy, you may remember we had a very good meeting with both leads and their security officers at the Church Festival 2 years ago in Neubrandenburg. I have met with both security guys several times since. And they are solid. I actually was thinking about making a trip to Schwerin to talk about our two Russians, to have a place where we can hide them a little closer to the border.

Fritz thought it was the best time to give his opinion. Although he was now in the area of the STUR, and Billy had, without hesitation, called the leader meeting, he still wasn't a member of their group.

So he started to speak, 'Listen, I am not yet an official member of your group. But I am also no longer the #1 at the RUUR. With that, I am hanging a little in the air. Yet I have thought about the situation for a while and have the following suggestion. I can get the two communicators I have in Sassnitz, and we place one of them in Bergen, which is easier to get there from both sides. Thus we have easy communication with the RUUR group. Another thing is that we should create a communication officer position, and he should be the only one programming messages and sending them. This position should also be the only person who knows the place of their own unit and a maximum of two other units. When a message FOR ALL is received, to ensure all groups have those, two additional communicators must be checked if the message is already there, and if not, it must be transmitted. I suggest that, as an example, the communicator for the exchange of messages with the Neubrandenburg group (NUR) the communicator is placed somewhen in the middle of the distance between both cities. And that is the structure we should keep throughout the country. Maybe with the improvement of technology, we can come to a point where I can build a more sophisticated communicator who can compress a data file and send it as a burst. And if I get better battery technology, I could increase the radio power without draining the battery with one transmission, and the communicators can transmit from one to the next. Since we are currently limited to a maximum distance of roughly 100 meters line of sight, we can't do this yet.

There was silence in the small basement room again while everyone hung onto his own thoughts. After a short while, Ralf spoke up and said, 'Fritz, first of all, you are one of us!' All nodded in agreement with Ralf. 'And I believe the idea of having a communication office, and only he is using the communication tool, is an important point to reduce the danger in case of a break-in by the enemy. But we should have a backup person, i.e., the security officer, who can spread the message when the communication officer gets arrested. What do you guys think?'

Leo said, 'I think it's the right way to go, but how do we get them placed? I could use my trips to get some of them in the right hands, but then I would know who has them and might endanger the communication system.'

'In the end, there will always be one who has that knowledge,' Fritz answered and continued, 'I have no problem meeting with the security guys from NUR and SUR and training them on how to use the system. I have already planned to visit my friend in the Leipzig area. And either on the way there or back, I will meet my Friend in the Berlin area. I am very sure my friend in the Berlin area has several contacts he trusts who would start a resistance group with him. They may already be working underground. And maybe I can convince my friend in the Leipzig area to get his bud out of the chair, stop yelling at the TV and start a resistance group himself.

'Ok, sounds like a plan to get it started,' Ralf said. 'I will get the SOs from NUR, and SUR instructed to meet with Fritz and let Fritz know when and where. Fritz, can you do your travel to the Leipzig area plan so that you can meet these two guys on your way somewhere around Neubrandenburg?'

'Absolutely no problem with that. Since this is planned as a personal trip to meet with friends, family isn't a part of it.'

'Great when do you plan to get on with the trip?'

'The week after next week.' I plan to leave on Sunday, which may make it easier for the guys to meet with me.'

CHAPTER 17

MONEY DOESN'T STINK IF IT IS FOR THE WORKER'S PARADISE

The conference room at the seat of the Central Committee of the SUP was filled with the smell of freshly brewed coffee and the aroma of very expensive cigars. The members were assembled on the special request of comrade Alexander, secretary of economics. He had just returned from a trip to Nicaragua and Cuba, and the freshly brewed coffee and the cigars were part of some gifts of the comrades of those countries.

Waiting for the Secretary-General to arrive, they chatted among themselves, talking about family affairs, and nobody was really spending thoughts on the nation's conditions. They all knew that comrade Bruno was working on the solution for that issue and already had a meeting scheduled for the next day.

The door opened, and comrade Werner entered with a package of papers under his arm. He took his seat at the table and immediately called the meeting to order. 'Comrades,' taken aback by the aroma of the cigars, looking at the large box with the top line of Cuban cigars, he said, 'wow, comrade Alexander, you made my day.' With those words, he grabbed one of the cigars, professionally cut the end, and lit it up.

He started again, 'comrades, we are meeting today because comrade Alexander, our secretary for economics, called me in the morning and requested this meeting. Although we already had an extraordinary meeting scheduled for tomorrow because comrade Bruno has some surprises for us. The reason is that he had a lengthy phone conversation with his colleague comrade Morishenkow yesterday. Comrade Morishenkow explained that, based on the changes in the economic structure of the Soviet Union, we have to start next year in January to pay for the oil and gas supply in convertible currency.' This message caused a murmur in the room, and the comrades looked at each other in disbelief. All started to speak simultaneously, 'That can't be true. Do they know what they are doing?' 'That would kill our economy!'

Comrade Werner knocked on the table and said, 'Comrades, discipline, please. We have to discuss the effects of that decision and potential solutions.' Pondering silence.

'Comrades, we need to find a way to get the needed currency; otherwise, we will not be able to survive the effects of that request. We have a little over eight months to create a steady stream of sufficient convertible currency through the export of products of our corporations.'

'Comrade Werner, you know as well as we all here that there is no product that we could export in such an amount that we would create the required amount of dollars or D-Mark,' comrade Alexander threw in the round.

'I may have a solution,' the low voice of comrade Frank startled all of them out of their thoughts.

'What, do you plan to sell our weapons, tanks, fighter aircraft?' comrade Juergen asked with a snippy tone in his voice.

'Please, comrade Juergen, no need for being cynical,' the Secretary-General said. And to the Secretary of Defence, comrade Frank speaking, 'What do you have in mind, comrade Frank? We don't have time and mood for jokes, and we need REAL solutions.'

'I think I have a REAL solution,' comrade Frank said, now a little louder and a little bit anger was recognizable in his voice. He was constantly accused by the Secretary of State Security, comrade Juergen of having no Army but deserters if not for the hard work of the SSP inside the Army units stop the defeatism. Now, he may have the solution in his hand to save the newly empowered comrades their skin. With a tone of gratification in his voice, he began to explain, 'several years ago, our military technology center (MTC) started to look into a target-finding system that could withstand the newest NATO electronic shielding systems. As you know, radar and electroacoustic target-finder are easily disoriented by electromagnetic waves, and heat-seeking target-finders are by refecting flares. Our MTC was not only able to overcome these disadvantages by using a raster-imagine technology which scans the environment for know patterns of the enemy's weapons but it is also based on the recently developed and successfully tested new 16bit microcomputer of the Keramische Werke Hermsdorf. It is our own design, and we don't have to pay royalties. Since it is completely based on ceramic materials, in combination with metallic shielding, it can not be destroyed by EMPs or disoriented by any kind of electromagnet wave.'

'Wait a moment, comrade Frank,' comrade Juergen jumped into his explanation, 'you are not suggesting to sell those wonder weapons to the class enemy?'

'Comrade Juergen, please let him finish. Nobody said something like that,' comrade Bruno interrupted the angry burst of comrade Juergen.

'Why do you think this system could solve our convertible currency problem?' the Secretary-General asked, now paying total attention to the comrade General.

'I know from research we did that many countries would pay about $ 1 million for such a system. With our current capacity, we can produce approximately 1000 pieces a month. That would give us $ 1.2 billion annually on convertible currency for a long time. And we have secure data that we would be unable to cover the whole demand no matter what.'

'If I understand that correctly, comrade Frank, we won't be able to produce more than 12,000 pieces of that...... ah, thing in a year?'

'That's correct, comrade Secretary-General.'

'Is it because it is so complicated to produce it, or is it just that we don't have the manufacturing capacities?'

'It's the lack of manufacturing capacities, comrade Werner.' By now, the General was becoming bold and started to address the Secretary-General by his first name. He was one of the most restrained men ever in such a high position that many of his cronies were wondering how he had ever achieved the rank of a General, let alone was chosen by comrade Werner to be the new Secretary of Defense. Only a handful of people, mainly family, in the whole nation know the truth behind that relationship. But that's a story for another time.

'Comrade Alexander, what would it take to increase the manufacturing capacity for that uh, what was it you named it, comrade Frank? Ah, yea, the target …. thing, to let's say, the double capacity, so 2000 pieces a month?'

'I have not the faintest idea what that ….. thing is, what raw materials it needs and what machines are needed, and maybe we have to import them. Perhaps even from the None Socialistic Economic Zone (NSW).'

'Comrade Werner, we don't need to increase production. Our experts calculated that the revenue of that system's sales is ten times the current inflow of convertible currency. And the money we would need to pay the Soviet Union's oil and gas supply can't be more than half of that revenue.' He did not realize that his statement about the possibility of making over a billion dollars a year from that 'thing' as the leader of the newly installed oligarchical dictatorship immediately woke up the greed in that guy. But he should have known since they had been acquainted for a long time.

'Comrade Frank, do I need to explain to you the basics of our communistic goals for the worker's class around the world?' he asked with a cynical tone and an expression on his face as if he had just swallowed a lemon. 'To fulfill the eternal objective of communism to free the oppressed workers' class from the dictatorship of the capital, we need exactly that. Capital!' His voice became louder towards the end of the sentence. So, as if he would start a speech to the masses, his cronies knew that that was about to happen.

Exactly knowing what would follow and avoiding a long monologue by his leader, comrade Walter interfered, 'comrade Frank, what do you think about taking it a step further? We can sell the systems we can manufacture to those countries who are not equipped to manufacture them and license out the systems for license production in exchange for royalties to those who can.' There might be considerable interest in license manufacturing these systems with the Chinese comrades. What do you think, comrade Werner?'

'Excellent idea, comrade Walter. I have to applaud you for always thinking ahead of all of us when it comes to money. Especially such we don't have,' he said with a broad smile. 'What do you think we could charge as a license fee for such a system?

Comrades Frank and Walter started speaking simultaneously, and the Secretary-General lifted his hand to stop them, 'Comrade Frank first.'

Now, even more encouraged, comrade Frank started, 'Comrade Werner, I believe we can easily ask for $50,000 to maybe even $ 100,000. The difficulty might be controlling how many systems a country has built in a year. And how do we ensure they are not refusing to pay when the invoice arrives.' All the time, while comrade Frank was speaking, comrade Walter had his hand in the air, eager to speak out.

The Secretary-General recognized him with a nod of his head, and he immediately said, 'Comrade Frank is correct to a certain degree. But there are tools in the international trading world to ensure payments, and we can always ask for a downpayment before we deliver any information. We can also include in the contract that the license requires them to use the main components of our design. The contract would also include that any re-design or copy of the system is a violation and would automatically initiate a specific penalty for each system built outside of our design with the same abilities.

The Secretary-General was silent for several minutes, collecting his thoughts for the following steps to be taken, and said then, 'Here is what we will do.

1. Comrade Frank starts building a team of his experts to create the necessary planning to start manufacturing the manufacturing of the ...... Thing ..... System. And please, comrade Frank, place it under the rules and regulations of the VVO (VerteidigungsVerOrdnung German for Defense Order System). We can't have situations as we have with normal manufacturing where everything fails for missing parts.

2. Comrade Walter, draft a potential contract frame for international trade for the license for that .... system and ensure that all the restrictions you suggested are included and enforced by international courts.'

We will meet again tomorrow because comrade Bruno is presenting his solution to the incredible counterrevolutionary situation, rampant corruption in our party, and our nation's economic leadership. Comrade Walter, can you have the draft ready to go over it tomorrow after we have handled the issue with comrade Bruno?'

'I will start immediately to put a framework together and have my experts working on the details. We should have a draft we can all discuss by tomorrow evening.'

'Conmrade Frank, what about you? Do you think you can have a list of factories involved in mass-producing the System by tomorrow and what needs to be done to get started?'

'Comrade Werner, we should be able to have all the necessary structure ready to start by the end of the following month. I am not sure we will have all the nuts and bolts ready and lined up by tomorrow. I need to meet with comrade Juergen to ensure we don't have any traitors in the extended teams working on the system's mass production.' That statement earned him an approving nod by comradeJuergen, the secretary of the SSP.

'Great, let's close the meeting with that, comrades. I know every one of you has his table full of work because we are in challenging times right now.' With that, the meeting was closed. The members of the Central Committee, which controlled every aspect of the lives of the people in the nation, filed out of the room. Several of them, not without taking two or three of the excellent cigars out of the box on the table.

CHAPTER 18

INTRODUCTION OF THE CLEANSER BUT THIS ONE DOES NOT CLEANSE THE HOUSE

It took Bodo just a few minutes to recover from all the new impressions, and he went into the office room and grabbed the phone to call home. Because of his position in the party's county leadership, he had a full phone line to his house.

After just one ring, Sarina picked up the phone and said, 'Hello.'

'Hello, my love, it's I,' Bodo answered. 'I know it's late, and I am tired as a dog, but I knew you would sit next to the phone, waiting for me to call.'

'Yes, I was sitting on needles and pins to hear you telling me everything is ok.' I am still not sure what this is all about and what it means for us as a family.'

'How is Nick? How did he react when you told him you had been called to come to Berlin?'

'I did not tell him much. I told him that you had been picked up to be at a critical Berlin meeting. Ah, I almost forgot to tell you. Nick said that about the time you left, he saw your brother driving by the sports field, and after about half an hour, he was driving back out of the village. And he said he believed that he thought that there were two people in the back of the car. I thought that would be strange because he wouldn't know anyone here. What do you think?'

'I don't know. And actually, I have no time to spend even one thought on that piece of shit called my brother. He is only of the same blood by birth. He is a traitor, and I may have some chance to deal later with him as needed. Now I am tired and need to sleep because tomorrow will be the hardest day I have ever experienced. Good night Sarina and give Nick my love.'

'I will, and please stay safe and call when you know more about what is going on and what this is all about.'

With that, she hung up, and Bodo placed the handset down with a deep sigh. Pulling out of the thoughts about his family, he went to the bathroom, got ready, and a few minutes later, he was deep in a dreamless sleep.

The alarm startled him out of that deep sleep, and for a few seconds, he had no idea where he was. He let his thoughts wander to the events of the last two days and couldn't help but get excited and still wondering if this was a realistic dream and if he would wake up in bed at home with Sarina next to him. Laying in bed, he looked around the room, still covered in darkness but lit up to the point that he could make out the different furniture and the shape of things by the street lights shining through the not completely closed curtains. With a look at the alarm watch, he realized that he needed to get ready for the day ahead and remembered that the car would be waiting for him at the garage at 8 AM. With that, he jumped out of bed and enjoyed the luxury of the incredible bathroom. All the amenities and unknown but excellent soap, shampoo, and towels were for sure not 'Made in GDR.'

When he entered the building entrance area where he arrived last night, his car had just arrived to pick him up. He greeted Dieter with a friendly 'Good Morning,' and Dieter said that he had the order to bring him to the office building of the Central Committee. After about ten minutes of driving, the guards stopped them at the entrance barriers. The guard approached the car, and the driver showed him his credentials. The guard then walked back to the passenger side, and Dieter said, 'He wants to check you out. You need to lower the window.'

The guard looked into the car and checked Bodo out, comparing him to a photograph in his hand. 'What is your name, comrade?' Bodo answered, and the guard walked back to the small man door he came out from. A few seconds later, the massive steel gate began to move upwards until the opening was large enough for the car to drive through and stop.

Dieter drove through the opening and, turning left, drove down into the underground garage. At a specifically assigned parking spot, having a large sign reading 'Secretary ICC,' he stopped and shut the engine down. Bodo exited the car and turned around, and he already had comrade Karl in front of him.

'Good morning, Bodo. I hope you have had a regenerating night and slept well.'

'I was so exhausted and overwhelmed with all that had happened to me within the last 48 hours. I slept like a stone.'

'Great, that can only mean that you are rested and ready for the challenges thrown at you today, 'Karl answered, laughing. They walked to the elevator, and Karl entered a particular sequence into the keypad. The elevator door opened, and when they were in and the doors closed, he had to enter the same sequence again. The elevator accelerated, and they stopped at their destination on the 6th floor. A large reception area appeared when the elevator doors opened. Karl went ahead, and Bodo followed down the wide hallway until they reached a solid-looking double door. Karl opened the door, ushered Bodo in, and followed. Bodo looked around and saw an impressive office. It was large enough to hold the working space for four women with comfortable desks and workspace for binders and file hangers. On the right-hand side was another large double-sized wooden door, and to reach that door, one had to pass the older women's desk, which Karl immediately introduced as Karin, Bruno's chief secretary.

'Bodo,' he said, 'this is Karin. Karin, this is comrade Bodo. He will be the comrade for the particular position we discussed the other day. Bodo, Karin is Bruno's right hand. Everything goes through her. She will get you access to Bruno when needed. The only exception is if Bruno contacts you direct.' And while working towards the door to Bruno's office, he said over his shoulder, 'Karin, is Bruno waiting for us? She nodded and answered, 'Yes, comrade Karl, I told him already that you are on your way.'

With that, Karl knocked on the door, and after the call 'come in.' was heard, he opened the door. He slightly showed Bodo in front of him into the office.

As they entered the large office, comrade Bruno was walking from behind his desk towards them and, with a stretched-out hand, greeted Bruno smiling warmly. 'It is so great to meet you in person, comrade Bodo. After all, Karl told me about you I was really curious to meet you in person..'

'I hope he did not exaggerate it, comrade Bruno. It is always challenging to keep up with the overestimation of abilities other people place on one's shoulders. I am just a servant of the communist party to the best of my abilities, and I hope I can better serve the party as a part of your department.'

'Oh, come on, comrade Bodo, you are much too humble. After Karl developed that little three-page framework for the new position we are about to offer you, I required a copy of your personnel file, and I can assure you I am much impressed. But come over here and sit down. Karin is on her way to bring us breakfast, and we can talk and get to know each other a little better.' While saying this, he had his hand on Bodo's shoulder and guided him to the comfortable seating area at the large window where he loved having breakfast and reading the party's newspaper, 'New Germany.'

A moment later, a knock on the door. The door opened, and Karin balanced a large tablet with dishes, coffee, and sandwiches on the table in the seating area.

'Thank you, Karin, this is great as always.'

I thought I would just bring some more sandwiches because our guest hasn't had breakfast yet.' Said it, turned around, and closed the office door behind her.

'Please, help yourself. How do you take your coffee?' Bruno asked while filling three coffee cups.

'Just black, comrade Bruno, just black. It's a habit I learned while working on the fishing cutter. The condensed milk was extremely sweet, I don't like sugar in my coffee at all, and the fresh milk was gone within a couple of days. So I got used to black coffee, and I believe real good coffee doesn't need anything in it. And, on a side note, this coffee seems to be the best I have ever had, just by the aroma of it.'

Comrade Bruno laughed out loud and said to Karl, 'why, Karl, you couldn't have found a better comrade fitting with us. All we need to know is that he likes the coffee different than we like it. That adds some diversity to the taste.'

While they had several different sandwiches, which were so tasty that Bodo occasionally let out a sound of excitement, they talked about general news and the overall situation, not to go into too many details. They seemed to have agreed that they wanted to enjoy their breakfast and have only easy themes discussed.

When they were done with breakfast, Bruno called Karin to remove the dishes and then moved over to the large conference table to discuss the issues of why Bodo was even there and the different aspects of potential solutions outlined in the three-page framework of Karl.

Comrade Bruno opened the discussion, 'comrade Bodo, you are a comrade who worked for several years now on the frontline of the party, and you know better than anyone here in Berlin what the real issues are and what needs to be done to get the situation cleaned. We, comrade Karl and I, understand that because I read your file, and Karl talked with you for a long time before he suggested you be the man for the complex task. You might ask yourself, why I? Isn't there anybody else?

There are so many experienced comrades in much higher positions, with many more years of experience in the party structure and apparatus. I don't even have a degree from the party university, which is usually the condition to move up even to a district position. I believe all these thoughts have gone through your mind over the last 48 hours since Karl left your office. Comrade Karl and I discussed the requirements somebody needs to fill for the position we are about to create. And don't think for a moment, comrade Bodo, that it is just a job. Suppose the Central Committee decides you are the comrade ready for this assignment. In that case, you will have enormous power, almost the same power as the Secretaries of the Central Committee have. Comrade Karl saw in you the character needed for this position and convinced me it is the case. You have to convince the Central Committee this afternoon the same way.

'Why I, comrade Bruno? I have asked myself that question a thousand times since I entered that car that broad me here. You are right. I believe there must be hundreds, if not thousands, of comrades with better education and more experience in the structure of the party than me. So, what lit up the bulb in comrade Karl's head?

'There are two reasons,' comrade Bruno answered. 'The first is actually comrade Karl's intuitive recognition of your genuine love for the party and its principles based on the teachings of Karl Marx and Wladimir Lenin. You are unwavering and have a steadfast stand on the principles of the basic rules for a successful finish of the formation of the worldwide paradise of the workers' class. Comrade Karl told me when he came back yesterday that he had never met a comrade with such an intense love for the cause yet, at the same time, such a hate for the traitors in our own ranks. That is the enthusiasm we need for this position.' He looked at Bodo and saw what he needed to see in his eyes: the absolute determination to prove everything that was just said. In continuing, he said, 'The second reason is because of me. We need all that comrade Karl saw in you for this position, and a critical addition to that is that the person who is called to fill that position is a nobody!' 'We want you to be able to work under the radar. We want that all of those who betrayed the party for their advantage have no idea and won't be able to find out who you are until it is too late for them.'

Comrade Bruno leaned back in his chair and let that statement sink in. All three were hanging on their own thoughts for a while until comrade Bodo spoke up.

'Comrade Bruno, comrade Karl, I appreciate your openness, and I can assure you that I will do my best to convince the other Members of the Central Committee that I am the comrade for that assignment. I have studied the three-page framework of comrade Karl, and I believe I can have a detailed outline of the whole organization, the program, and the material requirements completed by the end of the week. Today is Wednesday. If I can have a secretary by tomorrow morning, I should have all written out by Friday afternoon. Would it be early enough to present it to the Central Committee so I can go to work?'

'Let's see, it is time for lunch, and I want to invite you to a nice Russian-style restaurant in Berlin. You will love it.' After that, we will drop you at your apartment, so you can get some rest, and Dieter will pick you up at 4 PM for the meeting with the other members of the Central Committee. What do you think?'

'That sounds great.'

With that, they stood, and comrade Bruno called Karin through the intercom to have Dieter ready to drive them to the restaurant. The drive was just under ten minutes. Dieter drove through a gate in the back of the building and parked the car. Comrade Bruno and Karl knew their way around, and when they entered the restaurant, the waiter immediately recognized them and led them to a corner table in the back of the restaurant. A few minutes later, the chef appeared. He was a real Russian, which was easily recognizable by his accent. He knew both comrades, and after a few words of small talk, comrade Bruno introduced comrade Bodo as a special guest and said he would probably be more likely a regular guest in the future. The chef was delighted and presented them with the menu he would like them to get served. They explained to comrade Bodo that the chef was a professionally trained chef who had worked in a famous Moskau restaurant. As always, comrade Bodo would learn during the following minutes that they accepted the chef's suggestions because it was the best they could get in that restaurant. After finishing his service with the Red Army troops stationed in the GDR, he decided to stay in Berlin because he had found the love of his life here.

They had an excellent meal, and comrade Bodo was impressed that the restaurant had filled up with many ordinary people, so his first thought that this was a restaurant where only a few privileged party leaders could eat was wrong.

After the lunch was finished and comrade Bruno had paid for their excellent meal, Dieter drove them back to the guest house of the Central Committee, where comrade Bodo was greeted by the guard as if he had lived there for years. With his newly programmed code, he could enter the elevator and realized that the door opened right in a small hallway with only two doors. The left door was the entrance to his apartment, and the right one must be the door direct to the office. That door had no way to be opened from the outside. Curious, he went into the apartment, walked into the office, and saw that the inside of the door had a door handle. He also had a buzzer on his desk to let a person in.

He dropped his trousers and shirt and lay down on the bed to rest a little while. In about two hours, comrade Dieter would ring the bell to tell him he was there to bring him to his great show.

CHAPTER 19

THE COMMUNIST-STYLE TRANSPORTATION INDUSTRY PICK-IT-UP YOURSELF

Over the last several months, Leo had experienced an increasing number of transporting trips over longer distances and mainly to manufacturing places, he had never needed to drive before. Usually, he would drive to one of the several shipyards, which were part of the shipbuilding corporation of shipyards, and deliver or pick up items and special tools or parts.

Now that had changed. He was driving across the nation more and more to pick up deliveries typically transported by either the manufacturer's own transportation department or by Deutrans, the GDR national and international transportation company. Now again, he was standing in Billy's office to receive the instructions for a roundtrip through the country, together with the transportation permits and loading lists of the stuff he had to collect during his weeklong trip. Just as he was about to ask Billy how to pay for refueling, Billy handed him a strange-looking checkbook and said, 'Leo, these are the coupons for the fuel stations. When you have to fuel, enter the amount of fuel and the total price and sign it. Make sure that the copy is perfectly readable. It is your only proof. The original is handed to the fuel station clerk. The shipyard will then balance those checks.'

'Ok, Billy, I got it. But have you looked at the map and seen where you are sending me? This is almost a tour through the whole country.'

'So what, Leo? It is undoubtedly now the Soviet Union, isn't it?'

That's not what I mean, Billy. What I try to say is, at first, what is going on, is that we, as the receivers of goods manufactured, have to make sure we pick them up instead of getting them delivered, and secondly,' looking over his shoulders on both sides and bending over the table toward Billy while lowering his voice, 'isn't that a great opportunity to spread out some of these things, you know, these communist things Fritz had shown us the other night?'

Billy almost laughed out loud and answered, 'Leo, these are called communicators, not communists. And yes, that is a great idea. I will see if I get Fritz contacted and see what he thinks. As far as I remember, he had only a limited number finished and has planned a trip to visit group leaders he knows to hand those out. But, yes, great idea to use your increasing travel tours to plant them and then use them to transfer information.'

'See, Billy, sometimes even I have good ideas.'

'Oh, don't be silly. You are a smart guy, even though you were just a stupid paratrooper.' Both laughed loud because that was a common joke among both paratroopers. Billy had the higher rank because he went to the NCO school, which Leo did not even qualify for.

While Leo prepared his truck for the trip, he double-checked all the tires on the truck and the trailer and the breaks; Billy was on his way to find Fritz. That wasn't as easy as it seemed, considering the large shipyard and the unpredictability on which vessel Fritz was just at that moment working on the setup of the energy control computers and generator control systems. But knowing which one was the next to go onto test trial and the specialist, ironing out program errors in the controller programs, what Fritz had become renowned for within the short time he worked on the shipyard, helped to find him soon.

Entering the engine control room, Billy called out for Fritz, and he came around the corner of the controller cabinet fields. "Hello Billy, you are bringing me the replacement boards for generator 2 voltage control?'

'What, again, one that failed?' Billy said and sighed, 'I am almost out of new shipments of controllers to be cannibalized, and I have no idea when we will get repairs. Uh, good that you asked. I will just add that plant to Leo's country-wide travel.'

'What do you mean country-wide travel? Isn't he the transporter between the shipyards and only occasionally somewhere else?'

Billy sighed again and said, 'Yea, you are correct, but that changed a few months ago. I don't know why, but the manufacturers no longer have transportation capacity. So we must pick up our parts where ever we can or suffer extended delivery delays. They can only ship once a month because that is what the geniuses at the Central Planning Commission have decided. Monthly production plan, monthly shipment. So easy.'

Fritz looked at Billy, and Billy immediately recognized that Fritz was thinking about something he could not express at the place they were. Then Fritz grabbed his shoulder and said, 'Billy, let's go onto the deck; I need some fresh air.'

They left the engine control room, walked over to the chimney, and climbed up to the bearing deck. That place was not prominent, and easy to see that nobody else was on. Walking one round to ensure there wasn't anyone else, Fritz said, 'While you mentioned that Leo has to travel crisscross the country now more often, I had a somewhat stupid idea.'

'Let me guess,' Billy interrupted Fritz, 'having him placing communicators, messages and reading the responses?'

'Yea, you are reading my thoughts now?'

'No, it is just so that Leo had the same idea when I gave him the trip data and documents, and that's the reason why I was looking for you.'

'You should give the plan-jumper fellow of yours some credit for having great ideas,' Fritz said, laughing and turning toward the seaside of the harbor and leaning onto the railing, he said, 'I don't have enough units for him to place them yet, but he can investigate the route he is driving, record potential locations and when you guys schedule the next trip, he can start planting the units. What is the general route he is taking?'

Billy thought about it momentarily and answered, 'You know, I did not even think about it myself, and you are right. He had a brilliant idea to place the communicators creating a nationwide network. With that, everyone whom we train and who has a programmer can communicate with every group in the network.'

'Yes,' Fritz stated, 'but we must be very careful whom we let know about that. One rotten apple and the whole system are worthless.'

There was silence between them for a while, both hanging on their thoughts. While Fritz thought about the sudden discovery of a tool to create a nationwide communication network to organize the scattered underground resistance groups into a well-organized force for the final fight for freedom, Billy had his thoughts already focused on a strategic travel route for Leo's next trip.

Suddenly the bulkhead to the bearing deck opened and slammed into its stopper. A mechanic dropped an obviously heavy box onto the deck. Startled out of their thought, both looked at each other and, without saying a word, walked over to the box, lifted it together, and asked the guy, 'where do you need this monster?'

'Men, thanks a lot; that thing just ripped my arms out. Please place it in that frame; I must measure and build a lockable cover.'

Fritz asked, 'What is that for? It seems to be like a safe.'

The mechanic looked at Fritz and said, 'you are new here; everyone on the shipyard, at least those who work, knows this is for the distress missiles. It has to be solid like a safe, which is why it is so heavy.'

'Ok, get it. Yes, I m new here, just a few weeks, but I am definitely not a non-worker.' Fritz answered, and with a laugh, they shook hands, and he introduced himself as Hartmut, banned chief of the commercial fleet, and sentenced to work as a boy for everything.

'Wellcome to the club,' Fritz responded, 'whom did you piss on the leg?'

'Manfred laughed at the expression and said, 'If it would have been just that, I would still be on the tramp ship I was on for three years since I finished college and on my way to get promoted to be the chief engineer. No, not that easy, but I was in Egypt, Port Suez. We were waiting for the passage through the canal to be paid, which has become more and more of an issue in the last year and a half. We were in a restaurant and had some good food and some nice drinks, you need to know in these arab Islam nations where to get a drink, and mostly us Europeans are there anyway. And they do not give you much so that you can't get drunk, and they might be closed.'

He went over to the box, pulled out his measurement tape, and noted some numbers. Then he turned and saw them both still there; he said, 'So, you want to hear the whole story? I am not sure if you would appreciate it. But, I don't care because more damage to my life these bastard communists have already done is impossible.'

'Fritz looked at Billy and then back to Hartmut and said, 'you may not know us, but we are in the same boat. So what is it that these communist bastards did that you don't care about anymore?'

Hartmut was looking at them, then out at the seaside, and slowly began to tell his story. It wasn't much different from what many of their friends who had become members of the underground resistance went through.

Hartmut said, 'Sitting in that camel shithole, the bar we had been many times in his three years on the tramp ship, my friends and I were drawn into a discussion of the few locals who spoke English, and although both sides did not speak it very well, we could understand each other. The discussion soon went into politics, and we were astounded by how well-informed these people were. We began to criticize the oppression by the communist system and the restriction and the constant shortages of all kinds of things needed for daily life.

These Egyptians were aware of the shortcomings of communism. Although they had some restrictions because of Islam rules and regulations, they could live wherever they wanted. The average family could afford healthy and fresh food from the market, and they asked why we even put up with that oppressive regime. We explained the uproar of 1953 and the results and that the Soviet military backed the East German communists. That and many years of massive suppression of any disagreement with communist politics by the almighty STASI has broken the back of the East German people. We had not noticed that two men at a separate table had left the bar, and when they reappeared, they had 6 police officers with them.

We were arrested, together with the Egyptians, accused of planning an uproar against the Egyptian government. That jail we were in for two nights was a living nightmare. We never saw those Egyptians again. When we were delivered to the East German Embassy, we learned that these were paid provocateurs used to test the loyalty of the seamen of the great nation of the GDR. We were on a plane two days later, and the Interflug had a direct flight from Alexandria.

I was sentenced to 2 years probation, and when I could leave the prison, my wife was there. No, not to receive me and welcome me home to my family, no. She was there to hand me the divorce sentence decided while I was in prison. I wasn't even asked.'

His voice had become emotional, and he paused several times before he went on, 'the sentence stated that I had no rights to see my two children, and if I tried to get even close to them, my probation would be turned into real-time. So now you know the story, and I really don't care anymore what these bastards can do to me. Scripture says that we should not care about those who can destroy our bodies but be aware of those who can destroy our souls. Yes, I believe in my Lord Jesus, and I can only hope you do too because it is really all that counts. If you believe not and think I am a religious weirdo, having a college degree and believing in Jesus, so be it. Many much higher up believe that, so you must get in line.'

Billy and Fritz were silent for several minutes. None of the three sitting on the bearing deck uttered a word. All were in their own thoughts, recapitulating their own dramatic experience and how they got there where there was no care about what the world said.

Then, Fritz broke the silence and said, 'Hartmut, if you believe it or not, Billy and I have gone through similar trials, and we are believers. Fortunately, we have not lost our families, which is very harsh to experience. Maybe you can start seeing from this perspective that your ex-wife wasn't right for you. I know it sounds complicated, but it might be the best way to look at it. I am sure that your children when they reach a certain age, want to know about their dad and why he isn't with them. And her explanation won't fill the hole, and they will search for you.'

While Fritz was outing himself and Billy as Christians, Hartmut looked up at both of them and, with a little more joy in his voice, said, 'Really, you are both believers. Man, that is awesome. What church are you going to? I was at St. Mary last Sunday, but I did not like it. It seemed very watered-down preaching to me. And then these Monday folks. I can't stand their yawp. I believe they are highly infiltrated by those SSP bastards.

'We can connect you with people who lead a bible study, and they might be ok to add you to the group.'

'That would be awesome. How can I find them?'

'No offense, Hartmut, but they will find you. We need to be careful, and they will contact you in some way or another within the next two or three days.'

'No offense taken, I completely understand.'

They said good buy and walked down to the engine control room, where the apprentice with the replacement board was sitting in front of the panels and looked bored at the different elements on the Voltage control board. Billy said he would contact Ralf about the issue and left Fritz with his apprentice and the job of getting the computer-controlled engine system ready for the trial trip. Fritz instructed the apprentice to set up the correct levels of the generator voltage control board and began his re-programming effort of the computer controller for the energy control.

Going through the programming mistakes he knew already about was usually all he had to do to get the system to work correctly. When he started the test run, he recognized a severe memory overflow with no data from the different sensor boards, which he had disabled as usual at the first start. This indicated the typical memory board failure. With a smile on his face, he remembered the moment when he discovered the reason for that data overflow within seconds some weeks ago when he took over the late shift after all the "experts" had worked for two days and couldn't define what was causing the issue. They were all electrical engineers and electricians with no knowledge of electronics, which had. The combination of his electrical college and electronic master's degree was the key to many successful discoveries, and he had trained them to see those indicators immediately.

He shut the computer down and pulled the memory board. Calling the apprentice, he instructed him to walk to the office of the material handling manager to get a replacement board and not to forget to get a received that he left this board there. 'Don't forget the S/N on the receipt,' he yelled after him as he walked out of the control room.

He finished the adjustments on the voltage control and finest the last one when the door to the control room opened, and Leo walked in. He nodded in Fritz's direction, made a complete tour of the control room, looked behind the control panels, and returned to Fritz. 'Hi Fritz, looks like to damage more than you get to work, hu.' He said with a smirk. And continuing, he said, 'can you stop by at my place on your way home tonight? I guess you are by car today?'

"Sure I can, Leo. What's the reason? Something wrong?'

'No, we will have a grill party with our new friends, and Ralf, Billy, and Willi should be there too. We could maybe have an unofficial leadership meeting?'

'Why, yea, great idea. We have some stuff to talk about anyway. Especially your idea about the placement. Billy was here an hour ago, and we talked about it. I think it is excellent.'

'Ok then. I'll see you tonight.' With that, Leo left the control room, and Fritz was alone. He thought about his planned trip to visit his friends from the university who were on the same page as him and his vision of connecting all the underground resistance groups to a nationwide organization. They could expand when the existing and highly secured unground resistance groups had a solid, reliable communication system. His brainchild of a nationwide resistance movement mimicking the propagation of the Spider Plant became increasingly more real than he could have thought just a few weeks ago.

The rattling of the bulkhead startled him out of his thoughts, and the apprentice entered the engine control room. He handed Fritz the replacement memory board and said, 'I was instructed to tell you this is the last one functioning they have. None of the 14 memory boards sent out for repair have been returned yet.'

Fritz looked at the apprentice, whom he knew was a reliable comrade of the party's youth organization, as he once was himself one of those, and answered, 'Let me ask you a question, what was the slogan the party brought out at their last convention?'

And as if he was on an exam to get a good grade, he answered, 'Overtaking without catching up'!

'Great,' said Fritz, 'I see you learned your lesson for school. Why can we achieve such a goal?'

The apprentice did not hesitate again, 'The rotten capitalistic system is on the brink.'

'And what was the strategy for that goal they defined?' was Fritz's final question, stabbing the dagger of the logic insanity of that philosophy right into that young man's brain.

And again, like a shot from a pistol, 'Always be one step ahead of the class enemy!'

Fritz looked at him until he had his full attention and said, 'I was once where you are now, thoroughly indoctrinated with the absolute illogic philosophy that one can do what you just stated. You are a bright young man. Do you realize the insanity of the logic sequence of those three statements you probably memorized without even thinking about that?'

The young apprentice was baffled. It was clear to see on his face that nobody had ever talked to him this way. He knew about Fritz brake up with the party and his former leading role in the youth organization of the whole region, but this was the first time that he was attached to him for his praxis education and the first time that Fritz had talked to him directly about something else than work.

Looking back at Fritz with a doubting expression, he said, 'I'd never thought about it that way. I just want to get an excellent great, stay at the top level of the class, and learn as best I can.'

'OK,' Fritz said, 'let's put it all together, right?'

1. Overtaking without catching up!

2. The rotten capitalistic system is on the brink

3. Always be one step ahead of the class enemy

Answer me that last question, please, 'If the rotten capitalist system is on the brink, and we have overtaken them without catching up because we are always one step ahead, where are we?

The apprentice's eyes widened, his mouth opened, and one word came out, 'in the abyss!'

Fritz turned on his seat, placed the memory board into the computer slot, and said, 'That's the first accurate word you said in the last ten minutes. And that's the reason why we have 14 unrepaired memory boards, 12 motherboards, 18 ad-changer boards, and who knows how many time relays, overcurrent relais, voltage, current, and load control boards and who knows what else unrepaired laying somewhere because we are focused on correct political slogans, instead on having intelligent and brilliant people like you focusing on their daily jobs.'

The apprentice stood there, watched Fritz powering up the energy control computer, and waited for another outburst of Fritz criticizing the political system he had been told all his life was on the verge of victory over the rotten capitalist system. Fritz finished the setup changes he needed to make to get the new memory board recognized by the computer and activated the program.

'Let's see if we get it to work as it should, he said to nobody.' While the program started, the check sequences, spurring noise of some elements, and clicking of one or other relais were the only sound in the otherwise empty engine control room.

Then the apprentice suddenly said, 'Mr. Zipper, I have never thought about everything the way you laid it out here for me. I wondered how it happened that you were suddenly kicked out of all the leadership positions you were in a few years back. I was in high school and have been at several events where you spoke, and one of our teachers was actually at one of the training camps you held for youth leaders. I guess you came to that realization which I am starting to develop in my brain, that all of that is a huge big lie.'

The energy control computer ran through different number codes on its small display. Froitz, paying close attention not to miss a failure code, waited until that sequence was through. The computer became "Ready-Stage," then answered, 'You are right there. I was one of the big shots in the party. I was considered, at the age of 19, the coming star of the communist party scene. All that changed when I was challenged to use my analytical mind as an engineer to begin to think for myself.' And continuing in his explanation, Fritz said, 'Don't just jump to conclusions. Check it out for yourself. I might be completely wrong, but the decision must be based on your research results. Ask questions, and don't take a no for an answer.'

Fritz then told him to collect the tools and instruments because the energy control system was ready to be presented to the board engineer, who would have to sign off on the complete function test. But that was the job of another crew, and they; left the vessel and walked back to the workshop. He signed off on the apprentice's worksheet at the workshop and sent him home for the day. He then filled out the completion form for the energy control and monitoring system set up with all the values he had noted during the setup and test procedures. It took about twenty minutes, and several of his colleagues working on other vessels at different stages of completion walked in, dropped their tools, and said good buy for the week.

When he was done. He placed the report into the box for the transfer team and walked upstairs to their office. Opening the door and looking into the office, he saw there were two members in the office. He let them know that the report is in their box. He did not carry his report into their office because the rules were changed after the cleaning brigade trashed several reports lying on the desks. The setup procedure needed to be repeated, leading to several test trip delays.

CHAPTER 20

ANOTHER CONSPIRATORIAL MEETING AND A SURPRISING DECLARATION OF THE SPETSNAZ AMONG THE UNDERGROUND RESISTANCE

All steps finished to get the other to work; he walked out of the shipyard to the parking lot where his car was parked and got on the road for the 20 minutes trip to Leo's place. When he arrived, he honked twice short, one long, and twice short again to let Leo know he was there. The large yard doors opened, and Leo grinning from ear to ear, waved him in. Fritz parked the car next to Ralf's and Billy's and walked back to the gate, helping Leo to close it and lock it with that vast pole-sized squared timber.

"Is Willi not coming?' Fritz asked while they walked back through the big barn toward the garden where Leo had built a nice terrasse with a pergola years ago, which had become covered with ranked roses so that it was completely covered in the summertime, a nice place to sit. Now, almost mid-April with some almost summerlike days, and this Friday was one of those. It was still a little chilly, but a great place to have a barbeque and talk secretly with their newly gained friends.

They greeted each other, and Fritz was relieved that Oleg was healed entirely and up and joyful as a 20-year-old should be, even though they were deserters of the most brutal armed forces, escaped just at a hair's breadth with the help of patriotic Christians. Just as they were starting to place the sausages on the grill, they heard another honking signal, and Leo turned to open the gate for what needed to be Willi. Fritz walked with him, asking, 'Leo, can I use your phone because I need to let my wife know I am late?'

'Sure, just go in. Grandma is in the kitchen, and you know where the phone is.' When his grandpa died, nobody in the community where everyone knew him had the guts to take the phone away from grandma. Although that would have been a regular operation because of the country's constant shortage of phone line connections, and more so since it was a whole line phone, not split among 4 parties as was usually the case.

Fritz entered the house, and when Leo's Grandma saw him, she walked over to him, hugged him, and said, 'Fritz, so nice to see you. I heard a lot of great things about you.'

Fritz was surprised how she would even know and recognize her since he only remembered to have her seen when he and Leo were still in high school. She saw his surprised look and said, 'Oh, come on, Fritz, you don't think I could forget your face after it was at least once a week in the local newspaper my late husband used to read, complementing you as the coming start of the party in our region?' she said and laughed with her friendly laugh at him.

'I need to call my family, Grandma. Where do I find the phone,' Fritz asked and, holding her at the distance of his arms, added, 'you look actually younger than I had you in remembrance.'

'Uh, you charmer, you want to make an old lady blush?' she said, slapping him playfully on his arm. 'The phone is over there in the living room. Be careful what you say; we never know if some "rubber-ear" is listening.'

Fritz walked over to the phone, dialed his home number, and Karola took the call. 'Something happened to mom?' he asked because there was never a way to get to the phone before her. So they had the expression that she would have to be tied up to keep her from getting to the phone before anyone else.

'Karola laughed and said, 'no, she is in the garden playing vole. You are calling, does it means you are late tonight?'

'Yes, dear, we decided on short notice to discuss some stuff. I will probably be really late, so don't wait for me.'

'Ok, drive safe. You know, many deer are on that road through the forest at night. Love you.' And she hung up.

Fritz walked back into the kitchen, and grandma said, 'here, take the salad with you and tell Leo that the potatoes are almost ready.'

'Will do, grandma.' And with that, Fritz walked out to the backyard, where the barbeque was sizzling, and the smell of cooked meat was waving through the air. Fritz placed the vast salad bowl on the table and greeted Willi, whom Leo had let into the yard as the last missing of the group. While they were talking, Leo brought out the plates and silverware, and everyone grabbed a plate to fill the first load of salad on it.

A few minutes later, grandma appeared and had a giant bowl with steaming hot mashed potatoes in her hands. Everybody jumped up and wanted to help grandma, but she shushed them away, 'I am old but not fragile!' She placed the potato on the table and said, with a joking tone in her voice, 'Before you heathen all jump on to devour the food like a pack of wolves, let's say praise altogether. Dear Lord, in troubling times we know you are with us as promised. That knowledge gives us security and hopes that we will be safe. We thank you for the food we can put on the table each day, and we praise you, Father God, in the precious name of your Son, Jesus Christ. Amen!'

All around the table repeated Amen, and as predicted, they stormed the lined bowls and the plate with the sausages to fill their plates. It just smelled too good to wait. While they were all busy eating and chatting between the bite and chewing, Fritz leaned back in his chair and watched the two Russians. They ate and chatted with the group members as if they had always been part of them. Nothing would tell an outside person looking at the group that these two were, just a few weeks ago, the most wanted deserters of the Soviet Army. They didn't even have that typical Slavic profile that many people from that country had. They could easily go through as Germans if they could overcome the language barrier. He was istening a litten more intensively to the conversation Oleg had started with Willi, and he realized that Oleg started to sound more and more like the people he had met in the southeastern corner of the country during his first year in his Master's study. It appeared as if Oleg had an exceptionally well-pronounced talent for languages. Fritz listened a little longer, blending out the chatter of the others. Then, catching a break in the conversation, he asked, 'Oleg, did you train your German over the last days?

Surprised by being addressed by Fritz, Oleg turned toward him. He answered, 'No, Fritz, I have not specifically trained my German. Do you think it is getting better?' Before Fritz could answer, the whole group, which had heard Oleg's response, was now paying attention, and Fritz said, 'he, friends, what do you think? It appears as if he has a specific talent for language?' They looked at each other, and then Nicolay said, 'Think I Fritz being you on somethink here, Oleg and Afghans talking one week when he came to Afghanistan with their speech.'

'Nicolay, you are saying that Oleg was able to talk with the Afghans in their mother language after being one week in Afghanistan? Is that what you just said?'

,Da, da, you right, Fritz. Oleg speaking goot.' Only one week, right, Oleg?' Somewhat ashamed of being at the center of the whole group's attention, Oleg humbly answered, 'Da, Nicolay is right. Easy was for me to understand people. My talent is language. In school, I made voice of teachers come in other region of Soviet Union and comrades taught many. And after a brief pause, he added, 'Nicolay, I am saying now, or you?' Everyone's attention turned to Nicolay and then back to Oleg when Nicolay said in Russian, ' вперед, продолжать.'

Oleg took a deep breath and said, 'Nicolay and me had long discussion. We will stay if you will not send us away. We believe we can be many help with resistance in ground. Only if you do not love us we will go away. That is so.'

Silence! Only the crackle of the glowing coal in the barbeque was to hear. Both Russians looked around at their German friends. Their expressions indicated doubt, insecurity, and even fear that the Germans would say no. Suddenly Fritz realized that everyone was looking at him, and he, totally surprised, said, 'what are you all staring at me? I have nothing to do with this. I am not even a confirmed member of the SUR, am I?'

Billy, the leader of the Stralsund Underground Resistance, took a deep breath and responded, 'You are correct, Fritz. You are not yet an official member of the SUR. But, and this is a huge, gigantic but, Fritz, you are the most experienced, the most trained member of the underground resistance in the nation. You have gone through the most significant training of the communist Kaderschmiede. You know more about their tactics than anyone else in the underground resistance because no one else has that training and educational history as you have.'

'Oh, and that makes me now responsible for if our friends stay here or get to the border and try to cross it by risking their lives?' Fritz asked with slightly noticeable anger in his voice.

'Please, Fritz, don't misunderstand me. Let me elaborate on a thought I am chewing on since you were moved to the shipyard by our "friends," the almighty Shield and Sword of the communist bastards. I believe you are the key to a nationwide organized net of well-connected and organized underground resistance cells that can connect at a certain point to turn the whole country around and toward liberty. You could be the unifying figure and bring all the different groups on the same page.'

'Wow, that's all I can say. Billy, are you out of your mind, me, leading the national resistance? Me the former star of the whole Middle Germany communist youth organization and, as some of the people who promoted me thought, potential future Secretary General, me? I believe, if there were a chance, which I don't see ever happening, to have the top 2 of each underground group in one room, they would break the leg of their chairs and beat me out of the room.'

And after a short pause, he added, 'most people our age who have ever read the Young World newspaper know me as who I was and don't know who I have become.' At that point, Ralf jumped in. As the security officer of the SUR, he had connected early on in their existence with his counterparts in other groups and knew at least five personally. 'Fritz, do you have any idea how many people in the nation know about your "fall from grace," how many pastors have read a paraphrased version of the declaration of faith you gave at that party meeting? You don't, right?'

Now Fritz was shocked. He had never heard anything like that, not even thought about it. Besides the collision he had with the synod some years ago and the small village church they had in his in-laws' house once a month, he had virtually no contact with the official religious organizations in the country. He knew that especially the Lutheran

Church was infiltrated and that many pastors regularly wrote reports about their church members to their STASI case officers.

'I am stunned. In my wildest dreams, I would never have thought this would happen. And honestly, Billy, and all of you here around, I don't want that. I want to live a peaceful life with my family, work to earn my living, and be left alone. And yes, I believe it is a good decision Nicolay and Oleg made. But not because I think I needed them, but because out of fear for their lives if they try to cross that inhuman deadly border. And just a little historical lecture here. Does anyone know why most of the revolutionary movements, and I am not referring to communist or socialistic movements, in general, all changes of societal structures in history are correctly considered revolutionary movements failed?'

When there was no answer for a while, Fritz continued, 'the main reason for the failure was the centralized control of all activities. A centralized movement in its control structure leads directly to sluggish reactions and seldom to actions. The chain of command is too slow when a fast reaction to changed situations and conditions is required. And even if it takes action, the outcome is mediocre, mainly. That is because no plan, even the most genius, survives the first contact with reality.

Therefore, if and that is a gigantic if, I would even accept some kind of a leadership role in such an organization as the network of underground resistance needs to become to be successful in overthrowing this satanic government; it must be decentralized! It can't be centrally organized and controlled.'

That was when Billy joined the exchange and said, 'Fritz, I agree. But you need to understand that there is a much larger job, no, not a job; it is a calling for you. That is the main reason why I hesitated to ask you to join our group. We want you to be that unifying factor across all the different groups, which may have different ideas of what to do. Still, they all have the same goal, get rid of the communists.'

'I agree, Billy. And I am not really against organizing concerted actions and maybe even all groups together at some point.' Fritz answered. And going on, 'I just don't feel I am that guy to head the pack of wolves. And as I said before, I never thought about being that guy either.'

At this point, grandma, who was sitting there among them, smiling all the time and looking around the group of young men who were all at the age to be her grandsons, suddenly and with her typical calm and low voice said, 'Fritz, let me ask you, and you don't have to answer immediately or not at all, do you think that your outstanding and thorough education and training of the tactics of the enemy of our Lord could have been set up by God to have someone in his fighting force who was that way? That HE set up it so that you could learn how to lead his people to overthrow the domination of HIS enemies? You know the story of Paul of Tarsus, right.'

Fritz was shocked. Not because of Leo's grandma throwing in her opinion on the matter, but because when he had, from an ice-cold thinking communist youth leader, turned his heart to Christ, he had several times the flash of thought going through his mind that he was a modern type of Paul of Tarsus. But always when that happened, he immediately confessed his arrogant self-inflating sin and told his Lord that he was thousands of miles away from a Paul-type figure.

'I know the story of Paul of Tarsus, grandma, and I love his epistles because those are the instruction we are missing the most today. Most Christians can recite many verses which Jesus spoke when he walked on His earth, but few can recite Paul's. Many have never read Paul's epistles. But I tremble in awe when I think of being even named in the same sentence as Paul of Tarsus.'

Grandma looked Fritz directly in the eye and said, 'I am not trying to compare you to Paul. I am trying to say that you are in a similar situation as he was. Yes, less dramatic or glorious, but that doesn't matter. God called you out of the deep darkness, where He Himself may have sent you before, into His service to the Light. HIS Light. Not accepting what comes with it means denying that it was God who liberated you.'

For several minutes was silence at the table. The crackling of the two candlelights and the remaining glowing coal parts in the barbeque was the only noise in the growing darkness of that ending lovely Aril day, turning into night. Then, all of a sudden, Nicolay spoke and said, 'friends, hoping I allow to name you such, I ask you to give us a chance to stay. We not stay for safety. Da we have know that border crossing is dead. Not the reason we stay asked you. Reason is we fighters. Very special fighters. Very special training. We help you also very special fighter. Uh, not know words, Oleg much better. Объясните им это, da?'

Oleg looked around, and even though it had become dark and the candlelights did not produce much light, every face was turned toward Oleg, ready to listen to what he had to say. 'We, Nicolay and I laying wake long night when come to Leo's house. Wonderful home, clean and warm and even warmer with grandma. And we very thankful for have saved our lives. We thinking that giving back some of friendship and is only thing we know and are very good is fighting. Specialist in fighting. Idea is to have special group of 6 to 8 men command by Nicolay and Oleg where you have resistance group and train it to fight, we fight.'

Fritz immediately realized the implication of that idea even though it was kind of difficult to get the specifics of it with Oleg's still limited vocabulary. And while every one of the group was talking over each other about what Oleg just explained, without having understood the concept of the idea, Fritz already had the frame of the assignment of the two fighter specialists constructed in his head.

'Ok,' Fritz had to raise his voice to stop the cacophony, 'listen, here is what I believe that fantastic idea of Nicolay and Oleg brings to the movement. But first, I have to express our gratitude to our friends, and yes, Nicolay, you are friends. I believe that creating a fighter force at each of the underground resistance groups is necessary. If Nicolay and Oleg train those groups, we may be able to build a force that can be very useful when the demonstration hysteria crashes and the SSP forces are crushing the fantasts.

I am planning a trip through the country, visiting with some friends I know are running a group or at least have contact with one and supporting one. Nicolay and Oleg, you both develop a training program because all men have basic military training, adding special forces training is a huge advantage. I will think through the whole idea and develop a plan for implementing the training program for the different groups.

Looking over to grandma, he asked, 'grandma, if I am correct, you have been a German Language teacher in the past?'

'Oh, Fritz, that's so long ago, I can't even remember when I retired,' she laughed loudly. What are you thinking?'

I believe that you could start a German language class tomorrow. Being a severe teacher, Nicoley and Oleg could learn the language quickly and sufficiently. With the necessary intensity, Oleg could go through as a Sorbian from the southeast corner within a month of training. Not so sure about Nicoley, but that doesn't matter; he may consider a training session as a deaf and mute fellow.

Everyone agreed that this was a great plan, and with that, the group started to say their good buy. Since he had the longest drive, Fritz was let out first.

CHAPTER 21

THE BIRTH OF A CLEANSING ORGANIZATION

But Bodo did not find sleep. No matter what he tried, too many thoughts were constantly running through his mind. So, he went up. He dressed again and started to think over the presentation he had to make in front of the most powerful men in the nation. Writing down bullet points on small paper cards he had found in his desk drawer, he lined out the red line along he would go to tell these men what needed to be done to get the country back in order, to stop the protests and crush the counterrevolution in it's beginning if it was actually still in the beginning phase. He did not have all the necessary information yet, but he believed that the counterrevolution movement could already be in phase two, meaning they had started to connect and create a nationwide organization.

His experience with the head of the SSP station in Bergen was somewhat disappointing, and he wasn't sure that the new head of the SSP was up to date yet how corrupt his organization was in some parts of the country. He wasn't even sure that the SSP had the information he would need. He began to line out the operational structure with three locations, estimated the number of officers he would need, and wrote down the legal requirements he would not budge a bit from. They could find someone else for the job if these minimum requirements were not granted. Because he knew that if the party leadership did not have the guts to grant him the tools and legality he needed, this assignment was doomed to fail. He would not be the guy to take responsibility for not stopping the destruction of the first socialistic state in history on German soil.

He was formulating some of the statements he was to make in his mind when suddenly the intercom came to life, and the voice of Dieter asked, 'Are you ready, comrade Bodo?' Hitting the speak button, he answered, 'I am. I will be downstairs in a few minutes.' Donning his jacket, he pocketed the few postcard-sized notes he had made and was on his way to the garage. Dieter was standing outside the car, and when Bodo entered the garage, he opened the back door on the passenger side for him. A little startled by this type of service, Bodo entered the car and thought he might need to get used to this if he was confirmed for that position. After an already-known drive of about 10 minutes, they reached the headquarters of the Central Committee, and the same check procedure happened as in the morning. 'Are they checking you and your passengers every time out when you come here, or is it just because I am unknown?' Bodo Asked.

'Oh no,' Dieter answered. The guards will never let a car pass without knowing and confirming who is in it. 'Even when I drive in with the Secretary-General, what happens when his personal driver is sick or on vacation, even will be checked.'

He stopped at the main entrance portal with vast and large glass doors and a large and wide stair going up to them. On top of the stairs stood comrade Bruno, waiting for Bodo with a wide smile. He greeted Bodo with a short, brotherly hug and asked, 'Are you nervous? You don't need to. They are all very experienced comrades who may have been in similar situations years before and hopefully remember. Come on, let's get up there and get it behind us.'

With that, they entered the building, which opened up to a large atrium reaching three floors. On the left side was a reception desk with several security officers and secretaries, and very expensive-looking tiles cut out of dark green basalt with matching patterns covered the whole floor. The wall appeared to be covered with large plates, at least three feet by six feet size marble, and the walls were built to funnel the visitors towards wide stairs with a landing at half the high of the first floor from where the stairs separated to the left and right reaching the first floor. On both sides of the stair stood a bust; on the left, one of Karl Marx, and on the right, one of Wladimir Lenin. Bodo had stopped right at the entrance and was in awe about the majesty of the impression one got when one entered this marvelous ambiance of the nation's official seat of the 'government.'

Comrade Bruno stood at the side of Bodo, looking at him and letting him take in the impressive view with a smile on his face. He remembered very well the first time he was invited to enter this building. After a few seconds, Bodo looked at Bruno and said, 'This is just awesome. These basalt tiles must be worth a fortune. And the walls, all marble and so large.'

'These were gifts from our comrades in the Soviet Union. I learned that when the building was built in the early 1960ies, the comrade said they want to have the GDR leadership to have a representative building for visitors. Especially because there are many communist parties in countries where they are oppressed and persecuted, and even murdered. We want to show them the rewards if they just endure and fight till victory is theirs.'

'Yea, 'comrade Bodo said, 'I understand. We need to give them something they can tell when they get home that it is worth all the sacrifices.'

'But, let's get up there to the conference room where the rest of the Central Committee is waiting.'

He led them to the right side of the stairs, where a bank of elevators was. One elevator had a different type of call button, and when Bodo looked closer, it was a keypad. Comrade Bruno entered a set of six numbers, and the doors opened. Even the inside of the elevator was terrific. Wide blanks of dark ebony separated by small strips of polished white sandalwood gave the cabin a luxurious touch and a lovely smell. The doors closed, and the elevator went up to the sixth floor. The door opened, and there was a small hall with doors on the left and the right. Also, two reception desks with a secretary sitting behind each. They were busy typing something on what looked like a TV with a keyboard in front of it. Between the two desks was a large French-style door, and Bodo walked directly toward it. He opened both door wings and, with a loud voice, interrupting several individual conversations, announced the arrival of 'Comrade Bodo Zipper, guest of the Central Committee.'

All members turned to the door and watched comrade Bruno showing in a somewhat hesitant comrade Bodo. 'Don't be shy, comrade Bodo,' comrade Bruno said. These men are all full of expectations and want to know you.' They entered the room, and comrade Bruno introduced every member of the Central Committee to comrade Bodo. When they were through that procedure, they all sat down, and Bodo was placed next to comrade Bruno, who was considered his host and the guy who brought him into the secret place. And one could consider that room a secret place on reflection, that this was the room where decisions of enormous consequences were made.

'Comrade Bodo,' the Secretary-General opened the meeting, 'we thank you for taking the time to meet with us, and we are all very interested in hearing from you personally about your life and your perspective on the current situation in our country and the party.'

Bodo looked around, and as it was his usual attitude when he met a person for the first time, he looked each of them in the eye. He wanted to get a feel for the person. How far could he trust that what they said was what they thought and would do? It was a mixture of responses, and he registered every single one. He realized that in that whole round of the powerful men, only five were as genuine, at the edge of fanatism, as he considered himself. Genuine to fight with their life for the cause of the communist party and to set in motion whatever was necessary to crush the counterrevolution. But that was the majority. With the Secretary-General, the Secretary SSP, the Secretary of Defense, the Secretary Justice, and his host, the Secretary of ICC, he had the most powerful members on his site.

'Comrades, I consider it a great honor and, much more so, a huge obligation that comrade Bruno considered me to be here today to present myself as the potential head of a special office. An office that will cleanse the first socialist nation on German soil from the corruption that wreaked havoc throughout the country. In his three-page framework, comrade Karl precisely lined out the things that need to be done and the unlimited legality of the actions that the new office must apply. I am currently developing a complete strategic paper for the structure of the new office, which he gave the preliminary name 'Office for Investigation and Recovery,' and I like that name. I would love to have the whole strategy presented to this committee on Friday afternoon, giving me roughly 48 hours to complete it.

'Now, I will try to answer that one question that might go through your head since you heard my name for the first time. Why this comrade? What is so special about him that the head of ICC chose to use him for such a job with epochal proportion?' He looked around, and all he saw were expectant, maybe curious expressions on their faces.' Comrades, you all have read my personnel file. And you know I am very sincere regarding the communist party. I would give my life for the cause of the communist world revolution. I grew up in a rather poor home, with a drunk being my stepfather, who terrorized the family whenever he came home drunk. My older brother, Fritz, was my guide in that horrible world, and we chose to stay away from that horrible home as long as we could. The party's youth organization gave us a reason, and we enjoyed it. Fritz was always upfront. He, being one and a half years older, and I have to confess, equipped with an enormous ability to apprehend correlations much faster and more comprehensively than I, had a very steep career. He became a youth leader in our city and advanced very fast to the position of the leader of AgitProp. He was elected to the youth committee of the National Fishing Corporation General Director while in college and became the secret liaison between the SSP and the Youth Collective. While leading the Youth Brigade, he formed himself during his praxis education in the electrical department of the Fishing Corporation Sassnitz. He was my role model. I wanted to become what he was. It did not last.'

'What happened,' it was comrade Gerd Hollorek who asked, and it was clearly tangible that he, and several others, was captivated by the story Bodo told the members of the Central Committee because he had never experienced anything even close to that.

'I guess comrade Pieker knows more about the details than I will ever know, but he started to sabotage the basic rules for members of Youth Brigades. It is clearly listed in the statutes that no member of a Youth Brigade can have a relationship with persons defined as subversive elements of society. And among those are Christians. He refused to report such kind of relationships of members of the Youth Brigade to the SSP. Other breaches of the code of socialist ethics finally led to his exclusion from all his leadership positions. The topping was that he married a Christian woman. While she is a great and nice girl, I thought she might come around to our side and realize that her belief in God is stupid. It happened the other way around. After he was allowed to complete his graduation from university, my brother suddenly declared that he now believed in God and that this guy Jesus had rescued him from ...... who knows what. At that time, I had the Party University delegation in my pocket. With days left to start in Potsdam, I got called to the county's SSP. The officer explained the situation and said I could not be a student at that elite university under these circumstances. And I completely understood. The county party arranged the position of a major in a small village for me, and later, a long-time friend, a merited comrade, brought me into the party office of the county for the position of AgitProp. That's me.'

Comrade Werner let out a deep sigh because that story had caught his attention and said,' comrade Bodo, it was under a different party leadership, and I will officially apologize for the injustice done to you. I could guarantee you that if comrade Pieker had been in the position he is now and would have known about it, he would have made sure that this would have been immediately corrected.

'It is ok, comrade Secretary-General. I am not resentful against the comrades. They did what was best from their point of view, and the disappointment about my brother was enormous since they all knew him and had a great appreciation for his work for the party.'

'Thank you, comrade, for your understanding. It makes things easier when we can put personal issues out of the way. Now, let me ask you, are you aware of the seriousness of the situation, and if so, are you willing to do what is necessary to correct the mistakes many members of the party in leadership positions and not only there have made? And What would it take, in your opinion, to get our house in order?'

'Secretary-General and all comrades here in the room, I believe we are possibly at the second stage, or at least very close to it, of a well-organized counterrevolution.

'Wait a moment,' comrade Pieker interrupted, 'You really believe that the Monday night marches around churches with candlelights are the beginning of the counterrevolution?'

Smiling, Bodo answered, 'Not at all. Youth pastors organize those Monday marches around the churches with the support of the imperialist elements out of West Germany. They believe they can force you into submission to their demands of free travel. And I can only hope you are strong enough not to cave into those requests. I studied the history of this nation in detail. I read almost every single issue of the 'Young World' and the 'New Germany' from that time before the wall was built. We will not be able to survive the loss of highly trained, well-educated specialists. You just can't do that. You have to find a way to silence these marchers.'

'No, I am talking about the real danger, the underground resistance. It exists, it is very careful, and I know from comrades who are dealing with those indications that they are real. On an Island of just under 360 square miles with no way to get off, the only landbridge has been closed for weeks. Why do you think the two deserters of the Red Army Special Forces have not been arrested yet? They have help! And I know that many of our comrades have only their interests in mind. They are corrupt to the bone. Comrades, if you take a 50 D-Mark, hide it in a piece of paper and place it in front of a head of a department, and you say I need 20 bags of cement at this address, you will have it tomorrow. The person who did it correctly doesn't get those 20 bags and becomes angry. What do you expect? The people who are the real enemies of our communist party, those like my brother, use the disappointment of those people and activate them for their subversive actions. If the comrades in our party acted according to the doctrine of Lenin, they would be lights of the communist ideology, radiant examples of how people should work, giving their best for the cause. Suppose we want to ensure that the power of our party remains and that we are leading this nation to the next step, the establishment of a communist society. In that case, we must eradicate these elements of treason with their roots. Indicted, tried, and fried! No mercy! And I don't care if it is the First Secretary of the District Rostock or the head of the department of international trading, or, with all due respect, Secretary-General, your brother, or mine. If you don't have the stomach for that, If you are not willing to sign the death sentence for treason, even for your own brother, I am the wrong man for this position. I will drive home and work as the Secretary for AgitProp in the county until the socialistic system of this nation collapses, and I will bear the consequences of the last stand for it with my head high.

For several minutes there was silence in the conference room. And if it would not have been for the very low street noise seeping in through what Bodo considered a ballistic glass of the large windows, the heavy sighting of some of the Central Committee's members would appear as the sound of a storm.

After what seemed like an eternity, Secretary-General Werne let out another sigh and said, 'Comrade Bodo, this was some kind of a statement. I believe, speaking in the name of all Secretary of the Central Committee, that we believe that you are very determined and that there are not many with your conviction in our party these days. Would you please mind waiting outside to give us some privacy to discuss our opinions? The secretary will take care of anything you need. It won't take long.'

Comrade Bruno stood, going with Bodo through the door, addressed the secretaries to take good care of comrade Bodo for a few minutes, and went back inside.

The secretaries started to talk simultaneously, 'Comrade, what.' They looked at each other, laughing, and one of them continued,' Can we get you to drink or to eat? Maybe a sandwich?'

'I don't think this will take longer, and there is probably no time for getting the sandwich ever made. But I will gladly appreciate bottled water.' Bodo answered while walking towards the door with the sign for the men's room. Inside the room, he went to the basin, took his hands full of cold water, and swapped his face. His mind was racing a hundred miles an hour, and he thought, what have you maneuvered yourself into here, Bodo? You may end up shoveling coal into a heating system in the basement of a third-class health facility. What were you thinking? Threatening the brother of the Secretary-General could be found guilty of treason and executed. Oh my. I better get out there and face the music. Nothing to change after that. He stood straight up, looked in the mirror, and out loud, he said to nobody, 'And I will change nothing. What I said is what I am!'

When he exited the men's room, both secretaries, with big smiles, pointed to a small table with two chairs, and he discovered two sandwiches and a bottle of water with a glass placed there for him. He thanked them and sat down, grabbing one of the sandwiches topped with his favorite liverwurst. He thought that if I got punished in the next half hour or so, I should at least enjoy these sandwiches—kind of the last meal.

When the door opened, he had eaten both sandwiches and nearly emptied the bottled water, and comrade Bruno winked at him to join the Central Committee again. With a smile that immediately reversed all of Bodo's fear into excitement, comrade Bruno said,' We have come to a decision, and we would like you to sit down and listen to the assignment.

Bodo took the same seat next to comrade Bruno as he had before he was sent out and looked around at the members of the Central Committee the same way he had done at the beginning of their meeting. What he saw encouraged him to believe that they understood the situation and had gotten his message to the full extent.

'Comrade Bodo,' the Secretary-General commenced speaking, 'at first, I have to tell you that we heard your message loud and clear, and we are aware of the seriousness of the situation. As you can imagine, a meeting like this would never have taken place in this room under the chair of the, let's call it, 'old guard.' That is the reason why we established this new form of leadership. We have decided to give the assignment of cleansing this nation of all traitors to the cause to you. And we mean it. We mean cleansing and all, precisely as it is said—no regard to person or position. And here is your assignment:

1. You are considered an officer of the SSP with the rank of a Commander with all the rights, but you are reporting only to the Central Committee and no one else.

2. Your reports are asked to be done monthly and, if necessary, contact comrade Bruno to get a fast connection. He will instruct you how you can reach him at any time.

3. You will create an organization named the Office of Investigation and Recovery. You will be responsible for getting your officers, drivers, and other personnel hired, background-checked, and sworn to absolute secrecy. The SSP, Defense Forces, and Ministry of Internal Affairs are instructed to accept any order from your office you have authorized.

4. You will name a maximum of twelve officers of your choice to have the 'Authority to give Directions' to any officer in the departments mentioned above.

5. You and those officers will have complete unrestricted access to any databank and information available. That includes, per your signed request, our foreign institutions and scouts.

6. The immediate budget for your operation has been set to four million Marks. The Secretary of Economy has agreed to use the procurement department of the Ministerium of Foreign Affairs to purchase modern communication and office systems. We have to limit that to $ 1 million, you surely understand.

7. Secretaries SSP and Defense agreed to supply you with automobiles of your choice from their pool. Since you need excellent drivers, Comrade Pieker suggested the graduates from his academy of the class that finishes end of the month.

'Comrade Bodo, I can only imagine how loaded the day is for you. Comrade Bruno has been authorized to get you a house, and your family moved. Therefore we will close at this point and meet on Friday at 3 PM to get your general strategy outline for the operation. Comrades, the meeting is ended, and you are dismissed.'

CHAPTER 22

THE DEFINITION OF THE STRUCTURE OF A CLEANSING ORGANIZATION

Without saying a word, Bodo walked out of the conference room with comrade Bruno on his heels, trying to keep up with Bodo heading towards the elevator. 'Hey, comrade Bodo, wait for me. You are running away or what?' Bodo turned and, laughing, said, 'Sorry, comrade Bruno, I was so in my thoughts already at work about the strategic and tactical decisions which need to be made immediately that I completely forgot where I am.'

Bruno laughed and said, 'You can't outrun the necessary steps, and I guess you know that. First, we will go and get a nice late lunch. Then we will introduce you to your secretary, which will be at your temporary office tomorrow at 8 AM. Comrade Karl called me while you were outside and told me that Karin had agreed to sacrifice one of her assistant secretaries for your new OIR organization.' While riding downstairs in the elevator, Bruno further explained the next steps. 'Comrade Pieker had already called the SSP's headquarters and ordered to get a Lada with a tuned engine, and it is already equipped with the latest Nokia Cell Phone, 'Mobira Talkman, which we all use as you may have noticed in my car.' By that time, they were walking through the enormous and impressive entrance hall of the building towards the doors, and Bodo stopped in his tracks as if he had hit a wall. 'Did you say Mobile Phone, comrade Bruno, emphasizing every word? I mean, these things you carry with you and talk to people on the other side of the country? And no,

I have not noticed that you have one in your car. I thought it was a radio, which I understood when Dieter explained that it could contact whoever you needed. You know, the same way I used the radio from the fishing cutter to call home, connected through the base station on Land that funneled the radio cal into the phone network.' While walking through the doors down the stairs and entering the car, 'Bruno answered, 'No, comrade Bodo, it is an actual phone. It uses a specific frequency band as the European organization decided upon in 1982, and we were able to acquire a number of the Finnish-made Mobira just in January as an exchange for getting some high-ranking meetings set up between our Soviet comrades and the USA government.' While explaining this to Bodo, he grabbed the handheld from the holder between the two backseats and held it to Bodo. 'Here, call your wife and tell her to prepare for moving to the Berlin area. I already have an idea of where I would like to set you up. It is not far from the place where I live, and my kids are roughly the same age as your Nick.' While Bodo looked intensely at the handset and began to hit the keys with the number of his home phone, Bruno instructed Dieter to a specific Hungarian restaurant located in the famous street Unter den Linden.

'Hallo Sarina,' Bodo said after she picked up the phone and announced herself. 'Bodo, where are you? You sound a little like you are underwater, but I can clearly understand you. How are things with the comrades in Berlin? Have you had your meeting already? How did it go?'

'Slow down, my love, slow down. I am in the car with comrade Bruno and using his car phone. Can you believe I am calling from a car driving down the road, and you can understand what I am saying? Unbelievable when I compare that to our conversations from the cutter. But listen, I can't talk for a long using this essential phone, I will call later tonight, and it might be late—just upfront. It can happen within the next four to five days. We are moving to the outskirts of Berlin. Start to prepare everything for moving.'

All Sarina could answer was, 'Oh my!' where do I start? Oh my! 'Easy, Sarina, start packing all the clothing and stuff which can brake, so it is safe during transport. We will have a professional moving company from the party's Central Committee to move everything. So don't worry about the details. I need to hang up; love you, tschüss.'

Attempting to place the handset back into the holder, Bruno stopped him and said, 'I need it to call Karl to get the car from the SSP carpool for you and meet us at the restaurant. Hello Karl, can you get the car for comrade Bodo from the SSP carpool and meet us at the Hungarian?' Listening to his response of Karl he answered OK, sounds like a plan. See you there in a bit.'

A few minutes later, Dieter left the main street, named Unter den Linden, turned into a minor side street, and stopped in front of a large gate after a few meters. He honked the horn twice, and after a short pause, once again, The large gate opened a bit, and a man looked through the gap. He recognized the car and opened the gate fully so Dieter could drive in and park the car in the back of the restaurant. They left the car and told the man that comrade Karl was arriving in about thirty minutes. As on the day before, Bodo was just too astounded to be surprised that they walked straight through the back door, a long hallway, passing the kitchen on their left and a storage room on the other side, and entered the guest room through a door next to the bar. The restaurant was pretty full, and when a waiter noticed Bruno, he unusually fast walked towards them. 'Good afternoon, comrade Tecker. What a surprise to have you as our guest tonight. Is the booth in the back OK for tonight? And at his small nod of Bruno, he said, 'Please follow me.' It was a nice small place with a great view of the outside, but not so close that one could see them sitting there, and it was large enough to seat easily six people. While Dieter placed himself at the bar, and the waiter promised to send the chef over immediately, Bodo looked around, absorbing the restaurant's atmosphere. Everything was made from very dark, almost black wood. The tables, the chairs, and the walls were paneled to a height of about 8 feet. All were from the same dark wood.

'Comrade Bodo, this is an excellent restaurant with great food. But you must be careful. This waiter who serves us today serves me, Karl, or any of the central committee whenever we eat here. I suspect he is trying to get information about what we are talking about and sell it. But the SSP was on his heels for weeks and could find nothing to nail him. So we have never found any legitimate reason to name him a suspect, but my gut tells me he is not clean.'

'Good to know, comrade Bruno. Maybe he needs a cleansing from the new OIR?' Bodo said with a smirk, 'Sorry, pun intended.'

Bruno laughed loudly and said, 'I need to remember that line. It is awesome. Until Karl arrives, let me tell you a little about the facility I have in mind for you to move in. It is a very nice villa in the village of Karolinenhof and lies at the end of a cool de sack named Schappachstreet. There is one house between mine house and that one. That facility is something special, and I was fortunate that we could place a lock on it after that traitor ran away before the SSP could lay hands on it. The guy who owned it was a professor of vascular surgery. The absolute expert. He not only taught our Students at the Charite, but he also had teaching positions at several NSW universities. For several years we let him travel whenever he applied for a visa and used it as a propaganda tool. We knew he had his wife, which he dearly loved, and two cute little children here to whom he would return any time.

'What happened to him? Did he have an accident?' Bodo asked.

'I have to tell you, comrade Bodo, sometimes I wish I was as hard on our enemies as you seem. Especially with this guy. We gave him everything. We gave him the best education one can get, and he had to pay not a cent for it. We allowed him to buy that property because the Party owned it as an estate of an old comrade who died shortly after WW II. We made it possible for him to build that fantastic mansion by allocating building materials and a construction workforce, even though there was some resistance within the local party group. The next thing happened last year in the fall. He applied for a visa for a lecture at the university in Calgary. It was granted without any hesitation as all the times before. Nobody knew that his wife and the children were in Bulgaria on vacation. While he was lecturing at the University, they walked into the Canadian Embassy in Sofia and applied for political asylum. In the Bulgarian foreign affairs department for visa issues of citizens of the communist countries was a guy who had survived an accident because this professor was at the University in Sofia and saved his life at that time. He issued an exit visa for her and the children, and before her husband arrived in Calgary, they were on a plane to London. Our comrades at the SSP had no idea and learned about it when West German TV presented the family as the latest high-ranking refugees from our great nation.'

'Unbelievable sloppiness at the SSP,' said Bodo. 'Were there consequences?

'One of the consequences is that comrade Pieker is the new chef. It wasn't just that comrade Werner liked him; they had been connected for several years. He is a great comrade, and his heart is in the right place. He started cleaning his ranks and had much more work to do. That is why he was as enthusiastic as I was to create your new position and give the office as much power as possible. He, the Secretary-General Secretary of Finance, the Secretary of Defense, and I were the ones who voted to give you that enormous power even over the other legal entities and police or SSP in the country. He knows what is at stake, and he knows that his ranks are not clean.

'That is great to hear. We must work together on many cases where I need their expertise and capacities.' Bodo responded, just at the moment Karl appeared at the booth.

'Hello, comrade Bruno. Hello, comrade Bodo. I guess everything went as planned, comrade Bodo? '

'You guessed right, Karl. Otherwise, we would not sit here with a nice juice glass and talk.' Bruno responded. 'We were just talking about the property of that swine of a professor next to my home would be an excellent place for comrade Bodo to move in.'

'Why! I did not think about it. I had in the morning figured out where we could locate his headquarter office, and now you have the potential home almost in walking distance to that place.' Now you have me made curious, Karl. 'What? What did you find that would fit the requirements of the most secret operation close to Karolinenhof?'

'Comrade Bruno, do you remember the old Forrest Care facility off of the Adlergestell Expressway, just a few hundred feet before you enter Schlappachstreet? It has been closed for years now, but the buildings are in somewhat acceptable condition, and when we put our construction bureau on it and give it the top priority, it should be an excellent complex for the OIR headquarter.'

Oh, yes, I remember. This old Forrester's yard was renovated two or three years back, and then they closed it because they did not need it. I have to find out who has control of the real estate and see that we can just buy it.'

In the meantime, the chef appeared, and they ordered what he had on the menu for the day. When they were finished eating, Bodo wanted to take up the tab to pay, but both comrades Bruno and Karl immediately protested and told him that he couldn't pay for the meal until he got his first salary in his new position. So Karl took up to pay for their dinner. They left the same way they came into the restaurant.

When they entered the restaurant's backyard, the new Lada was next to the Volvo of comrade Bodo. It was black and had tinted windows, which was not usual in the GDR for a civil car. But because of the black body paint and the missing chromed lines, it did not really appear as unique.

'Are the tinted windows not somewhat peculiar? I want to be relatively unnoticeable.' Bodo stated a little insecure with his critics.

'That was what I thought when SSP presented this car to me. But then they showed me a training video they are using for the driver training. There is a section where the drivers must drive through a small village at max speed and then at average speed. After a few days, the people in the village are interviewed about a car driving through the village a few days ago. The only thing they remembered was that a black car many guessed but weren't sure about, a Lada, was driving far too fast. None of them remembered the slow-driving black Lada. And none had an idea that the second one had tinted windows. Many of them were absolutely sure that it wasn't the case.' Comrade Bodo, do you want to drive with me? After all, it is your future car anyway.

Bodo entered the Lada, and the first thing he noticed was the same mobile phone mounted at the rear center console. The carpool of the SSP had also mounted a front center console where the original Lada had just the gearstick coming out of the floor. He had no idea how they rearranged the gearshift system, but within a few meters of driving, Karl making a tree point turn, he saw that it was excellent work. The car was also severely tuned to the point that Karl had no problems hanging on the Volvo in front of them any time he accelerated. And all of this at a noise level that was almost unnoticeable inside the car. Watching Karl's driving skills for a while, he said, 'You're as good at driving safely, even at high speed, with maneuvering around hindrances as Dieter.'

'You have the driver position assigned to you, and you can participate in a driver's class with the SSP any time you want. I would insist you do it if I had the power to do that,' Karl said and smiled at him. 'Bodo, you haven't realized what powerful position you have been assigned, right.'

'Honestly, Karl, I still feel as if I am dreaming. About 48 hours ago, somebody, I had never heard of burst into my office on the Island, and now I am supposed to be as powerful as a Secretary member of the Central Committee. That is a lot to digest, Karl.'

'We are turning here into the Schappachstreet, at which end the House is comrade Bruno talked about. You will love it!' Karl was slowing down, and they stopped behind the Volvo, having its left turn light blinking. After two oncoming cars had passed, they turned left into Schlappachstreet and drove with a moderate speed through a very well-maintained area of more or less large houses. Some were set back from the street so far that they were barely visible through the vegetation growing along the fences surrounding the properties. When the end of the roughly one-eighth of a mile-long street became noticeable, Karl pointed to the left side and said, 'This is the house of comrade Bruno.' Since they drove rather slowly now, Bodo looked over and said,' Not much to see. That Conifer Hedge is a real nice cover. And the gate is solid, so I can't see anything.'

'That's the whole purpose. We don't want to give anybody a way to monitor what is going on on the property. It is a neighborhood where any unknown car would raise immediate suspicion when it parks alongside the street for a while. And here we are. This is the beauty comrade Bruno talked about.'

The Volvo had stopped in front of a gate that was even mightier than that at Bruno's property. Although the conifer hedge wasn't as high as the one there, it already covered the majority of the house, which was set back on the property for about 200 feet, and just about 100 feet off of the waterline of the river Dahme.

They drove up the not-well-maintained gravel road to the front of the house and exited the car. They joined Bruno, who was stretching out his arms, and called over to Bodo, 'What do you say, comrade Bodo? Did I promise too much?

Bodo was overwhelmed by the property's silence and beauty and could not believe that he and his family would live there. Such a stark contrast to the small half-sized farmhouse they lived in now.

'I am stunned, comrade Bruno. I have no idea how I deserve such a beauty of a property.

'You haven't seen the house yet. Come on in,' grabbing the keys to the house from his pockets. He unlocked the door. He opened the door and, with a gesture of his arm, invited Bodo to walk in. Bodo walked into a large entrance area, probably thirty by thirty feet. A centered wide stair went up to a landing at half the height of the second floor and spread from the landing to the left and the right, ending at an open hallway area on the second floor, not completely visible from the first-floor position. On the left side was a French-style door leading into an office space clearly defined by the beautiful, integrated bookshelves. The office was furnished entirely, and seeing Bodo's questioning look, Bruno explained, 'We left some of the furniture and the appliances as they were in the house because first, we did not know what to do with it, and secondly it was always considered to move a comrade in here with a particular assignment. We did not know at that time what the assignment would be, but yours justifies this.'

Walking further into the house, they entered a wide open area with what looked like very exclusive leather couches and chairs in front of an almost 30 feet wide window, opening the view onto a terrace with a waist-high stone wall around it and stairs on both sides and further down to the river. On the left side was a seating area with a huge table and 12 chairs around it, and on the right side was an open kitchen with all the appliances a modern West German household of the upper class would have. At the end of the dining area was a door leading to a room with a seating area, a washer and dryer, a closet, and a door that led to the outside. Bodo opened the door and stood right in front of a decently sized garden, which covered almost the whole side of the house up to the fence with a conifer hedge. Walking back through the dining and seating area to the right of the kitchen was an open space that connected the entrance hall to the seating and kitchen area. Although it wasn't furnished, Bodo thought it would be a great area for visitors waiting for him to come into his home office.

There was also a small powder room off the entrance hall on that side. The closed part on the right-hand side had a door leading to a somewhat large storage room equipped with shelves all around three walls. The fourth wall had another door, and when he opened it, it led to the three-car garage with a working area with workbench and tool cabinets covering one whole wall. They went back into the hallway and up the stairs to the second floor. Bodo turned around and looked down from the wide hallway area, which was open on that side, up to the enormously high ceiling. And a thought crossed his mind, how the heck would Sarina keep that cleaned?

Bruno, who had followed his gaze and said, 'Pretty high, right? How the heck can my wife keep that clean? Wasn't that your thought? We had the same issue, but there is a service company that we use once a month, and they come out and take care of it. They are also contracted with the Central Committee and other government buildings. They are not cheap but save, and you can easily effort them with your salary.'

The second floor had three bedrooms, all with separate bathrooms, and a master bedroom that was so fantastic that Bodo ran out of superlatives to express his impression. Although there was no furniture, it was huge. It had large window/sliding doors which opened almost the whole eastern wall of the room and led to a balcony that covered the whole wall. To the left were two doors leading to two separate bathrooms with directly connected walk-in closets.

They all went downstairs and out of the house. On the landing in front of that gorgeous Main door, Bruno asked Bodo, 'What do you think, comrade Bodo, will your wife like the house, or do we have to look for another one?'

Bodo burst out laughing like seldom lately, and when he caught his breath, answered, 'you are joking, comrade Bruno. Never in my life have I even dreamed of living in a house like this. And if I would not just have a walk through it, I would not have believed that something like that even existed. I don't know how I could justify such a luxury, knowing how many people live throughout the country.'

'Bodo, if you are in an exposed position such as we Secretaries of the Central Committee, or your new position, you need two things to stay sane. First, you need safety. And a house like this is a safe place. You can't live in a ten-story highrise with 45 families, with several traitors. Secondly, with an average o 10 to 12-hour workdays, you need a place where you can safely rest and scoop new power for the coming tasks' None of the members of the new leadership of the party lives in homes like that for free. We all pay for them.

We have agreed upon a rent with the finance department, or we pay down a loan, including interest, according to the official rate. You know that the average rent in our nation's capital is roughly 2 Marks per square meter, and with this house at approximately a little over 450 square meters, it will cost you about 900 Marks a month. We have not had someone moving in yet, and even though some comrades in positions with salaries could effort it, they did not want to sacrifice to pay the requested money. With your salary and your position, there is no doubt in my mind that you not only can afford the house but also will enjoy the place after hard work.'

'Comrade Bruno, excuse me when I am forthright with you. I have no clue what my salary is. And with that, I don't know if any money is left for food after I've paid for the house. I know that the budget for the operation of the OIR in total is four million Marks. Still, I have to calculate the salary for the officers, secretaries, cars, and all the operational costs, and I have no idea yet what is left for me as salary.'

'See, comrade Bruno, that attitude is part of why we chose you for the position. You always put the cause before your own needs. This brought the current members of the Central Committee together to send the Old Guard into retirement and try to do whatever was necessary to save the Republic. Your salary is not part of the budget for the operation. Your salary was decided long before your name, and the members of the Central Committee knew the personnel file. We thought a position like that needed to be just below the level of a Secretary of the Central Committee since you are not reporting to anyone else. You will have a salary of 4,000 Marks per month, which is a net payment. Since you are employed, the party will pay all taxes and social security. If you are traveling, you use the account of the OIR to pay for those expenses, as long as they are assignment related. This is clean and fair, and we believe you would agree with it.

'What can I say, comrade Bruno? I am again almost speechless, and that should tell you something. I accept the offer with great gratitude and will let my wife know what she has to expect.'

Bruno handed the keys to the house and the remote control to the gate over to Bodo with the remark, 'It's yours then, comrade neighbor. Enjoy! OK, let's get and look at the potential workspace comrade Karl found.'

They entered the cars, Bruno's Volvo in front. Karl had encouraged Bodo to take over ownership of his new car, and Bodo happily had taken the offer, now following the Volvo out of the gate and hitting the remote control, closing it behind them. After the short drive out of Schappachstreet, they turned right into the unpaved street leading to the abandoned Forrest yard property. In front of the large gate, allowing big trucks to enter, was a parking spot that could hold probably five cars. They turned onto it and stopped there.

Exiting the cars, even Dieter, this time, joined them. They walked up to a small man-sized gate very skillfully made out of dried-out branches. Karl took out a key, removed the lock from the locking bolt, and opened the gate. They walked into the yard, and while Karl closed the gate behind them, they looked around at the two dominant buildings on the property. One was a single-story, house-style building with a central entrance door and windows, and the other looked more like a barn or workshop. It had two large double doors riching onto the roof and a row of half-sized windows higher elevated from the ground than usual. They turned towards the house that seemed to be used as office space, and Karl unlocked the door with the same key. It had a decent-sized reception area, which led to a hallway to the left and right with open doors and presented office rooms that were large enough for four officers in each. At the end of the right-side hallway was a closed door, and they walked down the hallway, opened that door, and entered a rather large office. It was the right-sized office room for Bodo to have his office there and was large enough to have a small seating area and a conference table to seat numerous people for meetings.

They left the house and walked over to the barn. Opening one wing of the large barn door, they entered a space that could very well be used for the cars to be parked, and even basic service, such as oil change, could be done. They even discovered a pit that allowed work on the underside of a car. There was a waist-high separation wall with a small gate to the other section, where the second large door was the entrance too. They walked through the small door and opened the door which led to the other half of the barn. It obviously has been used to keep animals because there were four separate stalls on each side of a wide aisle between them. The stalls were all separated from the aisle by heavy iron rods from floor to ceiling and masonry walls in between the stalls.

Bodo could immediately imagine the whole building as a holding area for arrested people. Still, before he could comment on that thought, Bruno said, 'So, comrade Bodo, isn't that something? Not only did we find the best house for you and your family to live in, but we have the perfect property to handle the nation's enemies right down the road, almost within walking distance.'

'Comrade Bruno, you scared me here for a moment. You read my mind, and I hope that is not your general ability,' he said, laughing.

They all laughed, and Bodo finally put the last thought into the open, 'there is some work necessary because I need to have those 'cells' sound-proof separated, and this half of the barn needs soundproof.' With that, they left the building, closed the large barn door, and stood in the middle of the property, looking around.

Bruno laid his arm around the shoulder of Bodo and turned him 360 degrees to take in the whole scenery, and said, 'comrade Bodo, you think you could use this property as your headquarter? All this around us is a state forest, and the party will pay the rent for this property to the administration as long as we use it. The forest for miles around here does not need any maintenance for the next several years, which is why the Forrest administration abandoned this property.'

In the meantime, tired of all the new impressions which bombarded his brain, Bodo answered, 'I am lost for words for the extraordinary support for this new office operation, OIR. It proves to me that the new Central Committee is really interested in cleansing out the sewage that has infiltrated the rows of our party. I will see that I have the main steps of the strategic actions and the tactical basic written up on Friday morning, ready to present them to the members of the Central Committee.'

'Comrade Bodo, I am in joy with you knowing that we chose the right comrade for this challenging position and that we can give you the best possible starting conditions because we all understood your statement this afternoon about the party's danger in losing the power. I will have my office arrange all that is necessary to get you moved with your household as soon as maybe end this week. My office will also oversee the office space's furnishing and start the barn's construction. The construction could start tomorrow and should not take more than two weeks. And we will take care of restoring all the utilities and cleaning the house so that it is ready for you to move in. Now, Karl is driving with you to the guesthouse of the CC, and we will have a driver and a secretary for you available tomorrow morning. Sorry, there was no time to introduce her to you today, but the headquarters property was not on my schedule since Karl discovered it just this morning. Good Night comrade Bodo. I am looking forward to working with you.'

'Same here, comrade Bruno. We will make the country safe again.'

Bruno and Dieter entered the Volvo and drove off. Karl closed the man gate and locked it. He was about to hand the key over to Bodo, but then he stopped and said, 'Bodo, I think I will keep the key for now. I will get some duplicates made, and I believe we should do that for your house keys and the remote too. When you are ready to move in, all keys will be handed over to you. We will make sure that every copy is registered and counted for.'

'Sounds good to me because the guys working on the barn and offices and those on the house need to be able to get in.'

They went into the Lada, and Bodo drove back into the city and to the Guest House of the CC. It was a good hour's drive since the rush hour had already reached its highest level, and the increased traffic gave Bodo more praxis training himself with this powerful version of a commonly known car. While Bodo was driving, Karl made some phone calls arranging for the driver to be at the CC Guest House at 8 AM, meeting with him at the guard's office. They reached the Guest House of the CC at about 8 PM, and after they were checked, they drove into the underground garage where Bodo parked the car at one of the many free spots. Bodo stretched out his hand to say good night to Karl, saying, 'I am new to you, Karl, but we are roughly the same age, and in a few days, I will start an operation that will scare the living daylight out of our enemies, inside the party and outside. You brought me into this position, and I will always be there for you if you need me. I hope it is the beginning of a unique and long friendship, above-party relations, and beyond. The only issue that can break that bond would be the discovery that you are on the other side.'

'Thank you, Bodo. I can't tell you how I have waited for a day like this. I feel the same towards you, and let us fight the party's enemies together.' With a brotherly hug, they separated, and Bodo hit the code for his apartment floor at the elevator while Karl drove out of the garage.

Bodo went immediately to the phone and had his wife on within the first ring.

'you won't believe what I have experienced today, Sarina, and I am much too tired to give you the entire account. We will move into an awesome house beginning next week. It is directly on the river, has a huge garden and a master bedroom the size of our house. You will probably faint when you see the property first, and I have to carry you in,' he said with laughter in between the words.

'Bodo, don't scare me.' Sarina said, 'what do I have to pack myself, and what is the moving company doing?'

'I would suggest you pack everything that can brake, such as glasses and dishes and stuff you would usually be careful with when you move it around. I won't say anything bad about the guys who will do our moving because they are moving the top-level people's stuff. They can't risk breaking anything, but movers are movers, and that's what it is.'

'Ok, I understand. Are you home when we have to pack everything?

'I will try to get out of Berlin latest Monday or Tuesday next week. But I will call as soon as I am on the way. I want to be here at least to see the start of the construction work that needs to be done in the office and speak with the Architect before I leave, but that might not be necessary.'

'Good night, and I hope you can get some sleep with all these exciting things going on.'

'You too, tschüss!'

When she had hung up, Bodo walked into the bathroom and prepared a steaming hot bath. After done with that, he was ripe for the bed. I adjusted the alarm for 6:30 and was just about to fall into his bed when a thought shot through his mind. He walked over to his desk and ran through stored phone numbers to see if he could find a home phone number for Karl or Bruno. Unsurprisingly, both phone numbers were programmed, and he decided to call Karl, knowing that he was single and would probably be less interrupted at that time.

'Yes. Who is there?' was Karl's answer after the second ring. 'Excuse me for calling so late, and I hope I did not disturb you with something important?'

'Oh. Bodo, no, not at all. What can I do for you? Is something not alright?

'No, I was just about to lie down. I was really exhausted and about to go to bed when I thought you might be able to arrange some range instruction time for me at the SSP facility and get me set up with the handgun sometime in the afternoon. Would that be possible?'

'Sure, Bodo, no problem there. We can meet after your Secretay's work day is over and meet at the SSP facility. That's an excellent opportunity to test your new driver.'

'Great, thank you so much, Karl. See you tomorrow at the SSP' Just call when you have the meeting time.' He hung up went to bed, and before he even could look again at the watch, he was deep in sleep.

CHAPTER 23

THE STRATEGIC AND TACTICAL ORIENTATION OF THE OFFICE FOR INVESTIGATION AND RECOVERY

When the alarm went off at 6:30, Bodo was out of bed and had no issues finding himself oriented, in contrast to the day before. He got his bathroom activities done, clothed, and ordered breakfast from the guest house kitchen. He was reading his bullet points and started to correct here and there a little bit when there was a knock on the door. He went and opened the door, and a woman moved in a cart with a cover that contained his breakfast.

'Good Morning, comrade Zipper. Here is your breakfast, and we hope you enjoy it. Please feel free to call if you need anything else.' And saying this with a smile, she was already out of the suite.

With a sigh, Bodo removed the cloth and thought, who in the world shall eat all of this? He started with the eggs and butter toast. The Orange juice appeared to be freshly pressed from real oranges, not some powdered stuff deluded in water. He could not eat even half of it and covered the remains. Just when he was about to call the room service to remove the cart, he decided to wait to see if the driver or the secretary would want to get some of it. He returned to his desk and worked again on the line-out of the operation when the doorbell at the office door to the floor area rang. He closed the French door between the office area and his sleeping quarters and went to the door to open it. Outside stood the secretary and a young man. Bodo said hello and asked them into the office.

His secretary started and introduced herself, 'I'm Giesela, and I have been assigned to your office and the new agency, but I forgot what their name if it is. I am sorry.' I'm Gunther, and I have been assigned to this new agency,' with a smile on his face looking at Giesela, who was probably twice his age, added, 'I did forget the name also.'

'Oh, you are not sure if I am the right person you have to report to? Bodo asked. Then laughing at their baffled expression, 'It's Ok. It is even new for me, and I wonder when we will be able to say the whole name without thinking. Come in, and let's get to know each other.'

They took seats on the small couch table, and Giesela started, 'I have been working for the office of comrade Bruno Tecker under his personal secretary Karin for almost ten years. I was hired by comrade Tecker when we met at a conference at the Party University in Potsdam, where I worked for one of the teachers.'

'Are you disappointed that Karing sent you to this new agency' Bodo asked?

'No, she answered. I am actually curious and always interested in discovering something new.'

'That you definitely will. We have an assignment that has never even been thought of before, and you can be sure that you will be part of something interesting. I assume that you both have been sworn to absolute secrecy again, and it is no joke that your secrecy is a matter of life and death.

They answered simultaneously, 'Yes, comrade. We were sworn in again yesterday to keep all about this new agency, the Office of Investigation and Recovery, in short OIR, to ourselves,' Giesela inserted. This was the case with the office of comrade Tecker, the case anyway, but it seemed to be a lot more intense.'

'Gunther, what about you? You seem to be relatively young,' Bodo asked, turning his attention to his driver.

'Yes, comrade Zipper, I am 24, and I have served three years at the airborne regiment at the Island Rügen. After two years, I was sent to the special driver's course in the Soviet Union, where I was trained by a Speznaz instructor to handle not only all vehicles of the Warsaw Pact production but many of the NATO countries too. I graduated top class of 50 participants, and when I returned to the regiment, the General decided that I should be his driver. When I was discharged, I did not want to return to my regular auto mechanic job because I considered it boring.

'How did you end up at the SSP? As far as I know, they choose whom they approach to integrate into their organization, Bodo asked.

'I walked into their building in my hometown, Leipzig, and said I would like to be a driver for them. The officer fell almost out of his chair, and after about an hour with a captain, he made some phone calls and told me to report to the headquarter in Berlin two days later. I went to six months of additional training for personnel protection, and here I am. Comrade Zipper, I hope I can fulfill your requirements, and if I make a mistake, I hope you will give me a second chance.'

Giesela jumped in at that point and said, 'Me too.'

Bodo was startled and said, 'Who do you think I am? A monster?'

Both again almost simultaneously, 'No, comrade Zipper, no. It is just,' Gunter explained, 'We have been instructed to be 110 percent of our ability to perform; otherwise, we would be useless to the new office OIR!'

'Wow!' Bodo said. 'I am not surprised you got that instruction because it is a hundred percent correct. We have an assignment that has never been given to anyone before. I need every member of the OIR to perform at 110 percent of their ability. We will discover, investigate, indict and convict all traitors in the nation. No position, relationship, or connection will save the comrades or citizens who committed treason from justice. And just to be clear from the beginning, the punishment for treason is the death sentence.' And looking both of them straight in the eye, he finished, 'No mercy! You are definitely at the wrong office if you can't support that.'

They looked both at Bodo with determination and confirmed that they wer in complete agreement.

With that, Bodo stood and walked over to his desk. He grabbed his notes and told Giesela that he would like to start dictation for the strategy paper and Gunter to be on call at the crew-ready room at his disposal. And maybe he could use his skills as a trained auto mechanic to make it 'his' car, 'meaning whatever you think you can improve, let your fantasy fly, but keep me included in the decisions because not only am I a mechanic too, but I need to like the car when you are done,' Bodo added.

Over the next several hours, Bodo developed and dictated his strategic approach to the problem at hand. Starting with the definition of the issues that he believed were the critical points for the decline of the trust of the people in the party, the misery of the economic situation, and with that, the discontent of the people with their overall life.

Lining out the basic points as:

1. The Socialist Unity Party (SUP), as the leader of the Farmers and Workers in the first socialistic nation on German soil, had wholly abandoned the principles of a communist Party.

2. As the leading power in the nation, the SUP has absolute control over the economic, cultural, educational, and ideological understanding and direction of the newly developing society.

3. In that position, the SUP and its leaders are solemnly responsible for implementing and enforcing the laws for developing a communist society.

Analyzing the current state of the nation allows only one devastating conclusion. The SUP and its leaders have catastrophically failed to apply these principles in their daily work and thus created the chaos the nation is facing today. Corruption in the ranks of SUP and economically responsible comrades, from the low ranks of local country leaders, through the directors of local economic entities up to the highest ranking leaders of the party, i.e., District Secretaries, has not only led to the horrible loss of trust in the integrity of the party but also inspired the average worker and farmer to believe it is OK to steal, betray and destroy the economic basis for their personnel advantage. The results are clear to be experienced if one spends a day working among those workers and farmers

1. Material that has been ordered for a specific product does not arrive

2. People who are needed o fulfill a specific task at a specific time are not available on time

3. Material that is assigned for specific manufacturing processes is purposely devaluated to be sold for cents on the Marks to a college in response or expectation of favor and vice versa

4. Department heads include accounts of unfinished production into finished products to cover the misery of their own management incompetence

5. The Central Production Planning Commission has become an uncontrollable, inscrutable moloch that creates more chaos than planning security. The organization, with its hundreds of nationwide offices and thousands of workers, is one of the most considerable breeding grounds for corruption

6. Just one example to clarify that. The Central Planning Commission seems to be infiltrated with either saboteurs or the most incompetent people we can find. If the plan is that 100 alarm bells must be produced next year, they plan the material for 100 alarm bells: no spare parts, no extra production for potential failers or defects. Our workers are no robots. They make mistakes. They are still humans.

If we analyze the situation, we cannot avoid recognizing that the lack of control and leadership has led to the current situation. Sure, some individuals are slick and evil-minded and capitalize immediately on a situation when they realize there are no consequences for their evildoing. These are ordinary criminals. And we have those in our Party and leadership positions everywhere, even in the Police, Military. and even within the ranks of the State Security Police (SSP). And while those in economic leadership positions are usually treated as criminals, with some exceptions, those in positions in the SUP, the police, the military, or, even worse, the SSP are not just criminals. Those are criminal traitors.

The Office for Investigation and Recovery will investigate every trace of corruption, regardless of the person or organization it concerns. We will build cases for every suspicion we discover or that is brought to our attention by watchful citizens or comrades and meticulously investigate, interrogate and build the case to a point where a decision can be made.

A decision about guilty and the punishment for the crime/treason. We will also try to recover all still available assets, including potential such as being transferred to foreign accounts and return them to the people's assets of the republic.

To fulfill this enormous assignment, the Office for Investigation and Recovery needs provision with the necessary apparatus. The following (starting) structure has been considered:

1. The Office will have three locations,

    a) **Head-Quarters-Centrale is located (HQC) in Karolinenhof, formals Forrest Offices**
        i.   The area of operation for the officers of this location includes the districts Berlin, Magdeburg, Potsdam, Frankfurt

    b) **Regional Office North (RON) Herzsprung, property Black Lake**
        i.   The area of operation for the officers of this location includes the districts of Rostock, Neubrandenburg, and Schwerin

    b) **Regional Office South (ROS) Siebenlehn near Zellwald**
        i.   The area of operation for the officers of this location includes the districts of Halle, Leipzig, Cottbus, Erfurt, Suhl, Gera, Karl-Marx-Stadt, Dresden

2. Comrade Bodo Zipper leads the Office of Investigation and Recovery with the title Commander

3. Comrade Bodo Zipper determines his deputy and takes full responsibility for the integrity of the officer

4. He reports exclusively to the assembly of the members of the CC. His short connection is comrade Bruno Tecker

5. The office will have twelve sworn-in officers leased from the SSP but under the unrestricted command of the Commander of the OIR

6. Additional officers for research, investigation, and interrogation, 4 per office, will be assigned from police stations, having proven reliability and expertise

7. Each location will have two further secretaries

8. The SSP took the assignment to select and approve the office personnel.

9. Each approved officer, secretary, or other personnel assigned to OIR needs to be approved separately by the Commander, comrade Bodo Zipper

10. The Secretary of Economy, comrade Alexander Dietz, took responsibility for ensuring the construction and equipment of all offices

11. Secretary of Finance, comrade Walter Reichmann, has already cleared the implementation of bank accounts for the OIR and assigned the budgeted amount to the accounts

12. The necessary dollars for procuring office computers and other electronic equipment have been remitted to the department at the Ministry of Economy.

13. The headquarters in Karolinenhof will include the necessary premises to hold suspects and execute interrogations.

14. Secretary of Defense, comrade Frank Bode, and Secretary of SSP, comrade Juergen Pieker have approved four of the best suitable cars and four new SUVs for each location. These should be arriving within the next week.

It is planned to go active with all locations by the end of May at the latest. Although six weeks seem a short time to launch such a complex operation, the situation forces us to activate all resources to get the operation launched no later.

1. **The beginning activities focus on the review of already indicated instances.**

1.1 OIR will request all known files from the district offices of the ICC which indicate irregularities of comrades and economic leaders

1.2 The local OIR offices – as soon as operational – will start to verify the legitimacy of the accusations by evaluating of included evidence and interviews of the accusers

1.3 If sufficient evidence points to a high probability of the correctness of the accusations, the suspect will be arrested and, in secrecy, to the appropriate local office transferred

1.4 The suspects will be interrogated until a clear decision of guilty or not guilty can be determined

1.5 If the suspect is considered to have misappropriated financial or other values under his responsibility, the OIR has the full authority to use all possible tools to recover those assets for the republic/party

1.6 The OIR will create a complete and comprehensive report with an attached list of evidence in case the OIR can prove the accusations are correct

1.7 OIR shall then, based on that comprehensive report, suggest a case-related punishment

1.8 The OIR will present reports of that kind once a month to the assembly of the members of the CC or, in case of urgency, request an extraordinary meeting

1.9 The assembled members of the CC shall confirm the punishment with a simple majority; if the suggested punishment is accepted, it will be executed according to the law of the republic

1.10 If the suggested punishment is rejected, the OIR has another week to collect additional evidence to support the suggested punishment or present the case again with a different punishment

1.11 If the simple majority confirms the new punishment, it will be executed according to the valid laws of the republic.

2. **The second pathway of the investigation will be the evaluation of irregularities that have not been registered yet**

    2.1   Two specialized officers will begin investigating economic, political, cultural, or social inconsistencies at each location.

    2.2   They will focus on locally available new broadcasts

    2.3   They will accept spontaneous information from citizens through the newly installed post-office-box information line

    2.4   The subsequent procedures and process will be the same as described before

3. The third pathway of investigation is the analysis, discovery, and destruction of the underground counterrevolutionary organization

    3.1   Potential suspects who are already known to the agencies as rebellious will be placed under immediate and increased surveillance in close cooperation with SSP and Police

    3.2   While SSP officers will be integrated into active surveillance, police officers will only be encouraged to report more frequently about the activities they observe. Still, since no obvious criminal act is committed, they do not pay much attention.

    3.3   OIR will, in cooperation with the local SSP offices, create a 'watchlist,' which shall contain all names of persons who are potential candidates for recruitment by the counterrevolutionary subjects, such as:

    3.4   Persons who have voiced in school that they are in disagreement with the basics of the teachings of Marx and Lenin

    3.5   Persons who have commented negatively on decisions of the SUP

    3.6   Persons who frequently assemble with other persons of interest even when no adverse information is available about them at that moment

3.7 It is necessary to try to infiltrate any discovered group or suspected organization and to try to get accurate and detailed information about

   3.7.1 Structure of the group

   3.7.2 The leadership of the group

   3.7.3 Weak members – which can easily be turned into informants; the instruments used are not limited

   3.7.4 Potential connections to other similar groups

   3.7.5 All information about the ways they communicate

   3.7.6 No single group will be destroyed, and any activities compromising the infiltration must be avoided at all costs.

   3.7.7 If the cover for the infiltrator of a resistance group requires breaking the law, the Commander of the OIR has to be informed immediately, and he has absolute autonomy over the decision

The annihilation of the existing counterrevolutionary underground movement is the number one priority of the Commander of the OIR. With the public-promoted removal of corrupt leaders and their punishment in public, the discontent of the masses of workers and farmers with the party's leadership will soon diminish, and the social state of affairs will become more stable.

This will push some hardcore protesters into the arms of the underground resistance. Others will stay in protest and use the church organization to support the underground resistance. It is, therefore, essential to build a reliable information basis inside the protest organization and ensure that any person drifting into the underground resistance is immediately placed under 'Operative Personnel Control.'

This paper is the first line out for the Office of 'Investigation and Recovery operation and will be extended and more specified with the time of operation.

It was already after 4 PM, and since they had just a short break for some sandwiches at lunchtime, Bodo told Giesela that she could leave at that point and that he would expect her to be back the next day at 9 AM. She said goodbye and left. Bodo went to the bathroom, refreshed himself, and changed from his suit into casual jeans and shirt and a light sweater. Then he went to this desk, picked up the phone, and called Karl. 'Hi Karl, I am through with work today and wanted to know if you could arrange anything for me at the SSP range?'

'Hello, Bodo. I was about to call your driver because I wasn't sure if you were still in deep thought. Everything is ready at the range. The range officer is informed and has several guns ready for you to test; whatever you choose and feel comfortable with is yours. Get your driver and have him drive you there. He knows where it is. Ah, before I forget, he shall stop at department H2 of the SSP headquarter. It is on the way and will get you there. Your ID Card and all the credentials. By the way, with your special license plates,you are practically 'untouchable'!

'Awesome, thank you so much, Karl. I plan on leaving tomorrow after my presentation and getting home, but before that, I would like to invite you and comrade Bruno for dinner. Choose a nice restaurant. I am paying.' Karl laughed and said, 'I am more than happy to do that. See you tomorrow.' After getting off the phone with Karl, Bodo looked over the favorite keys of the phone on his desk, again marveling about the remarkable technology, and finally found a key named 'Fahrbereitschaft,' meaning motor pool, and hit the key.

'Motor pool here, a voice answered after the first ring.'

'Comrade Zipper speaking, let my drive know I will be down in about 10 minutes to be ready.' 'Yes, comrade Zipper, I will let him know.'

Bodo checked his wallet and grabbed the windbreaker he got two years ago for Christmas. He looked around his office and saw the printed papers of their day's work on his secretary's desk. He walked over, took them, and placed them on his nightstand, planning to read them when he returned. He closed the French doors between his bedroom and the office area and walked out of the apartment. The elevator was there in seconds, and when he arrived at the garage floor's drop-off area, Gunter was already there with the car for him to jump in.

'Gunter, We need to get to SSP headquarters department H2, I have to pick up some stuff there, and from there, we go to the shooting range. The range officer is waiting for me. I get told you know all the ways to get where we need to be.'

Yes, comrade Zipper, I know where we need to go. It shouldn't take long, probably 30 minutes or so.'

'Na, I believe that's a little too optimistic, Gunter. We already have rush hour.'

No problem, comrade Zipper, you will see. One of the advantages of the license plate we have as an SSP car is that there are no speed limits. And we got trained to drive fast and safe simultaneously because even if we have no speed limits, we don't want to injure a citizen.' What a noble attitude, Bodo thought and answered, 'OK, Gunter, get us there.'

They arrived just 25 minutes after they left the CC's guest house. Although traffic was already heavy, Gunter kept his promise. Gunter stopped at the massive gate of the SSP headquarters, and the guard checked his credentials in addition to having a look into the back of the car through the lowered window. He returned to the Guard shed and used a handheld radio to tell the operators to open the gate. After driving down a road and turning left after passing a three-story building, Gunter parked the car in front of a smaller, two-story building which was rather long stretched.

'This is the H2 department. They are responsible for all the documents one would need for the assignment,' Gunter explained. 'If you enter the building, comrade Zipper, right at the entrance area, is an officer, and he will know where you need to get your documents.

Bodo walked up the two stairs that led to the door and opened it. And, as Gunter said, there was an officer sitting behind a desk, greating him friendly and asking why he was there.

'Good afternoon, comrade, my name is Bodo Zipper, and I am here to receive my documents. I was told it would be ready for me upon my arrival.'

At the mention of his name, the officer with the rank of a staff sergeant jumped out of his chair as if it was suddenly on fire and saluted with exemplary precision, 'Comrade Zipper, I beg your pardon, I did not know who you were, I am sorry, comrade.'

'No problem, comrade sergeant, just next time when someone enters whom you do not know, I suggest being a little more upfront and respectful.'

'Yes, comrade Zipper. I will immediately call the case officer to come and get you to the office.'

After only a maximum of a minute, an officer of the rank of a second lieutenant appeared around the left corner of the hallway and saluted smartly. 'Comrade Zipper, welcome to our facility, and please follow me to my office. Everything you need on documentation is available. We received the back information and checkbooks for your accounts this morning,' he explained while walking to his office, and Bodo was beside him. At his office, a small room with the usual bureau furniture of the GDR government office, he offered Bodo to sit down and opened a somewhat large safe behind his desk. He took out a large folder with several plastic sheets which contained different parts. He handed Bodo a plastic card with his image, the seal of the Party, and all the data which identified him as the Commander of the 'Office of Investigation and Recovery.' He added several checkbooks with the name OIR Account and the number printed on them and two additional ones with his name and account number.

With a questioning tone, Bodo asked the officer, 'What is this about my account, a checkbook with my account number? How shall I understand that?'

'Oh, I am sorry, comrade Zipper. I was informed that your personal account had been upgraded to a national banking account, and the first salary has already been transferred. I thought you had been informed about that, and I apologize for the inconvenience that this may have created.'

'Not at all, comrade lieutenant. I was just surprised you placed a checkbook with my account number in front of me, and I had no idea what that was all about. So, does that means I now have access to my bank account wherever I am in our country?'

'Yes, comrade Zipper. Your personal account and the accounts of the OIR are accessible at any bank in the country, no matter where it is or what brand it is. Even the Trade Association Bank has to accept your checks and can easily clear them with the National Bank, which holds your accounts.'

'Great, that makes things much easier since we are working all over the nation and might be in several different places on the same day.'

'Now, here is something you need to be highly watchful about. These cards, and I have 36 plus one unique, so far allow your officers to use any fuel station in the country to fuel the cars they are driving. All they need to do is show the fuel station attendant the card, and he has to note the number on the receipt. You need to instruct your officers to get a copy for everyone. That is your only proof of correct usage.

The unique one I have here for you has your name and a unique alpha-numeric code. This card allows you to fuel anywhere inside the Warsaw Pact. Any fuel station attendant, even in Romania, knows no questions are asked. Fuel the car, note the code on the receipt, and they have to keep their mouth shut.'

'And that is it?' Bodo asked. 'I have to go ahead. I have some other things to get done today. I really thank you for the explanations and the work you placed into this.'

'That is actually all, comrade Zipper. All you need to do before your leave is to sign that you have received the documents according to my explanation.'

Bodo read every single sheet of paper with the list and description and number of items he signed up for and then signed the paperwork. He ensured that every item had his short sign on it. He asked for a copy of the signed paperwork, and the lieutenant copied all of them without any hesitation, and with a handshake, Bod left the office.

When he left the building, it had already started to get dark, and he was concerned that there was no way to have any shooting exercises today. Gunter had opened the passenger door already, and while getting in, he asked, 'Gunter, how far is the shooting range away from here? I am afraid we won't make it before dark, and there will be no shooting today.'

'No worries, comrade Zipper, the shooting range is right around the corner, and it is inside and underground.' You can shoot there as long as you can stand,' Gunter answered, looking back at Bodo with a smile.

'OK, that sounds awesome. Let's get there.'

They drove down the road they were on, rounded a few corners, and Gunter stopped at a small, one-story building. The building appeared highly secure, although they were inside the SSP complex, which was in itself a little town. Gunter parked the car, and they went to the door, and Gunter rang the bell on an intercom. A voice asked about their names, and Gunter answered. There was a buzz, the door unlocked, and both entered a small room. Another door opened with a buzz on the opposite of the room, and a sergeant holding the door open said, 'Come on in, comrade Zipper. I am ready for your exercise. Then, looking over to Gunter, he said, smiling, 'Why are you trying to increase your scores to 120 now, Gunter?'

'Does this means I have a sharpshooter as my driver?' Bodo asked. The range sergeant looked back at Bodo while leading them down the stairs and answered, 'He was one of the best shooters I have ever had in my 20 years. Comrade Zipper, I have trained many officers, many of whom were excellent shooters with one or two weapons. Gunter is a perfect shooter with as many weapons as we could hand him here.'

Bodo stopped in his tracks and, looking at both of them with an astounding expression, said, 'Is that so? Why am I even here? I may embarrass myself tonight. Oh my, what have I maneuvered myself into here, asking comrade Karl to get me range time.'

Now, both officers laughed, and all walked into the shooting area. 'I don't have to explain the safety rules to you, comrade Zipper. If I am not mistaken, you have served as a sergeant and a tank commander.' 'That's correct,' Bodo answered.

The range officer brought their attention to a table at the right-hand wall of the area, and they walked over. On the table were several handguns of different types, but all in 9mm Para, and two rifles placed. The first one was a Walther, the second one was a Glock, the third one was a SIG, and the fourth was a Smith & Wesson. He presented all of them one after the other and explained their pros and cons. Bodo took the first one in his hand, checked the empty chamber, and by pressing down the lever, let the slit slide forward. He weighed the gun in his hand to get a feel for it, imitated a pull from a holster three times, and pointed at the target, about 20 meters away. He repeated the same with the other three guns. He returned to the Glock and took it up again with his right hand and the Walther with his left hand. He compared both weapons in size and weight and placed the Walther back on the table. Turning to the range officer, he said, 'the Glock is lighter, although I understand it's not loaded yet, but what was it you said about safety?'

The sergeant answered, 'comrade Zipper, the Glock is currently the only handgun in the world, I mean of significant manufacturers as far as we know, that does not need a mechanic safety lever. It is designed to be inherently safe, as long as the trigger safety is not pressed in. Some people consider it a safety risk.'

What do you consider it, comrade sergeant?' He answered without hesitation, 'A security!' 'Explain your self please.' The sergeant thought about formulating his answer and said, 'Comrade Zipper, we are in a profession in which we have to consider every person approaching us a potential danger. Am I correct?' He continued, not waiting for an answer, 'when that situation appears suddenly, you are usually under stress. Your fine-motoric functions are compromised, and you need all your attention placed on the incoming threat. In that situation, you need a gun that you pull out of the holster, line up the sights, and press the trigger, and it makes bum!'

Bodo thought about that expert statement for a second and answered, 'I have to agree with all that you said, and I am choosing the Glock, not only because of that but also because this Glock 17 has a lot of cartridges in the magazine. Thanks a lot, sergeant, for the teachings on that. Let's have some training and fun.'

'And for the fun of it, we will shoot all of them, right?' 'Most assuredly, we will,' confirmed the range sergeant, and they went to the stands and loaded the magazines, of which there were 4 for every gun. The sergeant did not know which one comrade zipper would choose, and with that, he took out the same number of magazines for every gun. Both SSP officers were obviously familiar with all the guns and had no difficulties hitting the target at the death zones at the 20 and later at the 30-meter distance. Bodo was not used to any of the handguns they had there. Until he saw them at the table, he believed that all armed forces in the country were armed with the standard officer handgun of the military, the Makarov. It was the pistol he had learned to shoot as a sergeant and tank commander, and he was surprised that the SSP was using handguns from the class enemy. But he had not forgotten how unreliable the Makarov was and how imprecise.

After about two magazines with the Glock, which he had already decided to use as his service pistol, he was still struggling to hit the target consistently at the vital zones, and the range sergeant noticed his struggle. 'Comrade Zipper,' he finally addressed Bodo, 'May I explain the specifics of the Glock 17 to you and show you a little training trick that will help all of my students and myself to master this gun?'

'For sure, sergeant, I am getting frustrated. I am hitting, and the next shot I am missing.'

'Did you notice this weapon is much lighter than the others, even with more cartridges in the magazine? It is a striker fire system in double-action-only, which means with every shot, your trigger has to move the strike into position, and your mind automatically overcompensates for that. To overcome this normal reaction, you have to train your mind. Here, take this empty cartridge. Remove the magazine and secure your weapon.' Bodo did as instructed and showed the secured gun to the sergeant. Then the sergeant told him to go into a shooting position and placed the empty cartridge on top of the Glock's slide. Then he explained the exercise, 'The trick is to pull the trigger without the empty cartridge falling off of the slide. If you can get to the point where it doesn't even wiggle, you will hit exactly where the barrel points when you pull the trigger.' You can do this exercise wherever and whenever you have the opportunity to do so in a safe environment. Just make sure the gun is unloaded and safe.' If you do that as a regular exercise, within a few weeks, you will be as good as Gunter.'

Bodo was about to protest, but he interrupted him and said, 'See, comrade Bodo, I have been doing this here for over 20 years, and I know a talent as a shooter before he knows what he is capable off. You have hit the target with this weapon without any instructions on its specifics which are very disturbing when you don't know them. This weapon will make you an excellent marksman if you adhere to my advice.'

Bodo exercised meticulously with the empty cartridge on the Glock for the next hour and pulled the trigger. He reached a point where he could barely see it moving twenty times in a row and decided to fire another life rounds.

'I am back on the firing line,' he announced, so the others knew he was beginning to reshoot life fire. He got a confirming nod from both, loaded his Glock, and started shooting. The results were a stunning difference from before. Almost every shot was where he wanted it to be. After all, just one or two out of every magazine weren't precise enough—

that meant 15 out of 17 shots were precisely where he wanted them to be. Considering this opportunity a great chance to get really used to the gun, he extended the target distance and, after several magazines hitting the vital zones, including the head section, every single time, he was about to call it a day. When he stopped shooting, secured his gun, and turned around, both sergeants standing behind him clapping their hands. He looked at them with a questioning expression.

'Comrade Zipper,' the range sergeant said, 'I have the utmost respect for your achievement here in the last 2 hours. I rarely saw someone taking up a handgun, absolutely unknown to him, and firing with such precision even at 50 meters.'

'I just came to like the gun, and I have to repeat, I really like this gun.' It is almost a pleasure to shoot it. And again, 18 rounds before you have to change magazines is not to be underestimated.'

'Comrade Zipper, there are some other training sessions scheduled for you. One is to familiarize you with the MP5, and the second is with a special long-range rifle built by the manufacturers at the Suhl plant.' We won't be doing this tonight. It's just too late, but when you are back in Berlin and have time to spend three to four hours, call me, and we will find the spot for your sessions. I will clean your gun and the magazines, load them all, and put some extra ammo together for you. Gunter can pick them up tomorrow.'

'That sounds great,' Bodo said, and looking at his watch, Bodo was surprised that it was already after 7 PM. He thanked the range sergeant and gave Gunter a wink to get ready to leave. When he entered the car, he picked up the phone and called Karl's number. Karl answered the phone after the second ring, and they agreed upon a restaurant that wasn't that far from the SSP headquarters. Gunter knew it already and said it wasn't as fancy as the Bulgarian or the Russian, but it had good food and was more like home cooking. When they arrived, they had trouble finding a parking spot, and Gunter parked half on the walkway. Bodo started to advise against it because the police could punish them, as he knew from his hometown, but then realized that with the license plate, it would never happen. And Gunter stayed with the car since the group eating dinner together was far above his rank, so much above that he would be reprimanded if he walked into the restaurant with Bodo. The only time that was allowed was when Bodo officially asked him to watch his back, becoming his bodyguard.

Bodo entered the restaurant. He looked around and spotted Karl, Bruno, and another guy at a table in the far left corner. Walking through the crowded restaurant, he realized that most of them were probably officers or civil workers at the headquarters of the SSP since it was just around the corner. As he reached the table, they all stood up to greet him, and Karl introduced the guy as Joachim, one of the regional assistants of comrade Bruno. They spoke with low voices, although all the other people in the restaurant were loud enough and occupied by themselves. Yet, Bodo had learned early on that walls could hear. And nobody in the restaurant needed to know who they were, sitting among them.

'How was the shooting, comrade Bodo,' Bruno immediately asked as they were seated.'

'I have to tell you, comrade Bruno, I am amazed. I chose the Austrian gun Glock, and I have to say, I got pretty good with it in those few hours. They have a well-equipped shooting range in-house, and the range officer is a first-class instructor. Especially after he trained me on try shooting tricks, I practiced those for a while.'

'Did your get all the credentials you need?'

'Yes, I am prepared for the job now, and as soon as we get the people and locations set up, we can start. I am planning on going home tomorrow after the presentation and coming back with the moving trucks. It is planned for early next week, being back at Karolinenhof. I have already decided on my deputy and need him to accept. He is another hole in your organization, comrade Bruno, if he accepts my offer. If he does, I will send him to the location of the Regional Office North and have him scout the location and get me a report on what is needed to get that up and to run. And I would like to start collecting files of potential cases at the district offices in Rostock, Schwerin, and Neubrandenburg.'

'Wow, comrade Bodo, you are really full speed in it. I like that, and it confirms once more that we chose the right person. It will take a while until the facilities are ready to be usable, but I will have at least six potential officers for your office wedded and sworn next week, and you can interview them the following Monday if you like.'

'Sure, comrade Buno, that would be great. That would allow me to start the next steps in getting the southern regional office started.'

They talked about all that had happened during the day while they ate a tasty meal based on the regional cooking style and enjoyed their company. Bodo asked a little bit about Joachim, and he said he was married with two children and had been at the ICC reporting to comrade Bruno for four years. He had first served as a country assistant in the county Zeitz. Bodo interrupted, saying that this was a rather small county to get a lot of experience qualifying for the position. He looked at Bruno with a smirk, waiting for an answer from Joachim. That answer came soon, explaining that although comrade Bodo was correct, it was a small county but a hotbed of rebellion. It had the largest number of No-Votes for the party at the last election. He had a lot of investigative work done, analyzing the reasons, and had some decent results. But as in many other places, he was restrained from going after the corrupt people who had connections up to the highest levels of the party. He said he believes that his district assistant promoted him to the office as regional assistant because he wanted to have someone near comrade Bruno who would not cave in. And with that, he was now, for two months, a regional assistant—the youngest of all four. After finishing the dinner, Bodo took the receipt and paid for everything. They left the restaurant together, and Bodo was the only one who had his car right next to the door. The other had to walk down the road a few hundred meters. They said good buy, reminded Bodo of the meeting at the CC the next day for Bodo's presentation and walked away. Bodo entered the car and told Gunter to get him to his apartment.

After a short drive with little traffic, they arrived at the CC's Guest house about twenty-five minutes later, and Bodo was in his apartment in no time. Tired as a young dog, he used to say, he exercised his nightly hygiene and was soon in bed and deep sleep.

CHAPTER 24

WHAT CAN GO WRONG WHEN A DETERMINED COMRADE PRESENTS A SOLUTION

B odo woke up before the alarm watch went off and felt very well rested. Laying in bed for a few minutes, he let the events of the last three days pass through his mind, and he was still in awe about the speed with what had happened since Monday. Was it really only five days since this representative of the second most powerful man in the party, and within these few days, his life had changed entirely? Still unable to fully comprehend the impact of the last few days on his and his family's future, he got out of bed, into the bathroom, and prepared for the last day in the beautiful apartment he had used as a guest of the CC.

At precisely 9 AM, there was a ring at the hallway office door, and he went into the office, closed the door to the living space, and opened the office door to the hallway to let the secretary in.

'Good morning, comrade Zipper. I hope you have had a restful sleep.'

'Good morning Giesela. Yes, I am well rested indeed. Have you seen Gunter this morning?'

'Yes, he drove through the gate when I walked in through the main door. He must be at the motor pool to be ready whenever you need him.'

'Great. OK, let's go to work. I want you to start handling my daily schedule and organizing my calendar. Today I have to present the strategic structure of work for our office to the CC's members at 2 PM. We will review it in the next few hours to finish it and precise some of the points. I estimate that the presentation will be over in about two hours, and I will leave Berlin after that. I will work from my new home office and may be on the road a lot. Since the new office will not be operational for at least a week or two, I will see if comrade Bruno has a place for you in his building for the time being. Make sure you have my mobile phone number and don't hesitate to call if you have any questions. Please try to get comrade Bruno on the phone for me.'

Bodo was reading through the strategic paper she had tipped on that nice computer thing there on her desk and printed on that rattling printer thing, and she called the office of the ICC.

Giesela spoke into the handset and, after a few words, looked up and said, 'comrade Bodo, comrade Bruno is on the phone with one of the CC's secretaries, and Karin said she would let him know. Is there anything specific she should tell him?'

'No, just let her know I would like him to call me back at his earliest convenience.'

'Sure.' And with that, she went back to talking to Karin, and Bodo read the paper he would need to send out by courier as soon as possible to the CC's members. When he was done with the few corrections, he placed it on her desk and said, 'Please make these corrections and print ten sets. One set is for me, and the other nine need o be in sealed envelopes addressed to the nine members of the Central Committee personally. Do you know if there is an internal courier system?'

'There is one, but in my experience, they work somewhat awkwardly and never fast.'

'Ok, when you are done, call Gunter and have him deliver them to the members.' They need to have those envelopes by noon.'

'Yes, comrade Zipper.'

While he was thinking about the next steps to get ready to leave the apartment in a somewhat orderly fashion, the phone on Giesela's desk rang. After she announced herself and listened, she looked at Bodo, saying, 'I have comrade Bruno on the line. Shall I transfer it to your living room phone?'

'Bodo immediately realized that she was well trained, not even get tempted to listen to a conversation between the power players of the nation, and answered, 'Yes, please.'

He went into the living space, closed the door behind him, worked over to the small site table, sat down on the comfortable leather chair, and picked up the phone that had just started to ring. 'Comrade Bodo speaking.'

'Comrade Bodo, Karin here. I have comrade Bruno for you on the line. Please hold while I connect.' There were a few clicks, and then he heard Bruno's voice.

'Comrade Bodo, how are you this morning? You wanted to talk with me. What can I do for you?' I hope you have gotten some well-deserved hours of sleep?'

'While I was reviewing my strategic paper for the OIR in the morning and thinking about the next few days ahead, I thought there would be no functional office available for at least a week. Maybe you can prepare a small office for Giesela somewhere in your building until we have everything set up at the new headquarters?'

'Oh. No problem, not at all. I will let Karin know, and she will take care of it. Although she seems still a little crumpy about losing her most efficient second in line, she will be happy to help.'

'Super.'

'And since I have you on the phone already, I would like to tell you that the Secretary of Economy has already ordered the construction material funding for the house and the headquarters, and the secretary of Finance told me in the morning that the money for all the work has been assigned under the LVO act as enacted by the members yesterday. That means that the construction crew is already out at the headquarters, and I have sent out Karl to make sure they know what we discussed during our visit. They will start with the barn first, which means there will be no work on the office building until you are back, in case you have some special requirements. We will have all utilities and secure phone lines ready at the house by Friday morning. Give Karl a call as soon you arrive, and we will have the SSP phone crew install the phones wherever you want them.'

'Great. Many thanks for taking care of this for me, comrade Bruno. There is so much to think of and organize; it just takes some additional hands-on to get everything done. I wish sometimes I had a magic stick to get it all set up in one second. But it is a whole new organization that needs time setting it up.'

'You are right, comrade Bodo, but you must thank Karl for most of it. He seems to be extremely energized by the idea of the new office, and I am almost afraid he might apply to be transferred over to that operation. When you look at it from his perspective, he came up with the general idea to have 'outsider' installed as a 'cleanser.'

'Oh no, I don't think Karl is even considering that idea, comrade Bruno. He is so excited, as you rightly suspect, because he is as frustrated with the status of our party and happy that there are comrades in power now who are decisive and took the chance to start the necessary action years ago. He has a much broader future in your department. Between you and me, if you are honest with yourself, comrade Bruno, you consider him your successor when you decide to retire.'

Bruno laughed and said, 'comrade Bodo, you seem able to read minds. He has shown the potential to lead the ICC into the new future. But aside from joking, you are correct. And that needs to stay between you and me. I just don't want to get him heavy-headed and blow it. And yes, I am thinking about retirement as soon as you have some success cleaning up the mess of our communist party and getting us back on track. It is time for you, the younger generation, to take over leadership positions. And believe me, many other members of the CC think the same. We all know that we waited too long to send the 'Old Guard' into retirement, and we won't let that happen again.'

'Thank you for your open word, comrade Bruno. I will do whatever is in my power to secure the historic eternal power of the communist party of the workers' class for the German people. And I understand that the enormous power given into my hands by the members of the CC is only for that reason given. I won't disappoint them.'

'Well said, comrade Bodo. I am confident that you will do the right things to get it done. I'll see you in the afternoon at the meeting. Tschüss.'

'Tschüss, comrad Bruno.'

Bodo hung up the phone and walked back into the office where Gisela was about to finish printing the papers for the CC's members. 'Comrade Bodo, you need to sign them, and then I can pack them and bring them down to Gunter, Giesela said when he entered the room.

'No, I don't want you to get down. Let Gunter come up here so I can instruct him, Bodo answered and sat at his desk.

After the printing and sorting were complete, Giesela came over to his desk with the signature folder. All copies were sorted, and the last page with the date and the line for his signature was laid on top. Bodo was thinking for a moment and was starting to sign the last page and then went to initiate every single page of the strategic paper. Giesela was standing at the side of his desk, and when he saw her questioning expression, he explained, 'Giesela, you have typed all of the paper, and you certainly understand what it means. Right?

Giesela answered with a somewhat hesitating low voice, 'Yes, comrade Zipper.'

You worked for several years at the office of the ICC, and you must have realized the frustration of comrade Bruno and many other great comrades about the dangerous path the party was going down, right? 'Yes, comrade Zipper.'

'You have been chosen to be my personal secretary by someone who places an enormous confidence in me that I would not misuse the power given to me by the unanimous decision of the assembled members of the Central Committee. The assignment is to cleanse the party, all related organizations, and the economic structure from the corrupt traitors who led the country on a downward spiral of moral desolation and at the edge of a counterrevolutionary situation. The mean attitude to have success in that assignment is 'NO MERCY.' The main rule for success is ABSOLUT SECRET and total TRUST among the 'Office of Investigation and Recovery's' members. We may have to do things that we don't like, and we may discover things that may be disgusting, and I may have to write suggestions to request the death sentence for people we all may know, but it must be done, or this nation is destroyed in a few years. Can I place my complete TRUST in you, comrade Giesela, that you are up to the task and willing and able to be silent about all you may see and hear for the rest of your life?'

'Comrade Zipper, I have been sworn to these exact requirements when I started for the office of comrade Tecker some years ago. I was frustrated over the last years the same way as many other comrades, asking ourselves over and over again, what are the leaders doing about this? But I understand this is a step up the secrecy I have experienced so far, and I agree entirely with the assignment given to the OIR.'

'I appreciate your openness. For the future, as an instruction, whenever I have to sign papers, I want to have it in such a way that I can initialize every page and sign the last one.'

'Understood, comrade Zipper.'

While he finished initializing and signing, Giesela placed the signed papers in to the envelopes and placed a small sticker at the opening. He initialized those stickers and thought that this was a suitable procedure for the safety control of papers transferred. He would later learn that there was a technique to open those seals easily and would immediately change the sealing of secret documents.

A few minutes later, Gunter opened the door after he knocked twice, and Giesela called, 'Come in.'

'Gunter,' Bodo called him over. 'I want you to deliver each of these envelopes to the addressee as written. Do not, and I repeat, do not hand any of these envelopes to any secretary or assistant at their offices. I want you to insist that you must deliver them personally to the Secretary of the CC himself. State your position as the driver of the Commander of the OIR, and in case you have trouble, call me.' Are we clear?'

'Yes, comrade Zipper, totally clear.'

'Ok then. We are leaving Berlin right after the meeting with the CC's members. And I need you to be back latest at 1:30 PM to get me over to the Central Committee for my meeting. Ah, and before I forget, make sure you are ready for travel for approximately a week, including today.'

'Yes, comrade Zipper, I will be back in time and ready for the trip.' With that, he grabbed the bag with the envelopes and left the office.

Bodo turned back to the secretary, who was waiting for his next instructions and said, 'Giesela, I don't have anything else to do for you today. Consider it an early Friday off. Be at the ICC office on Monday as usual, and Karin will show you your interim office until we have the headquarters office building ready. Do you have the means to get out to Karolinenhof?'

'Is that where I will work at the new office,' she asked, somewhat excited. 'I am living in Grünau, and that is not far away. I have to see if there is a bus route or another connection. But it should be easy to get there.'

'Great,' Bodo answered and closed, 'I wish you a great weekend, and we will be in touch Monday morning.'

Giesela said, 'Tschüss!' and left the office.

Bodo took his copy of his strategic action paper and read it over again. He was satisfied with his work, especially since he had Giesela add the names of all nine members of the Central Committee to be signed on the last page. All of the Central Committee's Secretaries had to sign the assignment they had placed on his shoulders. He had two reasons for it and would explain if there was a question. First, he needed to ensure that, if a change in leadership happened, he could prove that he did not usurp this powerful position under any circumstances. Secondly, he needed to ensure that none of the members could later say, I wasn't really into it.

Satisfied with his preparations, he placed the documents into his briefcase, cleaned up the desk, and ensured there was nothing that did not belong there. He walked to the living area and packed his belongings into his suitcase. Before he was even aware of how the time flew by while he was thinking through all of this, slowly packing his stuff, the doorbell rang, and when he opened it, Gunter was outside and told him he was ready to go.

'What is it already that late? 'Bodo asked nobody. He grabbed his suitcase and handed it over to Gunter. He turned around and had a last look throughout the apartment to make sure he did not leave anything of his stuff. When he was sure he had everything, he turned around and followed Gunter into the elevator.

Gunter placed the suitcase in the trunk next to his own small one while Bodo entered the car and grabbed the phone. It dawned on him that he had not called home since yesterday afternoon and wanted to say a brief hello to Sarina. She picked up the phone after the first ring. She must have been sitting right next to it, he thought, smiling. Gunter was starting the car and driving out of the secure area, and he said, 'Hallo honey, how are you?'

'Hello, Bodo, you did not call yesterday evening, and I was a little concerned all day today.'

'Nothing to be concerned about. It will be late, but I should be home tonight. I am just horribly busy and on my way to the last meeting before we turn around and drive home.'

'Bodo, I have to tell you the movers arrived today, about an hour ago, and they started packaging already. They are very nice and really take care of the stuff, wrapping everything twice into blankets. I am surprised because I remember the last time we moved furniture up here, those guys did not know how to handle things safely and damaged more than I remember. These guys from Berlin are totally different, and I am satisfied and relieved about their professionalism. If you know who their boss is, you should say a good word for them.'

'Sarina, slow down. I will see if I can find out who that is. Do they have accommodation? Where are they staying? Most of the vacation homes are still closed up out of season.'

Oh, no problem. I called Eckhard, and although he was still angry that I was leaving, he was ready to open his summerhouse on the cliff for them. I was just over there to ensure it warms up nicely and it is all fine for them to stay there.'

'Sarina, I need to hang up, but before I do so, can you arrange for my driver to get to stay there too? As I said, we will arrive late, but it shouldn't be a problem since at least five family-style apartments are in that house.'

'I will talk with Eckhard and let him know that he can make even more money out of season.' On a side note, who is paying for that? As you know, his apartments aren't cheap.'

'Don't worry about that. All costs are covered. I will talk to you later, honey.' While Bodo was placing the handheld back into the cradle, they were already approaching the gate of the CC's building. They were in the garage a few minutes later, getting through the security procedure fast.

At the entrance hall, leaving the elevator, Bodo was greeted by one of the secretaries at the reception desk, 'Comrade Bodo, I have the honor to escort you to the Secretaries' meeting room. They are awaiting you.' Bodo thanked her, and after they entered the elevator, she entered the code for the sixth floor, and soon they were at the target floor. He stepped out into the small reception area and was friendly greeted by the two secretaries who were the same as last time. One of them stood and went to the conference room door, knocking and opening it. She put her head through the gap and announced the arrival of comrade Bodo. Bodo heard the voice of the Secretary-General, 'Get him in,' entered the room, and greeted all the members with a friendly, 'Good afternoon, comrades.'

They all answered with a friendly nod, and some said good afternoon, comrade Bodo. After Bodo had sat down, the Secretary-General, having Bodo's strategic paper in front of him as all the others as he could see, opened the meeting with, 'Comrade Bodo, we have all read the outstanding strategic operation description in your paper. We all agree that we want you to start the operation as soon as possible. Even though we did not have your paperwork in hand before this morning, the impression you made the day before yesterday was enough for us to set some of the necessary steps in motion, as you have already noticed. Based on the punishment procedure, one question is left to be answered.'

'Secretary-General, what would that question be?'

'During the discussion, it came up that, in case the second punishment suggestion is rejected, what happens with the accused person?'

'That will just not happen. I assure you that if we present a case to you for punishment, the accused person is guilty, proven beyond the shadow of a doubt, that there is no logical reason to decline the punishment. I just hope it doesn't come to the point that we end up back where we are starting.'

Comrade Hollorek cleared his throat and said, 'What do you mean by that? I don't understand. Do you mean you will never make a mistake, and some innocent people are presented for punishment?'

Bodo was about to lose his temper. Did he not clarify at the last meeting that he did not care about the relationships and acquaintances of the persons he would investigate? And did his paper not clearly state that two independent investigations would take place to collect all data about the case for both guilt and innocence? He took a deep breath and answered as calmly as possible, 'Secretary Hollorek, I understand your concerns about justifiable punishments related to the law. But what has that approach brought yet to solve the issues? Read the strategic operation paper completely and understand my approach to the problems on hand. You will understand that there is only one way that this assembly would be tempted to reject a revised punishment, and that is for precisely the same reasons that we need this OIR, Relationships, and Acquaintances!'

Bodo leaned back in his chair and looked around the members of the Central Committee. This was the last moment where all his efforts to create a powerful and nearly unlimited force to secure the absolute power of the communist party could be stopped by the doubters. The restoration of a party structure that would agree with Lenin's principles for the victory of communism needed this force and an unconditional commitment to them.

He saw many of them nodding their heads, that absolute commitment to using all possible tools, and only the Secretary of Justice, had a doubtful expression on his face. Bodo looked over to Bruno, the Secretary of ICC. As the head of the Internal Control Commission, he had the power to suggest the removal of even the Secretary-General from his position. However, all members had to agree to that to be executed.

Since nobody said a word, probably waiting for Secretary Hollorek to answer Bodo's statement, Bodo proceeded, 'I have my personal copy here, and there are all names of the members of the Central Committee listed with a line for your signatures. Comrades, the objective you are about to assign to me is an enormous responsibility and, at the same time, temptation. You have equipped that office with enormous power, and the person who is the commander of this office needs the undivided and hundred percent support of the Central Committee as a whole. If you cannot sign this paper, I am not your man. You have to look for somebody else.'

There was silence in the conference room. Bodo thought about the proverbial needle dropping on the carpet.

Then after a while that lasted only a few seconds but felt as if it were minutes, Secretary-General cleared his throat and said, 'comrade Zipper, would you mind giving us the room for a short moment? I promise it will be quick.'

'Of course, comrade Secretary-General, of course.' With that, Bodo stood and left the room. In the reception area, he walked over to the small table but then thought other and went into the bathroom. With a deep breath, he throws some cold water into his face and thinks, if these guys get cold feet now, all is lost, and I will see that I get a job as a mechanic somewhere. Because under the current circumstances, this government can't last longer than a year, and if this collapses, there will be blood in the street. The counterrevolutionaries will have as less mercy on the communist comrades as he, himself, will have on them.

As he left the bathroom, one of the receptionist women said, comrade Zipper, they just a minute ago announced that you are welcome back into the conference room when you are ready.

Bodo walked into the conference room, sat down at his seat, and looked around, and he noticed that the Secretary of Justice, comrade Hollorek was no longer there.

The Secretary-General looked at Bodo and explained the situation, 'comrade Bodo, let me begin with the declaration that all of us in this conference room are here because we believe there is a way to secure the socialistic republic. We are also aware of the extraordinary situation that has developed over the years of negligence of the basic principles of party leadership. All of us here have been in power for less than three weeks. We are the group that brought a majority to vote the former leader into retirement. Unfortunately, comrade Gerd Hollorek believed that a bit of paint-over could clean the wall, so to speak, and was not in favor of using a steel brush to clean out the rotten parts in our organization and throughout the nation. We all unanimously voted him out of the Central Committee. After he doubted that the constitution covers the installation of your office, we had to ensure he was not running around and broadcasting it to the world. He will be under house arrest until further decisions.

As you can see on the paper in front of you, we have all signed the strategic operation outline and wish you total success. However, you should not need help, maybe advice, since you are now mighty. Don't hesitate to call any of us if you need advice. I directed the communication experts to program the direct phone numbers of all of us into your mobile phone, and it will be the same with your office and home phone.

He stood and walked over to Bodo, who stood as well. He gave him a brotherly hug and said, 'Welcome, comrade Bodo, to the few men who hold the nation's fate in their hands.

All members clapped and stood and came around to hug and congratulate Bodo, who was overwhelmed by the sudden brotherly friendliness he had not felt so far among these powerful men. With reference to his long trip home, he thanked them again for their trust in him and the affirmation that he would not disappoint them; he walked out of the conference room, leaving the members of the Central Committee with their next headache-causing agenda.

He said good buy to the receptionists, entered the elevator and was soon at the carpool area, where Gunter was waiting for him at the car.

'I know it is non of my business, but to know if you have been confirmed, comrade Zipper, is existential for me too.' He stated with a smirk.

Bodo entered the car without saying anything, and when Gunter was driving out of the secured area onto the street, he said, 'Do you know how to get to Rügen?'

'Sure, comrade Zipper, does that means you have the job? And do you keep me as your driver?'

Bodo, now laughing, answered, 'for the first question, yes, I am now officially the Commander of the Office of Investigation and Recovery. And for the second question depends on how fast you can get me to my family safe and without interrupting my thinking or sleep.'

You won't be disappointed, comrade Zipper. You will be delighted.' And by the way, the handgun with the holster and the spare magazines are in the case between the seats. I picked them up when I was delivering the envelope to Secretary Pieker.

CHAPTER 25

WHILE MOVING TO BERLIN EXPERIENCING SOME STRANGE OBSERVATIONS

Gunter hid the accelerator, and soon they were flying through the afternoon traffic of Berlin. With the sudden movement to the left and right because Gunter had to pass some more slow-driving cars. Those weren't really slow-driving. They were just in the way of Gunter speeding through the traffic as fast as it was safe for him, with the engine's enormous power allowing him to accelerate and pass more frequently than others. Bodo started to sort his thoughts and was thinking about the next steps. It was so much to do just to get the whole organization set up and going. He had the place for the northern regional office in mind and thought he might already have the right guy for running it. Still thinking about all that was necessary to do, he noticed that the driving became more consistent, and looking up from the notes he was penning down, and realized that they were out of the city limits and had hit the Autobahn. Realizing that they were driving at a very high speed for GDR laws and regulations, he was wondering about the still usable conditions 44 years after the war's end and 55 years after being built. He almost admired the quality of the work but immediately threw that thought aside. Thoughts like that would conflict with his conviction, and he did not allow them even develop into something other than a fleeting thought.

He grabbed the mobile phone's handset and keyed his friend Reiner's number, hoping to reach him still in the office. It rang three times, and Reiner picked up the phone, 'Hello, comrade Worser speaking.'

'Oh, comrade Worser it is,' Bodo said, mimicking an old man's voice, but there was no way to trick Reiner. He immediately recognized Bodo's voice and responded,' Bodo, you old fool, where are you? I was looking for you at the office now and then, hoping to catch and squeeze you about that strange visitor you had last Monday. But you wer like vaporized.'

'Hahaha, Reiner, are you sitting?'

'Yea, why?'

'Because of what I have to tell you, I don't want you to drop on the floor and hit that head and cause more damage to it than it already has. I want you to find someone to take over your position at the county office and prepare yourself to work for me in a new function. I will meet you at your office on Monday and explain everything. And don't even think for a second you can say no. You have been for much too long rested your bud on a half-sized position at the party's cost.'

'Wow, Bodo, come on, I need a little more than your insults to give up my warm office, the great pay, and the high appreciation I get from our county's leadership.'

'If these are all your arguments against a job change, you are definitely the only person in the whole nation I can use for the position I have to offer you. And just one additional reason you can't say no is that it comes with doubling your paycheck. And if you say yes on Monday, which is still before mid-month, you already get that new payment for this month.'

'OK, Bodo, you are telling me I have until Monday to decide if I want to accept the new job knowing nothing about it?'

'Oh, come on, Reiner, that's beneath your education level. You have three nights and two whole days to think about it, and you know all I can tell you over the phone, and that's your paycheck.'

'OK, Bodo, you got me there. I am looking forward to our discussion on Monday. When do you think you will be at the office?'

'I will be there at about 8 AM, and if you see Peter, let him know I need to talk with him too. Maybe he can join us, and to avoid further back and forth, Bodo hung up. Just as he had disconnected the call, his phone rang and released the button. He heard Karl, 'Hello, Bodo, can you hear me?'

Yes, Karl, I hear you five by five, falling already back into the radio communication rules of his time as a tank commander.'

'Bodo, I heard from comrade Bruno that you are planning on stopping in Rostock, Schwerin, and Neubrandenburg?'

Yes, I am. It will probably be on Wednesday or Thursday, depending on when all the packaging is done. Why do you ask?'

'When I was there last week, a secretary stuck out of that district's party headquarters trash pool that it was like an air raid light at midnight. I want you to interview her and see if you can use her in your office. You need more than just one secretary there; she would be a good fit. That's my feeling, and I am seldom wrong with that.'

'Oh, I can confirm that. I'll do that because I am slowly getting scared that I can't get the people fast enough as I need them.'

'One other thing, I had a little confrontation with our rep at the district office ICC, and I told him that he would have only one last chance to keep his place if he had all the files with complaints, sleeping in his cabinets had ready for delivery within a week. If you pick those up while you are there, please evaluate his usefulness for the position under the new wind blowing through the party now.'

'Thanks a lot for the heads up on that, Karl. I will check and let you know. I wish you a great and restful weekend, Karl, 'and they ended the call.' Feeling the exhaustion the stress and demands had placed on him over the last several days, combined with the rhythm of the tires running over the Autobahn plate cuts, slowly had him drifting off into sleep.

Gunter noticed a short time later and watched out that he avoided the worst potholes not to wake his boss up from the well-deserved nap.

Driving a powerful car with no need to keep speed limits based on the license plate they had, Gunter turned onto the Rügendamm a little after four hours of driving. When they rattled over the liftable part of the 55 years old steel construction, Bodo woke up. He looked around at the familiar structures, and although already dusk had begun, he could make out the massive steel beams holding the part that could move upwards to let vessels pass through it to the harbor of Stralsund.

This passing always reminded him of when he, with his brother Fritz was rummaging through the stuff at the old manor house attic and found these old newspapers from the 1930ies. And especially from 1934, reporting about the world's first complete welded steel bridge was praised as an achievement of the despised National Socialistic dictatorship. Again, one of those thoughts he hated was coming through his mind if he couldn't immediately focus on something else. So did he now. 'Gunter, you know where we are?'

Yes, comrade Zipper, the Rügendamm. We just crossed the balance bridge part.'

'Great, we may have another hour and a half to my home, so let's get going.'

They drove on, and there wasn't much traffic at all. And in almost no time, compared to the longer part, they finished off the rest of the trip and turned into the driveway of Bodo's property. Bodo instructed him to park closer to the barn because the space in front of the house was blocked by two large moving trucks with identical trailers.

He stepped out of the car, told Gunter to follow, and walked around the moving trucks toward the door. Suddenly the door flew open, and his son ran out and jumped into his arms, yelling, 'Hi daddy, great that you are back. We missed you so much.' He gave him a big hug, kissed his head, and then turned to his wife Sarina, who stood with a smile, waiting for the son to release his father. Then, she moved in, hugged and kissed Bodo, and said, 'it was some time with not really knowing what was going on. You have a lot explaining to do, Bodo.'

'I know, love, I know.' Turning to Gunter, who stood at a distance to give them some privacy, he added, 'This is Gunter, my driver, and he needs to get a place to stay for a couple of days, as I told you over the phone. Could you drive with him and show him where it is so he knows the way and can drive you back here?'

Sarina looked at Gunter, stretched out her hand, and said, 'Welcome, Gunter, and I have a better idea. The movers are inside eating dinner right now with us, and why don't you just join us? They can drive to the apartment house together when all are finished.'

'That sounds great. Gunter, go ahead and follow my wife. Let me get the suitcase and the phone out of the car, and I will be with you.'

Bodo walked back to the car, took his suitcase out of the trunk, and opened the door to the passenger department. He lifted the lock at the center console in front of the two formed backseats and lifted the mobile phone from its holder. Then, he opened the center console between the two backseats and took out his Glock 17 with the shoulder holster and the spare magazines. He threw on the shoulder holster and then the windbreaker over it to cover the holstered Gun and was satisfied with how well it was sitting and the gun was hidden.

He grabbed the phone and the suitcase and walked into the house. On the large kitchen table were his family, joined by Gunter and three men who wer the movers. They said, 'good evening,' almost simultaneously, and Bodo answered, 'I will be right with you, just putting away the stuff. He entered the bedroom, placed the suitcase into the corner, took his gun with the shoulder holster off, and placed it into his nightstand drawer. Walking back into the kitchen, he sat down, and Sarina filled his plate with food. That was when he realized how hungry he was; he hadn't eaten anything since breakfast.

Looking at the three men who were about to move their household to the new place in Karolinenhof, he said, 'What company are you working with? I did see the DEUTRANS sign on the truck doors, but I had no idea that DEUTRANS has a moving department.

'One of them swallowed the bite he had just taken and answered, 'we are with DEUTRANS, and we are a separate department with just a few trucks. We are all sworn and background checked by the SSP. But we specialize in moving mainly for government or party officials to ensure that there is not much talking going on when a high-ranking member moves to another place.'

'Oh, I did not know that. Always learning something new,' Bodo answered. 'What do you think when you are finished loading up? I learned from my wife that you are taking good care of our furniture and everything.'

'We think we can move out of here Tuesday night or, I think, better Wednesday morning,' looking at the other two guys who nodded, 'because then we can drive straight through and would be at your new home Wednesday night. We all live in Berlin and could get home for the night, be back, and unload on Thursday. Unloading always goes faster than loading, so we should be done Friday around noon.'

Sarina jumped in and explained, 'We talked about the sleeping situation for the last night here, and I thought for that one night, just having the mattress on the floor with some blankets should be a big deal. They can load those in the morning and drive off.'

That sound like a good plan,' Bodo said, confirming the setup and the timetable. And adding on, 'It would allow me to get the visits I have to make, and you can get to our house. But I won't be making it there on Wednesday night. Let's talk later about the details.'

When they were done with dinner, the movers and Gunter said good night and went out to get to their sleeping apartments.

Sarina took Bodo by his hand and said, 'While I show you around what they have already packed and how great they did, you can tell me what is going on.' Nick was just tailing and listening to his father's explanation about the craziest week in his whole life. When he started to explain the new house and where it was, Nick couldn't hold back any longer, 'dad, you said it is directly on the river? What river is it? Is there a beach? Can I swim there?

'Slow down, son. Yes, it is on the river Dahme. And if you didn't sleep in geography, you know roughly where that river runs. And there are all kinds of watersports possibilities. But we have a huge garden directly next to the house, and we will definitely use that opportunity to grow healthy food. As I know your mom, she will love it, and she will also love your unlimited help,' he said, looking at Sarina with a smirk.

'Och' was all that came as an answer.

Bodo saw that they had the living room furniture already wrapped in several layers of blankets and secured them with tape. They had started to prepare blankets for the dining room furniture, and it appeared as if they could get that room done on Saturday. Most of the work was in the kitchen. All the dishes and glass items need to be securely packed, which could take some time. The movers had brought boxes for the delicate items and clothing, which were still not touched. So, Bodo could see why they estimated finishing on Tuesday.

After they had put Nick to bed, Sarina and Bodo sat in the kitchen since the living room was no longer usable. They had brought the TV into the kitchen, placed it on a small side table, and Bodo switched it on to get the late-night news broadcast. Just then, as the TV was up and running, the signature sound ended, and the speaker appeared. As always in the GDR news broadcast, he was very formal in his expression, and his voice was as lethargic as humanly possible. Bodo did not even register how robotic that whole appearance had to be received by any normal-thinking human being who was not yet entirely deceived by the communistic indoctrination. For him, it was exactly as it had to be done. A news broadcast had to be absolutely emotionless presented. The speaker started to read the news from the pieces of paper in his hand; it wasn't really news. It was again the repeated message that the farmers of the tremendous socialistic agricultural collectives fought the fight they did every spring, getting the planting and sewing done, braving the elements. It was followed by almost the exact wording, only that the farmers and agricultural collectives were now replaced by the miners and the tremendous socialistic coal mines where the weather was always the reason for not enough coal produced, and any extra ton was heralded as the outmost achievement only possible in socialism because of the firm conviction of the miners. Neither Sarina nor Bodo paid much attention to the announcements until a meeting of the Central Committee of the SUP was mentioned. They were suddenly attentive and listened to the speaker's announcements.

'The members of the Central Committee of the Socialist United Party of the German Democratic Republic hold their weekly meeting today. Among many essential decisions, they decided on the following changes and additions to be announced.

1. Comrade Gerd Hollorek resigned from his position as the Secretary of Justice based on health concerns. The Central Committee will decide until the next scheduled session who would be the best replacement.

2. The Central Committee has installed a new office directly reporting to the Central Committee. The new office is instructed to investigate corruption inside and outside of the party.

3. The Central Committee calls upon all citizens, members of the Party or not, to report cases of corruption they are aware of in written form to the following address OIR, PO Box 68 Berlin

4. The Central Committee declares those letters absolute secret, and any person who interferes with mail addresses that PO Box would be committing an act of treason. The statement includes the note that the punishment for treason is the death sentence according to the constitution of the republic.

Other announcements followed it, but both of them didn't listen any longer. 'Wow, that is something,' Sarina said. 'They are telling the people they can denunciate corrupt people with name and address, and if any of those corrupt assholes interferes with the process, it is a death sentence. That is colossal. And what is that OIR? Is that the new office they have installed?' Since Bodo did not answer and was apparently deep in thought, she pushed him on the shoulder and said, 'Bodo, is this perhaps the new job you have? This new office? I can't believe it, really?

'Calm down, Sarina. Yes, this new anti-corruption office is my new job. I have been appointed commander of the Office of Investigation and Recovery. I have an incredibly powerful position when all is built up, and I can finally realize what should have been done from the beginning. That was why I was in the last week in Berlin; that is why we are moving there, and it is an enormous responsibility. We often talked about the party's conditions and the country as a whole and how it has deteriorated into a swamp of corruption at the highest levels of the party and economic leadership. How many times have I come home in the last several years, frustrated and angry about the situation that destroyed the nation? How many times have I pointed out that the basic principles of the Leninistic-Communistic revolution are disregarded, and that leads to the destruction of the party? And nothing happened. Only more complaints about me and my work were filed, and my carrier in the party was blocked. Now, five minutes before the collapse, a brave group of comrades have taken control, and they know what is needed. Yes, Sarina, I am the Commander of this new office, and I will do what is necessary. No mercy to the traitors.'

She looked at him and finally hugged and kissed him passionately. Then she said,' I am happy for you and proud of you, Bodo. I have seen over the years how these treasonous actions of your brother and all the others have eaten you up on the inside. Now you can get it back to them, and you might even be appointed in time to save the socialistic society of the german nation. I am on your side, Bodo, all the way.'

Bodo took a deep breath, 'I know, Sarina, we have had so many discussions about what should be done, and I was at a point where I believed it would never happen, and shortly the communist movement would lose everything we had accomplished. And even at the last minute, it seemed like it would not be completed again. That one comrade, the secretary of justice, did not resign. He was removed. It was an eight-to-one decision of the Central Committee. He was not with us on this assignment, and the secretaries decided he needed to go. This new Central Committee has the same opinion I have. I have the total support of the remaining members of the Central Committee, and I have it in writing. One is either with us or against us. There is no middle ground, and those who are against us need to be eliminated!'

Said that Bodo got up from the chair, turned off the TV, and said, 'come, honey, let's go to bed. I am tired as a young dog. I have some necessary paperwork to do tomorrow, and I hope to finish it so we can have some family time on Sunday.'

The following day was somewhat fresh, but the sun came through and quenched the morning fog fast, and with the starting of a light breeze, it looked like it would be a nice fresh spring day.

The men arrived with Gunter soon after Bodo and his family had finished breakfast. They had breakfast at the apartment because that was included in the price. The mover men resumed packing, and Bodo took a cup of coffee and walked out to the barn. He opened the barn door, looking at the motorcycle, and he got a nostalgic feeling. That was now a part of the past. He might as well sell it before the move to Berlin. He had no idea how he would be able to sell it there. He heard steps behind him and turning around, and he saw Gunter approaching slowly.

'Comrade Zipper, I would like to know your plans for today. If you don't need me, I would love to visit some friends from my service with the parachute regiment in Prora.'

Bodo thought for a while and answered, 'I thought about doing some paperwork and spending the day with my family and relaxing. So, yeah, why not. I don't need to remind you that we are here undercover for the public. Although the new office was officially announced yesterday in the news, nobody knows that it is me, and we want to leave it at that. Always remember that many people here on the island know me very well. How would you get to meet them?'

Gunter answered, 'if I can use your phone, comrade Zipper, I could call my friend in Glowe, and he could pick me up. He would also bring me back on Sunday morning if that is OK with you.

'Yea, that should be fine. Catch your friend down at your apartment instead of getting up here' No need for him to see all that is going on.'

'Yes, comrade Zipper, no problem. See you tomorrow morning because we have to see a friend. I need some convincing to do.'

'Yes, please be here at 8 AM, we have some work. Yea, 8 AM is OK.'

Gunter said good buy and walked to the house. Sarina showed him where the phone was, and after a few minutes, he reached the bakery where his friend worked as the baker's son-in-law. His friend was excited by the surprise visit and promised to be there in a maximum of 20 minutes. Gunter thanked Sarina, said good buy, and walked down the driveway, walking to the apartment to wait for his friend.

Bodo looked a few minutes longer at the motorcycle, and it hurt him that he had to get rid of it, but it was time to move on. He had a new responsibility and all that was needed to move around much more safely. He was walking back to the house in his thoughts about how to sell the bike in such a short time when one of the movers startled him out of his thoughts, 'comrade Zipper, I noticed that nice bike in there when your wife showed us around, and I was wondering, are you taking the bike to Berlin?'

'You know, I am thinking about selling it, but I just don't know how to get it done within the few days I have left.'

'Would you mind telling me the price, comrade? I might be interested in buying it.'

'You know, the AWO425s is a rear bike. And this one is special because it has been upgraded several times. I have upgraded it to the 350ccm version, and the guy I bought it from had already included all the available modernization. I guess you need to have at least 5.000 Mark at hand to have me even think about it.'

'Oh, that is expensive, and I might have to think about how I can get it together. I may need some days, maybe even a week. How much time could you give me, comrade?'

'You know what, since I am pretty sure I can't sell it here in those two to three days before we leave, see that you get it loaded up safely and when we are in Berlin, and you have the money, let me know, and we have a deal. But if I get it sold before for more than that price, I am sorry, but I have to see for myself.'

'Oh, I understand. I will see what I can do. It is really a nice machine. Would you allow me to take a short trip with it?'

'You have the bike driver's license?' Yea, then go ahead and drive it around. But be careful, the police officer in the village knows me and might stop you and ask you about it. Tell him to call me if that happens. Here is the key.'

With a big smile, the guy pushed the bike out of the barn, put Bodo's helmet on, and started the engine. The low growling sound of the idle engine was music in Bodo's ears, and again, a kind of sadness overcame him that he had to let it go. As he turned toward the house, Sarina stood there, looking at him with a typical woman's expression. She knew it all. 'You really let someone foreign to you drive the bike? 'She asked, smiling. It looks like you are ready to let go, but it still hurts.'

'Yea, kind of,' Bodo answered with a deep-drawn sigh. 'I believe it is time to sell it since I now have any car available I need at any time. And since we are on talking car, what about this, let's drive down to Sassnitz and have a nice lunch and coffee somewhere, walk the mole and have some time as a family?'

'That's an excellent idea, and I am sure your son is even more excited.'

CHAPTER 26

SEPARATING FROM A PLACE WITH LOTS OF MEMORIES IS NEVER EASY, EVEN WHEN THE PARTY CALLS

They went into the house, called Nick and when he appeared they told him to get ready for a trip to the city. He was really excited and was ready in no time, leaving his partly finished homework as it was on the small desk in his room. He was investigating every piece of the car and was wondering about all the little gimmicks. The phone found his special interest, and Bodo had to remind him several times not to play with it. When they reached the city, Bodo parked at the large parking lot at the Rügen Hotel, and after a short look at the watch, he said it was time for lunch. Since he was really hungry for lunch with fresh fish, they did not leave the car. Instead, he drove down Hafenstreet and along the Strandpromenade. Parking there was a huge problem, even outside of the season. But getting increasingly conscious about his new status, he parked as best out of normal traffic and shut down the engine.

'Dad, you are parking illegally completely where you parked the car,' Nick announced, agitated. 'I know, son, but my new position allows me to have some privileges. 'With the announcement, let's get some real fresh fish lunch today,' he opened the door and stepped out.

They went to the 'Gastmahl des Meeres,' and again, off-season, there weren't many people in line to be seated. A few minutes later, one of the waiters appeared, and to Bodo's and the waiter's surprise, they were former classmates. Not knowing the position Bodo had been appointed to, not even knowing what he was doing at all, since they had not met in years, he may have assumed Bodo was still a mechanic on one of the cutters of the Fishing Corporation in town. But an old classmate was always welcome and got the best place in the restaurant that was free. They chose their meals and were excellent serviced, and Bodo did not spare a big tip. When they were done, they enjoyed the still lovely and sunny, although a little chilly weather, and walked the whole mole up to the head where the green light tower of the harbor entrance was. On the way back, they passed several people they knew, and some of them greeted friendly, while others looked demonstrative in the other direction. It did not get unnoted even by Nick, but he did not say anything until they were back at the car.

When they reached the car, a police officer was walking up and down the road next to the car, and when Bodo approached the car, he immediately walked toward him.

'Is this your car? He asked. Bodo thought for a moment to play a little game with the officer whom he remembered was at the same school he was but some years behind him, but he thought it was not the time to do so.

'Indeed, I am driving this car, comrade constable. Something wrong with the car?'

'Not with the car, at least I hope, but with the parking. You must have noticed when you parked the car that this area is a total parking-restricted area.'

'Is that so, comrade constable? So let me ask you a question, did you check the license plate?

'Why would I do that? You are parking in a non-parking area, and it doesn't matter what license plate the car has.'

'Comrade constable. I want to spare you embarrassment and suggest you use your nice little radio and call in the license plate. It might be saving your day.'

With a deep breath and a kind of strange look at Bodo, he hit the button of his radio and asked for the license plate of Bodo's car to be checked. The answer came within less than 30 seconds, loud and clear, that it could be understood by the whole group, 'Leave that car and the people with it alone! I have that car on the list: UNTOUCHABLE! Do you understand? Do you copy?'

With a startled expression mumbling an excuse, the office confirmed that he had received the message and walked away.

They all entered the car, Bodo started the engine, turned the car around, and they drove off. Only then did Bodo notice that a small crowd had assembled while they had that little confrontation with the police officer. Driving out of the harbor area, he saw the police officer standing at the entrance to the fishing corporation, and he realized that he was a part of the forces guarding industrial properties considered important or potential ways for traitors to leave the country illegally. He made a mental note to call the commanding officer and have him send the officer's file. A potential future member of the RON. He was the type of officer that noticed irregularities and acted upon them, even if he did not get the necessary information first.

While they were driving up the cobblestone road, passing the Red Army Harbor command building, he said, 'Sarina, or Nick, is there any news about those Speznas of the Red Army that fled a few weeks ago?'

'Sarina answered, 'No, they don't have them caught yet. Rumor is that the authorities believe that they have probably tried to swim through the Baltic sea to Danemark. They could have gotten over to Hiddensee and, from there, the shortest passage. After all, they were Speznas and might have thought they could make it.'

'I don't think so,' Nick threw in. It is more than 50 miles, and even if they were that good, you could easily lose orientation in the water if you don't have a compass. I believe they had some help and were brought off the island long ago.'

Bodo had decided to use the backroad through the gorgeous forest of very old beech trees to test the car's ability on that winding road. It was an excellent feeling accelerating at the engine's full power and then breaking down to get through the next curve only to accelerate again full.

While doing so and having no difficulties or getting even a little agitated, he looked over to Sarina and saw that she wasn't agitated either. Instead seemed to enjoy the excellent car. He asked Nick, 'Is that what you are talking about among your friends at school?'

'Yes, dad and my friends ask me all the time if you know anything about it.'

'I have to tell you, Nick, that I do not know more about the current stand as everybody else. But I agree with your assessment that they are long gone and have not been on the island within a few hours, or somebody had somehow hidden them and smuggled them off the island.

When they arrived home, he stayed in the car and told his family to go ahead, and he had to make a phone call on his secure phone.

After just two rings, Reiner picked up the phone. 'Reiner Worser, whom I am speaking with?'

'Hallo Reiner, I thought I better give you a heads up that I will be at your place tomorrow at about 11 AM.'

'Bodo, why am I not surprised anymore that you have something in mind with me that I can't reject yet don't even know what it is? What is it this time?

'I need to speed things up a little bit and have to head back to Berlin on Monday. Since I need to get some documents from your office, I need to talk to you tomorrow, and with that, your time to decide is just reduced by a little less than 24 hours. But it doesn't make a difference since you sleep most of the time anyway.'

'You are my new boss if I take the position?'

'Sure, why are you even asking? It is about time you get a boss who shows you what work means. But joking aside, I will be there at about 11, and we can talk about everything. Did you talk to your wife already?'

'I did, and since the kids are not in school yet, she is not against a new place if it is not in Berlin.'

'I can confirm that, at least.'

'Ok, then, See you at 11 tomorrow at my place.'

Bodo ended the call, and leaving the car, he locked it and went into the house, where movers were almost done with most of the remaining furniture. They had just started to pack the dishes and other easily breakable items in special plastic boxes.

Sarina looked at her husband, 'They are almost done. If all goes as they said, they could be finished tomorrow around noon.'

'Why, that's great. They could start moving and be at the new home on Monday night. My schedule is somewhat cramped. I need to stop at Rainer's office in the morning, at the office of the ICC in Neubrandenburg, Schwerin, and Rostock, and from there, I will drive directly to our new home.'

'How are we getting there? Are you not dragging us through half of the nation on your collection tour? Now, it would be great to have time in all three cities, but I guess there is no room for us to have a shopping trip with your timetable?'

'No, that won't be an option. I promise you that there will be plenty of time for you and Nick to drive into the city and go shopping. I thought about getting you on the Interzonen-Train from Sweden with a separate cabin for you and Nick, and you will have a very nice traveling to Berlin. I will arrange the pickup for you both in Berlin, and they will get you a nice apartment until I can pick you up. What do you think about that?

'I like that much more than being crammed into the car for hours one end. And Nick probably has more fun than sitting hours in the car, either. Yes, I think it is a better way to get there.'

'Let me make some phone calls and get the arrangements done. And you will love the place. It is like a luxurious hotel, including breakfast service to the room. And you are in the center of Berlin. If you want to go somewhere, you can call a car service. I'll arrange that all for you both.'

'That sounds awesome. I will go and tell Nick,' and with that, Sarina was out of the door. Bodo went out to the car and took the phone inside the house. Walking through the empty rooms, he was looking for a spot where he could sit down and make the phone call or calls needed. In the room, he had used as his home office was still a chair and a small desk where the movers had placed the landline phone on to avoid having it on the floor. He placed the phone box on the table, sat down, grabbed the handset, and hit the button connected to his secretary's home number. It took several rings until somebody picked up the phone and announced,' Franzia.'

He realized this was not his secretary, so he asked,' May you please get Giesela Franzia on the phone for me? Comrade Zipper needs to talk to here.'

'I will get her. Please wait a moment.' After a few minutes, Giesela grabbed the phone and said,' Giesela Franzia, whom am I speaking to?'

'Comrade Zipper here,' Bodo answered. 'I need you to do me a favor because you know all the people who need to be involved better than I do, and therefore, I needed to interrupt your free time on a Saturday. I need a reservation for my son and wife for the Interzonen-Train tomorrow from Sassnitz to the Berlin Station, where it stops. I need somebody to pick them up there, and since the house is not ready, they need to get accommodation at the Guest House of the CC, probably till Tuesday. I want you to stay home on Monday and be near your phone, so I can reach you if needed. Any questions? Did you get all of this? I was probably talking much too fast.'

'No, comrade Zipper, I am pretty well with short-hand writing and have everything.'

'Call me back with the train schedule information and let me know if there are any issues. Call me immediately if things need to be changed. Do you have my mobile number?

Yes, comrade Zipper, I have your mobile number. I will call you as soon as I have the train information.

'Great, and again, sorry for interrupting your free time.'

'No need to be sorry for. I am used that things like this can happen.' With that, she hung up.

Bodo went to work on some of the strategic ideas he was running through his mind and made a list with bullet points for the things that needed to be done for the RON.

About one hour later, Giesela called back and gave him the ticket numbers to be received at the ticket office. And she confirmed that Sarina and Nick would be picked up from the train station in Berlin by comrade Lenner personally, and he had already arranged dinner for them, including comrade Bruno. Bodo thanked her and called Karl immediately to thank him for his engagement in the affair.

'Karl Lenner, whom I am speaking with?'

'Hello Karl, I just got the message from my secretary that you have arranged everything for my family and I wanted to say thanks for it.'

'Bodo, nothing to thank for. You will be very busy for a long time, and the family has to stay back through that period. I thought it would be the least we could do to improve their moving experience. And Bruno actually had the idea to invite them for dinner. So, lean back and enjoy your cross-country trip through the northern part of the nation.'

'It might be such. You know as well as I do that the streets in the northern area aren't very well maintained. That's why I chose to go Neubrandenburg – Schwerin – Rostock and then use the Autobahn down to Berlin.'

'That's what I thought when Giesela told me your route. Have a safe trip, and we will stay in touch.'

After Bodo had hung up, he looked for his family and found them in the remaining kitchen. Sarina had, in the meantime, explained to Nick how they would be traveling with the Interzonen-Train to Berlin, all in their own cabin. She had also arranged with the movers that the remaining furniture in the kitchen and the bed in the bedrooms would be loaded last, on Sunday.

'I just talked to Karl – you will meet him in Berlin, and he will greet you at the train station. All is arranged for your accommodation until we can move into the new house. I suggest you both go ahead and pack the travel bags because I need to drop you at the station in Sassnitz at 9 AM.'

'How would Karl, who is that at all, identify us at the train station in Berlin?'

'Karl is the guy who fished me out of the forest of withering trees, the fighting reserve of the SUP, and he is the right hand of comrade Bruno Tecker.'

'Comrade Bruno Tecker? You mean that Bruno Tecker?'

'Yes, that Bruno Tecker, the head of the Internal Control Commission of the party and the second, most powerful man in the country.'

'I know, dad, the most powerful man is the Secretary-General, right?' Nick threw in, to show that he had learned his lessons in Political Science.

Bodo looked at his son, smiled, and said, 'I am not really sure anymore who is the most powerful man within the new structure of the country's leadership system.' Sarina and Nick looked at each other, then both turned to Bodo, and with wide and stunning eyes, they were just silent. Both understood what Bodo just had said without saying it.

Sunday morning, Bodo woke up at 7:30 and heard Sarina already working in the kitchen, using the little stuff left to get breakfast together.

Laying awake in bed for a few more minutes, he listened to their laughing, and although he could not understand what they said, it appeared to be as if they both were talking in joyful expectation about the train trip to Berlin and the two days they would spend there.

He finally stood up, did his hygiene, and went into the kitchen after dressing. They both greeted him, smiling and talking, and he was with his thought already again at work. 'Bodo,' Sarina said, 'where are you? You are not here with your mind. Come on, sit down, and let's have breakfast. We have all our stuff together, the movers will be here in a few minutes, and then we have to leave for the train already.'

'Yea, I know. There is so much to do. I am already thinking about how to get everything started. I need 48-hour days.'

At that moment, the doorbell rang, and Gunther was there when Sarina opened the door. He greeted all of them, and Nick gave him a high-five. Bodo was looking with a questioning expression. Nick turned around and said, 'Dad, your driver, comrade Recker, I mean, is a real funny guy.'

'OK, get ready. Gunter is driving because we will visit somebody after we get you on the train.' When we finish that, we will come back, do the last check, and send the movers on their way. I will ensure all is loaded and the house is secured.

They grabbed the travel bags, and Gunther went out with Sarina and Nick and loaded them all in the car. Bodo went over to the movers and said, 'We will be back at approximately 2 to 3 PM, and I guess you might be done by then. We can double-check everything and get you guys on the way.'

'Oh, sure, comrade Zipper. We should be done, and getting out here at that time, would definitely get us at least half the way to Karolinenhof. I plan on staying overnight at Prenzlau and be at your house approximately early in the afternoon.' We will start unloading but won't be able to get much done.'

'That's great,' Bodo said, 'I will be arriving really late. It would be nice if you could just place the bedroom furniture in the Masterbedroom so that I have a place to sleep. My wife will be there on Tuesday at approximate lunchtime, and she will direct you with all the things where they need to go.'

'Does that means we do not need to be there before noon?'

'No, no need for that.'

'Great, that would give us time to get a larger crew together and be done latest that evening.'

Bodo confirmed the general agreement and said, 'Good, then, see you later.' He went to the car, where the family was already in the back seats and Gunther in the driver's seat, to get going. He entered the car and said, 'all ready?' Not expecting an answer, he turned to Gunther, 'Do you know the way to the railway station in Sassnitz?' Gunther confirmed that he knew the way, he started the car, and they were on their way. After a short drive of about 15 minutes, they arrived at the train station, and Bodo went into the building with his family. As promised by Giesela, the ticket office had the tickets for Sarina and Nick, including the 1st class reservation tickets. The woman behind the desk immediately recognized Bodo as a former classmate and from several meetings where he had spoken in his function as the Secretary of Agitation and Propaganda. She asked, 'Bodo, how come you have your family traveling at such a luxury and only with a one-way ticket?'

Bodo thought about how to answer the question because he did not want the whole city to know what was going on or run on rumors. After a moment, he signaled her to come close and then, with a very low voice, said, 'Nick won a writing contest, and they will come back by bus later the week. We really don't want to make a big deal out of it. You know what I mean?'

'I understand entirely, Bodo. I will keep that to myself, for sure.'

'Thanks,' Bodo answered, took the tickets, and walked over to Sarina and Nick while thinking, yea, that's precisely why I did tell you the lie. Just at that moment, the speaker came to life, and a barely understandable shrill voice announced the arrival of the Interzonen-Train from Malmoe. Bodo grabbed Sarina's bag, Nick took his bag, and they walked out onto the platform. The train stopped, and the first-class wagon was almost in front of them. The doors opened, and a few people looked out, but the only ones who left the train were the officers from the border police and custom and the conductors of whom were three at the train. The one for first class stepped out directly where Bodo stood with his family, and

Bodo went to him. 'Comrade, I am placing my family in this cabin,' he said while showing him the tickets, 'and I will be out immediately.'

'Sure, no problem. Just see that you are out soon because we have only 5 minutes stopover here.'

Bodo went into the train, helped Sarina and Nick up the steps, and right behind the door for the walkway was the door for their reserved cabin.

They embraced, and he kissed Sarina, kissed Nick on the head, and with a goodbye he moved out of the cabin, almost colliding with one of the conductors coming from the back of the train. He stepped out of the train where the conductor was still looking up and down the train. 'The conductor looked then at Bodo and said, 'comrade, you must have a very special position.'

'Why is that,' Bodo asked.

'I have been running this Interzonen-Train now for eight years, and I have never seen one of our citizens having a seat in the 1st class, let alone a whole cabin reserved for them at the last minute possible.'

'Comrade, let's say that I have some strings I can pull to get things done, and if my family tells me later that they have been treated well during their travel time with this train, I may pull some strings for you.'

With that, he turned around and was about to walk back to his car when the conductor asked, 'how would you do that? You don't even know my name?'

'As I said, I have some strings I can pull. You will see.'

Bodo decided to stay until the train moved out of the station and maybe wave to his family again. And there they were, both standing at the window in the walkway. The train slowly started to accelerate, and he waved until he couldn't see them anymore, turned around, and walked out to the car.

He entered the car, gave Gunther the home address of Rainer, and they drove off. It was about 11 AM when the car stopped in front of a multistory apartment house on the outskirts of Bergen, where Rainer had a two-room with bath and kitchen apartment, as the code defined it in the GDR. He told Gunther to stay with the car and that he would take the phone with him. At the entrance, he looked for the bell with the name Worser and hit the bell. A few seconds later, the electrical lock sounded, and the door was unlocked so he could enter. Stepping into the stairway, he immediately saw Reiner standing a few steps above him at the door to his apartment.

'Hello, Reiner. I did not know that you were living on the first floor. That makes moving easier.' Bodo greeted him with a wide smile.

'Come on in; no need for the whole house to hear what you have to say.' Reiner answered. Bodo walked up the few stairs and entered his friend's apartment. It was the first time he was there because they had moved in about a year ago, and he had never had time to visit him at home. Hi wife Corinna, which Bodo had known since he was Reiners best man at their wedding, greeted him with an embrace and winked them into the living room. They sat down, and Corinna asked if they wanted a cup of coffee, and both confirmed. She brought it in and filled their cups. Then she asked, 'Bodo, do you want me to stay in the other room while you are talking?'

'Oh no, just the opposite. I need you to be a part of this as well, as I need Reiner. If I remember correctly, you are a certified secretary, aren't you?'

Corinna answered, 'yes, that's true. I worked until our child was born four years ago at the office of internal affairs here at the county district office.'

Bodo explained that everything they were about to discuss had to stay between them. He talked about his recruiting by the Central Committee, explained his position, and that he needed Reiner to be the head of the North Regional Office. He explained the meaning of the position and the benefits that came with it and painted the enormous responsibility that was attached to it in no uncertain terms. After about two hours of questions and answers and back-and-forth discussion of ideas, already strategizing the work at that office, Bodo went to the bathroom to release himself from the amount of coffee they had consumed. When he returned, he said, 'So, we are clear in the overall function you have to fulfill, Reiner, and if you both decide to do so, Corinna can be employed as your secretary, which would increase your income even if she works only half a day. As soon as I am settled in my home, I will arrange everything for you to get moving. We will see to get a decent house for you in Wittstock, and from there to your future office will be about 15 minutes drive, that's the area we are looking for a location.'

'You think we can get a real house?' Corinna asked with a joyful expression.

'Yes, Corinna, you will have a real house for you and your family. I will see if I can get something you might really enjoy. He stood with a, 'you will hear from me within the next two or three days,' he said goodbye. Reiner escorted him out, and Bodo reminded him to make sure he could react on a moment's notice when he called him. It was about two in the afternoon when they were back at his place, and he was surprised that the movers were already closing their trucks to prepare for the trip. They were not sure, though, about the sleeping arrangements for Bodo and waited for his decision.

While they were in Sassnitz the other day, he had developed the idea to sleep at the Rügen Hotel instead of getting no sleep on a mattress on the floor. He told the movers to wait a minute, walked out to his car, and called Giesela. This time she picked up the phone herself, and he said, 'I need you to call the Rügen Hotel in Sassnitz and make a room reservation for two singles tonight. I will be there in about one hour and a half.'

She called him back about ten minutes later and said, 'Sorry, comrade Zipper, that it took so long, but I had to get the manager on the phone to make sure they understood that this wasn't a late fools-day joke. Because they seem to know you very well, they would not take my reservation.'

'I am sorry for the stress they put on you. They should not have done that. Anyway, many thanks again, and have a great rest of the weekend. I will not bother you again.' With that, he hung up and walked back to the movers. 'You can close up everything and move out. We will stay at the hotel tonight, and you can start your trip.'

Bodo walked around the empty house for the last time when the trucks had left his property. Considering all the memories connected to it, he became a little heavy-hearted. The thoughts about why he even had moved here in the first place caused his anger to rise again. His brother, that traitor, had caused his career to be wiped out. Now, he was in an even much better position than he had ever dreamed of. And if he would even find the slightest sliver of evidence that Fritz is involved in the uproar in so many cities of the country, he would use his new position to remove him as an obstacle for all time. After his walk-through of the house, he locked the door and went to the barn. He opened the small door and walked into the empty space, which now appeared double the size when he used to work there on so many things, mainly his bike. Again, he heaved a deep sigh, remembering all the hours and the many successful improvements he had made to his bike in the years in this very place. He left the barn and locked that door, also. Deep in thought, he walked over to the car, entered the passenger back seat, and said, 'Gunther, get us to the Hotel in Sassnitz. I have a reservation for us for tonight.

'Yes, comrade Zipper,' Gunther confirmed, and, realizing that his boss was somewhat melancholy, which he could completely understand, he drove out of the property. Bodo didn't even bother to look back. He had closed that chapter of his life and was now entirely focused on the new assignment. Nothing would stop him now from erasing all the parasites and traitors from the face of the German Democratic Republic, which he considered the only legitimate state on German soil.

Within a short trip, they entered the city, and Bodo stopped him and told him to enter the underground garage when Gunther started to turn onto the parking lot. The gate was closed, and Gunther stopped. Bodo stepped out of the car and walked up to the main entrance. He entered the hotel and walked to the front desk, where two young women looked expectant at him, and one of them asked, 'good afternoon, what can we do for you?'

'I have a room reservation for two rooms. My driver is at the garage door. Would you please open the gate for him?'

They looked at each other as if to say, what does this guy think who he is? Then the silent one so far said, 'we can't do that. Only specific people can park their cars in the underground garage.'

'I understand, but I am more than special, and please ask your manager before it becomes a problem.'

She shrugged her shoulders, grabbed the phone handset, and dialed a number. After talking a few words, Bodo could not understand. She hung up and said that the manager would be here any moment. When the manager arrived, he asked Bodo for his name, and everything changed on a dime. He ordered the two women to open the gate immediately and see to it that the rooms were more than ready.

He guided Bodo down to the garage where Gunther had just parked the car and was about to get the luggage out of the trunk.

Then, the manager accompanied them to the highest floor, number seven, and showed them to their rooms on the side of the hotel. He handed them the keys and apologized for the inconvenience, which he excused that the women didn't know who Bodo was. Bodo told him that it better stay that way and he should make sure that their curiosity did not cost him his job. The manager hurried to the elevator and was probably happy that this event had not created worse reactions.

'Gunther, I don't know what you are about to do, but I will use the time to get some work done, and later I will get some dinner. There is a nice bar up on the eighth floor but don't forget, 8 AM breakfast and an extended driving are ahead tomorrow.'

'I will be down at 8 AM, comrade Zipper. Good night.'

BUILDING AN UNDERGROUND COMMUNICATION NETWORK UNDER THE WATCHFUL EYES OF THE SPP

Fritz was preparing all the stuff he needed o his trip to his friends, including Monday's stopover at the Neubrandenburg area. He did not yet receive the exact meeting location with the two guys. It wasn't even confirmed yet that the SUR guy could get to the same meeting. That would not be good because then Fritz would need to drive over to the west side of the country to get to a separate meeting with the SUR guy close to Schwerin. Otherwise, he could just drive straight north along the east side of the nation and pass Berlin on the east instead of having all that far detour on his way home. He had taken four days off, and with God-Friday and Easter Monday being official holidays, he could have the whole week for his trip and the following Monday for resting.

Two weeks ago, they decided to move in with his mother-in-law. She lived in that old farmhouse, and with all the stress they had with Fritzs' removal from the NAVY Base and her mother struggling to live alone on that large property, Karola had asked if it would be possible to move there. Although it did not improve the travel situation for Fritz, it had some advantages. First, he was away from all the people in his hometown who knew about his 'fall from grace,' as he usually called his break with the party in power, and secondly, it was a much better place for the children since it was a huge farmstead with a large garden. And the whole village was surrounded by large forests. The house was large enough to have one half for them and the other half for her mother. They cooked and ate together in the large kitchen with the attached small dining room, the former office when her grandpa was still operating the collective agricultural years ago. It was a great help that Leo usually had the truck parked at his place, and with that, they could move their belongings on the weekend with just four trips from Sassnitz to the small village of Juggenhagen, near the Island Usedom.

He loaded the communicators and programmers into shoeboxes, two sets each to a total of 10 units, and packed them into a larger carton on top of which he placed books until the box was filled. For someone looking at the carton, this would appear as if it was loaded with books. All of them were technical literature from his time at University, and he thought it would make sense if someone asked since he was visiting friends from his time there.

On his way out to the garage, Karola asked him about a specific shirt she was ironing at that moment, and he said, 'I will be right back, honey, just putting this box in the car. Then we can go over the clothing I am taking.'

When he came back into the room, she had already packed most of the clothing into the travel back and had two button-up shirts lying outside. 'Which one do you want to take,' she asked, pointing to them. 'I'll take the dark blue one. In case I need to wear the jacket, it fits best with it. Most of the time, I am with my friends, and jeans and other shirts with a light sweater should do it.'

His mother-in-law looked through the open door and asked, 'How long will you be gone, Fritz?'

'I plan to be back on Friday night to be back for the Easter weekend, and I hope there is not too much traffic because of Easter.'

'Great. I asked because I thought you could stop at the nursery in Jarmen and see if they already have their great white asparagus. I would love to cook us some of it coming weekend.'

'That's a great idea. I would love to have some asparagus. I can already taste it, 'Fritz answered, and all of them laughed. Karola's mother was a master in preparing asparagus in several ways, and they all longed for the asparagus season every year. That specific nursery in Jarmen was always the first one of several in their area, which started to sell asparagus end of April.

Finishing up the packaging, Fritz placed the travel back in the hallway, and it was time for dinner.

The family sat around the table, and Fritz said a short praise thanking the Lord for the food and travel save for the following days. He helped Karola tuck in the kids, and they all said their little goodnight prayer together.

'I need to get a hold of Ralf because I have not yet heard where and when the meeting with the two guys around Neubrandenburg should take place.'

'As always, Fritz, be careful what you and he is saying on that spy phone,' Karola said. 'Always, and as you know, Ralf is the most scared guy,' he responded and walked into the dining room where the quarter phone was.

As a leader of the electrical department of the shipyard, Ralf had a phone line at his apartment since it was necessary to reach him immediately in case of an emergency at the shipyard. After the third ring, he picked up the phone, and Fritz apologized if he had interrupted his dinner.

'No, all OK, Fritz. I was just in the bathroom, which is why it took me to get to the phone. You know, my wife hates this thing like the plaque and doesn't even hear it ringing anymore,' he joked. I guess you are calling about the address for the books to drop off tomorrow?'

'You guessed right.'

'It's at Stargarter Strasse 55, and they are there until noon. After that, they have to leave.'

'Great, that fits with my plans.'

'Have a safe trip, Fritz, and let's hear from you when you are back.'

Fritz hung up and went to the living room where Karola and her mother were sitting watching the news broadcast of the GDR TV called 'Current Camera.' It must have just started because when Fritz looked at the wall clock, it was just a minute after 7:30 PM. In his usually unemotional tone, the speaker read the news from a piece of paper.

'The members of the Central Committee of the Socialist United Party of the German Democratic Republic hold their weekly meeting today. Among many essential decisions, they decided on the following changes and additions to be announced.

1. Comrade Gerd Hollorek resigned from his position as the Secretary of Justice based on health concerns. The Central Committee will decide until the next scheduled session who would be the best replacement. He is taken care of by the best specialists in our country, and the Central Committee wishes him a soon recovery.

2. The Central Committee has installed a new office directly reporting to the Central Committee. The new office is instructed to investigate corruption inside and outside the party.

3. The Central Committee calls upon all citizens, members of the Party or not, to report cases of corruption they are aware of in written form to the following address OIR, PO Box 68 Berlin

4. The Central Committee declares those letters absolute secret, and any person who interferes with mail addresses that PO Box would be committing an act of treason. The statement includes the note that the punishment for treason is the death sentence according to the constitution of the republic.

Fritz wasn't sure that he correctly heard what was said there and when he looked at Karola, he realized that he had precisely heard what he could barely comprehend. Even though he could not know what the new agency would do and what powers would be transferred to her, it sounded scary. Knowing the structure of the party and the several different tools of correction and investigation the CC already had, such as the Internal Control Commission and the SSP, this new agency must be a new combination of both, making it the most powerful and with that most dangerous entity in the nation.

Blending out the ongoing messages of the newscast, he asked his wife, 'did you get that?'

She answered, still somewhat shocked, 'I can't believe what I just heard, but if that is true, they just announced that there is a new agency that is even more powerful than the SSP. That is unheard of! Combining the power of investigation of both political and economic corruption.'

Thinking about the other part of the announcement, Fritz added, 'Adding the special PO Box and declaring interference with those information mails as treason means they mean business.'

'You know I support everything you do, Fritz, and although I don't exactly know what it is you are doing, I am scared that this new agency will be so well equipped with whatever they need to get not only the corruption under control but also to discover the resistance and their leaders. Be careful, Fritz, for the sake of our children.'

'I will be as careful as I can, and with the electronic, I have worked for the last years so hard on, it will be even safer to do what is necessary to bring this evil and godless regime down for the sake of the future of our children.'

'I know, it is just so scary with all that is happening.'

With that, they checked after the kids again and went to bed. The next day would be a long day for Fritz, and Karola's nerves would be strained for the next week until he was safe back from his trip.

Early on Monday morning, Fritz woke up without waking Karola, and while getting a cup of coffee, he went through the pieces he was taking with him on his trip in his mind. Suddenly the door to the bedroom opened, and Karola entered the kitchen. She grabbed a cup, filled herself a coffee, and sat next to Fritz. Leaning against his shoulder, she said, 'please be safe out there on the road. Try to call when you find a phone to let us know how you are doing.'

'I will definitely try, but I must also be careful when I call. The phone can be listed and, with that, monitored. I don't want these people to know where I am at any time.'

'I understand, but it would give us peace of mind, knowing that you are ok. It is a whole week you are out.'

Karola was trying to reconnect with friends when she moved out of the village to see if they could help get some needed materials. They were talking about things on the plate with the garden and the improvements he had in mind for their living. About an hour later, the children were awake and came running into the kitchen. Jumping onto Fritz's lap and started to talk simultaneously. Fritz grabbed both, one left and one right, and carried them into the small dining room, where they would have breakfast together. After a few minutes, Karola's mother came out, and together, they prepared breakfast while Fritz played with the kids. They enjoyed a simple yet good breakfast based on food one could get in an economy that was a central micromanaged communist government.

Fritz said goodbye to his family and drove off. Since he needed just under 2 hours to drive to Neubrandenburg, he was sure to be there long enough before the time and could ensure all was safe. After an uneventful drive, he entered the inner ring around the city's center and drove to the point that gave him access to the center. Through Wollweberstreet, he reached Stargarder Street, and when he reached the Marktplatz, he could park and walk to the meeting point. He bought the parking ticket and ensured it was clearly visible behind the windshield. After a good look around, he noticed the red-brick building on one side of the Marktplatz, which was, as in almost all cities, the SUP's headquarters and their armed force of power security, the SSP. After realizing that he was staring at that building for too long, he shook off his thoughts about his experience with some of these people in his past and turned around, walking slowly and very conscientiously to the address where he should meet NUP and SUP #1. The Schwerin group had the same abbreviation as the party in power. While walking, he thought it was nice that they named the underground resistance groups that way.

CHAPTER 28

A SUDDEN DISCOVERY TEARS OPEN OLD WOUNDS

A few minutes after 8 AM, Bodo entered the hotel's breakfast area and was glad to see that Gunther was already there. He chose to order some eggs and toast and coffee.

'Good Morning, comrade Zipper. How did you sleep?' Gunther asked before stuffing the next piece of toast in his mouth.

'Not too bad, but thanks for asking. Are you ready for an awful lot of driving today?' Bodo answered just as the waitress placed his breakfast in front of him.

'Oh, I am fine and ready. Actually, I missed driving more than just a few kilometers for the last several days,' he answered, smiling.

'OK, then, here is the tour for today. We are starting as soon as we are done with breakfast, first stop in Bergen. Then we drive directly to Neubrandenburg and from there over to Schwerin and Rostock.

'Hm, sound a little bit criss-cross to me, comrade Zipper. What is the reason for that?'

'Yea, you would usually go Rostock first, then Schwerin, crossing over to Neubrandenburg, and then straight down to Berlin, but since Rostock Berlin is all Autobahn, it's much better to go the way, I'd say.'

'Uh, I did not think about that. You are right, comrade Zipper. If we hit the Autobahn from Rostock, we will make up for all the slower driving between Neubrandenburg and Schwerin.'

'Ok, you are ready? Let's get on the road.' They grabbed the luggage and went to the front desk, where Gunther took Bodo's luggage and said, 'I will come around with the car at the main entrance, comrade Zipper.'

Bodo took the invoice and wrote a check for the amount using the new checkbook for the OIR agency.

When he walked out the door, Gunther came around the corner, and Bodo entered the car, and on their way, they were.

About 30 minutes later, Bodo entered the office building of the county's party leadership. He went direct to Reiner's office. Reiner was already waiting for him and had a box with case folders ready for him. 'These are severe cases of potential corruption and treason, Bodo, eleven in total. I hope we are at a crossroads here and going in the right direction. I am ready to be on your team, and Corinna is with me.'

'I am happy to have you, Reiner. I know I can trust you with my life, which is the most important parameter we have to look for when choosing people for our new agency. Do you know if Peter is in his office?'

'Yea, he should be in. I saw him a few minutes ago.'

'Thanks and stay tight, you will hear from me soon. In the meantime, whenever you have some time, check out where in Wittstock you think is the best place for you both to get a house and let me know.'

'Sounds awesome. Will do.'

Bodo walked over to the office of his old friend Peter and knocked on the door. 'Come in. Wow, look whom the cat dragged in. Where have you been, Bodo? Haven't seen you in over a week now.'

'Slow down, old man. I am here to drag you out of this office and get you into a position where you are finally a benefit for the cause of the implementation of the communist world order. I am about to tell you a secret, and I know you can keep it because you have nobody who would believe you, even if there would be one you could tell.'

'What? What has bitten you? Are you drunk? No, it can't be. It's too early. So what are you talking about, Bodo?'

'Peter, I don't have much time, but I guess you have gotten the news about the new agency?'

'You are talking about the, what was it, office of Investigation and Recovery? The Central Committee placed a lot of power on whoever is leading that office.'

'Yes, and that would be me.'

'Come again. I mean, I am deaf now. You? You're kidding, right?'

'No, Peter. It is me, and I will honor that calling with all that's in me. And I want you to be my chief officer in that agency.'

'I am too old for jokes like that, Bodo.'

'That's the reason I want you to be it. I have the most respect and trust in you to be on my side, no matter what, and you will have my back at any time. I know I can leave the office for days in a row and come back, and all is as it should be because you are in charge. I don't know anyone else I could trust with that function.'

'Bodo, I don't know, that's a huge move for me. How much time do I have to think about it?'

'None. I need your, yes, now because I am already on the road. I will arrange for you to get an apartment close to the headquarters office within the week, Since you are all by yourself, it should not be a big deal to move, and the movers are really nice guys whom you can trust completely.'

'Man, Bodo, you have a way of convincing an old man from being totally helpless. What would my specific assignment be?'

'As I said, chief of office operation. That means I don't want to have to do with anything that has to do with the operational situation of the three offices we will have. And since all are at the earliest beginning, you have a free hand to set it all up as you see fit.'

Peter sighed deeply and said, 'I see you are helpless without me. I have to make sure you don't screw this one up. When do you think I need to be ready to move?

'I would say by the end of the week. I would like to have you down there by Monday next week.'

"OK. I will be ready. Bodo, many thanks for the trust. I can only imagine how much this position puts on your shoulders, and I will do my best to ensure that the cleansing of the party from all these traitors and parasites is going as fast and successful as possible.

'I have the most respect and trust for you, Peter, as a comrade and friend. We will fulfill this calling of the party to the point. See you in a week.' Bodo embraced his friend and walked out to ensure he did not see how he became emotional. He looked into the office of Reiner and told him to get the file box to the car. He had to have a word with the county's party leader on his way out. Walking up to the second floor, where the leader's office was, he knocked and entered the secretary's office without waiting for a confirmation. She looked stunned at him and asked, 'Bodo, what are you doing here? There is no meeting, and the County-Secretary has no time for visitors right now.'

Bodo walked to her desk and said, 'Tell him I am here, and he will have time.'

'I don't think so,' she answered. Bodo pressed the button on the intercom. Although she tried to get his hand off it, but the voice of the County-Secretary was already there, 'What is it?'

'Comrade Bodo is here and said he needs to speak with you. I tried to stop him.'

'Let him in' and make sure we are not disturbed. By nobody!'

Bode walked over to the door and went right into the County-Secretary's office, closing the door behind him.

Looking at the County-Secretary, and seeing his slimy smirk, he thought, 'your days are countable on the one hand.'

'Comrade Bodo, great to see you're back. I thought you had been sick. I have not seen you in almost a week or so. Am I right? Come sit down. What can I do for you?'

'Comrade Secretary, I am just here to say goodbye and to let you know that I am taking comrades Worser and Wille into my new office. I hope you will find acceptable replacements for the two comrades and my position, but I am not sure you are. I am sure the District-Secretary has already informed you about my new position since I know how close you to are. Time is getting short. I suggest you try to get things in the county in order if you still can.

Bodo turned around and left the stunned County-Secretary behind. Outside of the building, Gunther was talking with Reiner, and when Bodo closed in, Reiner turned around and said, 'Bodo, can you believe that we had the same drill sergeant at the Army even though we were years apart with service.'

'I don't wonder,' Bodo answered, 'That is a special breed of people being able to rip you apart and put you back together in the way the Army needs you for the specific function. We need to get on the road, Reiner, but we must stay in touch. Gunther, are you ready? I told the knucklehead upstairs that you and Peter are already out of here. You can both stay until you move, or you can stop working for his corrupt rabble until you move. You are on my payroll from today, so it is your decision.'

Bodo took his seat in the car, and they drove off.

'Comrade Zipper, where in Neubrandenburg do you actually want to go?'

'The county party office. If I remember correctly, it is at central Market Place, and they should have a reserved parking area in front of the building. It would be best if you got almost entirely around the center on the circuit to enter the city center for the Market Place.'

'Got it, comrade Zipper.'

Bodo took the first of the files out of the box Reiner had prepared for him to use the time while they were driving to look at the human scum he had to deal with in his new position. And he was aware that there might be enough denunciations that were completely incontinent, based on the envy of the person who accused the other for some base motives. But right, this one showed him that Reiner had done a great job in pre-screening the cases because it was the accusations of corruption of the County-Secretary himself. The list of incidences was long, and there were not only witnesses listed, but some of them had actually presented evidence; diverted money to build a beach house at one of the most beautiful beaches on the Island, ordering to bypass laws that secured the dune landscape from being destroyed by unlawful construction projects— allowing the construction of other beach homes for friends, such as the District-Secretary under similar circumstances, circumventing the laws. And much more. Now he regretted that he had indirectly warned that scum of a party leader and thought about immediate action.

Dialing the phone number of Reiner, he had him on after the first ring. 'Reiner, I need you to start working for me immediately. I made a mistake, indirectly letting that bastard of a County-Secretary know that I am on his heels.'

'What do you need me to do?'

'I will arrange everything for his arrest, and I need you to take intermediate control of the county party leadership. I'll call you again in a few minutes.'

Bod hung up and hit the call button where the phone number of Jürgen Pieker was stored. After the second ring, the voice of Jürgen Pieker came through, 'Pieker, who is there?'

'Comrade Pieker, Comrade Zipper here. I am in a very peculiar situation. I bid farewell to my former County-Secretary and could not avoid telling him to get his stuff in order. While driving to my next appointment, I looked at his case file and immediately recognized that it was a huge mistake to let him know I was on his heels. He is as corrupt as you can be, and I have a lot of evidence.'

'Ok, get it, comrade Bodo. It's easier, and since we are on the same power level, it seems appropriate. Can I call you Bodo?'

'Sure, comrade Pieker, sure. No problem.'

'No need for Pieker in return Bodo. Just call me Jürgen.'

'OK. Thanks, Jürgen, it is indeed easier. So here is what I need to happen. The County-Secretary Rügen and the District Secretary Rostock need to be arrested a.s.ap. The current County-Secretary for the ICC, which will be my future head of the RON, has been authorized by me to take intermediate control of the county party affairs of the county Rügen. Please inform the SG about the District-Secretary issue and have a replacement authorized there too. I am on my way to Neubrandenburg. After that, I am in Schwerin and will arrive in Rostock shortly after noon. I hope all is arranged when I arrive in Rostock.'

'Be assured, Bodo, I will immediately order our respective offices to execute the arrests. Do you have any specifics for their handling?'

'Yes, no communication to anyone outside the CC about the fact. As soon as my facilities are ready, they will be transferred. Keep both in solitary confinement and treat them well.'

'Ok, got it. Drive safe, Bodo.'

'I guess that is a given since I have one of your best drivers,' Bodo said and hung up.

He called Reiner and let him know what was decided with the head of the SSP and that he should await the officers shortly.

Meanwhile, they had reached the outskirts of Neubrandenburg, and Gunther notified him about the fact. Bodo instructed him to follow the ring along the former, almost wholly preserved medieval city wall until the sign for the left turn into the inner city appeared. They drove up to the Market place, and while driving along the parked cars to the front of the administration building, Bodo suddenly startled Gunther by yelling, 'Stop!' And then immediately followed by an almost as loud command, 'Don't! Drive on!'

'Comrade Zipper, what is the matter? What happened?'

'Park at the building. I need to think that through. I will explain in a minute.'

Gunther drove to the reserved parking area at the front of the administration building, where the District Party head their offices and partly governmental departments used offices.

'Gunter, the Skoda with the license plate AN 98-06, which we passed, driving through the parking lot, is the plate of a potential counterrevolutionary. I will see that I get an SSP crew to monitor his movements, and I want you to stay with it if it moves out before they are here. I will tell them to contact you for details. Having a slight idea of why this car is parked here is essential.'

'Yes, comrade. I understand.'

Bodo left the car and walked into the building. He looked for the sign indicating the different offices and found the party's offices on the first floor. He walked up the stairs and opened the door with the sign SUP District Headquarters. Closing the door behind him, he found himself in a somewhat larger reception area where several women wer sitting on desks, hammering away on typewriters or speaking on phones. One of the women looked up from her papers and asked him, 'can I help you?'

"Yes, I am comrade Zipper, and I need to see your District-Secretary ICC (DS-ICC) immediately.'

'One moment, comrade Zipper, I'll see if I can get him on the phone.' She dialed a number, and after a few seconds, she spoke into the phone, explaining that he was there for the DS-ICC. She covered the handset microphone and said, 'the DS-ICC said that he is occupied right now, and if you would come back later in the afternoon, or better make an appointment, he would be much obliged.'

Bodo was at the edge because he had seen his brother's car in that parking lot, not knowing what he was up to. He was probably organizing another turmoil for the communist party. Now that DS-ICC, feeling important, told him to come back later, all he could do not explode was to take a deep breath and slowly let it out. He took out his ID Card and a business card. 'Tell him what you are reading on my ID Card, please.' he placed the business card in front of the woman and held his ID Card close to her eyes, saying, 'tell this comrade that he has 2 seconds to confirm my visit now or he is toast!'

The woman's eyes were on the ID Card, reading it to the DS-ICC, her hand holding the handset beginning to shake, and her voice almost broke in fear, 'Paul, you better be here in a second, this is the Commander OIR, and I guess you don't want him to come back in the afternoon.' Since she was highly agitated, her voice had increased, and suddenly the room was totally silent.

'Did your workday suddenly end?' Bodo asked, looking up and into the room. I guess you go all back to your work.

'Uh, there he is—the extremely busy DS-ICC. Great that you could separate yourself for a few minutes from your important work. Can we get to your office, please?'

'For sure, comrade, for sure, please follow me.'

In his office, which was not that usual, janitor-sized room where the desk, the file cabinets, and the chairs filled all the available space, he offered Bodo a seat at the small coffee table with two comfortable chairs. 'Please take a seat, comrade. Shall I ask my secretary to bring you something, a coffee?'

'No, first, I needed a phone connection to the SSP office five minutes ago. Then we can talk about why I am here, and the rest we will see about.'

'Sure, give me just a moment.' He hit the button on the intercom and told his secretary to get the SSP on the phone immediately. A few seconds later, the phone rang after the DS-ICC picked it up and heard who was on handed the handset over to Bodo.

'Hello, comrade Zipper, Commander OIR here. Who do I speak with?'

'Lieutenant Ross, the officer in charge, what can I do for you, comrade Zipper?'

'I need an immediate surveillance set up for a car parked on the Markt Platz parking area with the license plate AN 98-06. My driver is in our car in front of the administration building, license plate BE 99-01.

He has some more details. I want to get a report about his travel route until he gets back home. Persons identified he meets and, if possible, what is discussed.'

'Ok, I have all noted down. One last question, what about photos?' Bodo was now really on edge. What kind of amateurs was working for the SSP?

Comrade Ross, the whole nine yards! Why are you asking?

'Oh, comrade Zipper, we have differently equipped teams according to the severity of the assignment.'

'OK, comrade Ross, get the show rolling before he leaves the city.'

'Yes, comrade Zipper.' And he hung up.

'Now to you, comrade Paul? What was so important that you couldn't even get five minutes to talk to me?

'Comrade Zipper, I apologize, I did not know it was you, and you know how that is. Some people come to the office all day long and have something to complain about.'

'Yes, I know. But does it come to your mind that some of those complaints may be justified, and the comrade is coming to the only department of the party that they know is responsible for the order inside the party? Did it ever cross your mind that this is why the department you worked for is named the Internal Control Commission?'

'Comrade Zipper, I have hundreds of cases where I have to verify whether or not those are actually cases or if somebody just wants to revenge against something he found unjustified against himself.'

'That's why we started this new office. And that's why I am here. Your Regional Assistant should have sent you instructions to pack the ten most critical cases together and hand them over to me. Did you get that message?'

'Yes, comrade Zipper and I have all ten cases in this box.'

See, comrade Paul, it wasn't that difficult to give me the time to get me out of your hair.'

'Again, comrade Zipper, I am very sorry about that misjudgment, and I promise I will be more receptacle to the comrades in the future. Now that I know I am not just filling papers that are then rotting away in the file folders, I am really excited that there is a force that can fight the rotten corruption going on for much too long.'

'OK, comrade Paul, I will keep that in mind and return to that any time I can use your help.' Shaking Pauls's hand and saying goodbye, Bodo was out of the office. When he reached the car, his first concern was the surveillance team, and he asked Gunther, 'have the SSP guys taken over?'

'Yes, comrade Zipper, they were here about ten minutes ago, and after I instructed them about the car, They set up the teams. One is right in the second row behind the Skoda, and the other team is at the exit. They said that there is only one exit they could use that car first when the Skoda leaves the area.'

'Sorry that we came in after he had already left the car. We have no chance to know where he is and whom he is meeting with. Let's get on the road.' OK, we must trust the SSP comrades, that they know how to do their job.

Gunther started the car and drove out of the parking lot. After a few minutes, they were on their way to Schwerin, and Bodo started to dig into the Neubrandenburg box of files with cases of potential treason. He opened the first file, almost with a certain fear of another act of irrefutable treason, but it wasn't clear, and a lot of the information was daring. He went on to the next and then the third one, and although all were reasonable legal cases, non were as extreme as he had seen within a few minutes with the cases of his home, the island Rügen.

He was startled when the mobile phone rang, and picking up the handset, Karl's voice sounded in his ear, 'Bodo, what did you do to my DS in Neubrandenburg? You scared the living daylights out of him, hahaha! Joke aside, he should not have tried to block you, though. But I want to let you know he is one of my better DS in my assigned region.'

'Karl, I have to tell you, I have to apologize for being a little too harsh, but I wonder how many of DS-ICC I may discover who is not really up to their tasks.'

'Bodo, I agree to a certain degree, but somehow the DS-ICC are not adequately trained correctly. I am unsure how I could pinpoint it, but some skills are missing. That is at least my opinion since I gained more knowledge working directly with comrade Bruno.

'Karl, I see where you are going. I think there is some work coming down the pipe for you.'

'What are you talking about?'

'I have an idea, and I believe your boss will really like it.'

'Wow, wow. Waite a minute. I smell something there. Bodo, I will get some additional work when you have an idea.' What are you thinking about?'

'Let me chew on it a little bit, and maybe at the end of the week or early next week, we may sit down with comrade Bruno and talk it through.'

'OK, let me know when you are ready, and I will get us the time at comrade Bruno's schedule,' with that, he hangs up.

'Comrade Bodo, we are at the SUP House in a few minutes. Do you want me to enter the underground garage?'

'Yes, please.'

Over many years, the administration of the party district was spread out over the whole town because there was no building available to house all the departments. Then, four years ago, as a gift for the sixtieth birthday of the First District Secretary (FDS), as his title was, and to honor his fight for peace and against fascism during national socialism, the Old Guard of the party allowed the building of a central facility for the district administration of the party. It was one of the most impressive buildings outside of Berlin, and just building the two-story underground garage was challenging because of the high groundwater level. They entered the driveway leading down to the underground garage and were immediately stopped by a uniformed guard of the people's police.

Bodo lowered his window, and it was apparent that the police officer was not appreciative that he had to walk around the car to the passenger side. He bowed to look into the car and said, 'This is prohibited territory. It can only be entered with a special allowance. Tell your driver to back up, and park the car on the street.'

'Officer, can you read this ID Card, please!' Bodo said and held his ID Card close to his face, which was now almost inside the car, his eyes locked onto the mobile phone and the unusual interior of the car. The police officer, startled out of his stare, looked at Bodo's ID Card. It took him a few seconds to process the information he read, and with a sudden movement of his head out of the open car window, he saluted and yelled towards the gate, 'open the gate, authorized car!'

Bodo closed the window, and Gunther drove down through the gate and found a free space near an elevator. He shut off the engine, looking back at Bodo, and asked, 'Comrade Bodo, should I come with you, or shall I wait here?'

'Please stay with the car, Gunther. I should be back here within a maximum of twenty minutes. Try to get some rest.'

Bodo went to the elevator and was almost ready to hit the button for the main floor when another police officer, very agitated, came running towards him, 'Comrade, you are not allowed to use the elevator. You must use the stairs. Only the FDS and his deputy are allowed to use the elevator. Bodo took out the ID Card, placed it under the nose of the agitated Police officer, and said, 'I assume you are able to read. Please get the elevator open for me. That is all that is required of you right now. And by the way, don't even think about harassing my driver.'

'Uh,....uh, I am sorry, comrade. Yes, sure, here you go, comrade.' The elevator door opened, Bodo selected the ground floor button, and the doors closed. When the elevator doors opened at the ground floor level, multiple eyes off receptionists and security guards were looking at him as if he was an appearance from another world.

Bodo walked into the somewhat impressive entrance hall, and feeling a little reminded of the entrance hall of the CC Guest Building, he asked with a loud voice, 'Can someone show me to the office of the DS-ICC?'

'I can, comrade.' one of the women behind the reception desk said and, passing him, walked into the elevator. Bodo entered the elevator after her, and she hit the button for the third floor. After the elevator had just moved a few meters, Bodo hit the stop button and turned to her. When he saw the scarred expression, he said, 'No danger, comrade. I just want to get some answers before we get to the floor. Why is nobody allowed to use the garage or the elevator beside the FDS and his deputy?' She looked at him, still unsure what to make of him, and finally said, 'there were three or four incidences that the elevator was occupied by one of us, and the FDS had to wait for it. And the spot in the garage where he usually has his driver park the car was occupied by someone. The FDS was furious, and the official order came a few days later.'

'Thank you so much,' Bodo released the stop button, and the elevator moved the rest to the third floor. The elevator doors opened, and the first thing Bodo noticed was, that the woman had moved behind him. Then he looked out the door, and there stood the FDS. He was puffed up like he would explode any second and was about to start a tirade against Bodo. All Bodo did, was place his ID Card in his face and say, 'Before you talk yourself out of your position, comrade, take a deep breath and show me to your office. After the FDS had read and processed the information on Bodo's ID Card, he shrunk about five inches and said, 'I apologize, comrade Zipper, I had no idea that you would come to our town today and that it was you how stirred up all that commotion down there. Please follow me to my office.'

Bodo turned to the woman who guided him so far and asked, 'what is your name, comrade?' Again, somewhat scarred, she asked back, 'Me? My name?'

'Is there anybody else in the elevator? 'Bodo asked and smiled at her, hoping to take some of the tension from her, which worked.

'Oh, my name is Elsa Mitterer, comrade …?' 'Zipper, comrade Zipper.' Bodo responded. 'I just want to be sure that there is no aftermath for you, helping me here to get my job done. You may go back to your work, comrade Mitterer.'

Turning towards the more and more stunned FDS, Bodo said, ' let's get to your office, comrade. My time is really limited.'

At the office of the FDS, which was as plentiful as Bodo thought it would be after what he had experienced so far, he explained that he wasn't actually there to meet with him. But since he was obviously free to receive him at the elevator, they may also use the opportunity to know each other. The First District Secretary excused himself again for the mistake and expressed his appreciation for the changes which have taken place within the party leadership in such a short time.

Bodo listened to his jabbering, and after a while, he interrupted and said, 'comrade, I am not really here to make an introduction visit that might happen later. I am here to see your DS-ICC.

'Yes, yes, I heard that. I told the DS-ICC, to wait until I talked with you, and he is waiting for me to call him in.'

'Comrade First Secretary, you may be informed about the changes that took place over the past several weeks with the party's leadership and the organizational structure change, but it appears that you have not entirely processed what that means. I am going to the office of the DS-ICC, and you stay here and finish your important work for the benefit of the people in your district.'

Bodo stood, walked out the door, and left the FDS and the secretaries in his reception area dumbfounded behind. He walked down the hallway toward the elevator, where he had seen the sign on the door for the DS-ICC, and knocked on the door. Hearing the come in, he opened the door and entered the office.

Bodo sat down on one of the visitor chairs in front of the desk and looking around he was impressed that the DS-ICC at least at this facility had a decent office. Not really representative, but he could have visitors and discuss issues. The DS-ICC was obviously astounded that he did not get called to the office of the FDS but seemed to be eased that he wasn't.

'Comrade, I am only here to get the files with the most crucial potential corruption cases in your district. I did not want to get in touch with your FDS, especially since I am not sure if any of the old-guard survivors are not involved in one or other of the corruption scandals that have been covered up and brought the people to revolt against the leadership of the party.'

'Comrade Zipper, I am absolutely speechless. I was informed that somebody would come to my office to collect the most critical cases, but I had no idea it would be you personally. And I have to apologize for the FDS.'

'No, comrade, don't apologize for a comrade, acting as if he was an Emperor. I felt he would have thrown me in jail if it wasn't for my credentials and position.' Is that what I experience here, the everyday situation? I need your honest answer, and I promise you that it will not be used against you.'

'Comrade Zipper, in that box,' pointing to the corner where a box stood, 'are the twelve most critical incidences of which I did get information from concerned citizens and comrades. Three of them involve the FDS, at least to some degree.'

Bodo looked at him and could not avoid being concerned about the safety of this comrade. He asked, 'does the FDS know why I am here and what I would collect today?'

'No, comrade Zipper, not to my knowledge. He wouldn't have even been aware that you were here if it had not been for the garage and elevator. And I am not criticizing you, comrade Zipper, for that. It was time that this issue became public a long time ago.'

'Ok, I am leaving now. I have a long trip in front of me. Here is my business card, don't hesitate to call if you believe it is necessary. And I mean it.'

'Goodbye, comrade Zipper, and good luck cleaning up the mess!'

'Nothing to do with luck, more with determination, comrade. We will be in touch.'

Bodo left the office and hit the button for the garage on the elevator. When the elevator arrived, he was not much astounded that several people walked out and walked down the hallway, smiling at him. It looks like you have made the first change in this admin here, Bodo said to himself while riding down to the garage, balancing the box on his shoulder. At the garage, Gunther was outside the car, talking with one of the police officers. When he saw Bodo coming out of the elevator, he shook hands with the police officer, walked back to the car, and opened the trunk.

'No, thanks, Gunther, I will take it into the car. Maybe you can place the other two boxes into the trunk?'

Yes, comrade Zipper. Are we ready to leave?'

'We can be on the road when you are ready, Gunther.'

'I am. Let's go.'

After all, that happened this day, Bodo was actually at a point where he wasn't very interested in opening another can of worms. But he had no chance. It needed to be done anyway, if not now, then later, and who knew what could be missed in the meantime. The enemies were warned, so much was sure. The arrest of the two powerful comrades out of their offices must have shaken the tree, and the rotten apples would fall no matter what.

'Gunther, what is your estimation to reach Rostock?'

'Approximately 2 hours, comrade Zipper.'

'Can you speed it up a bit? Let's take advantage of our special license plate because I need to return to Berlin tonight.'

'No problem, Comrade Zipper, I am on it.'

Bodo opened the box and took out the first folder. To no surprise, it was named Case FDS. It was clearly visible that the FDS Schwerin did not have enough to build a very attractive and modern building for the party's administration. He had no issues diverting masses of construction materials for a very nice villa on the outskirts of Schwerin and even used some of the money to buy the property. And not only that, the property was perhaps illegally confiscated and then for pfennig on the mark sold to him by the district court.

'Gunther, slow down. Stop when you can.' Bodo looked out and realized that they were almost out of the city. He took a page out of the file and held it up front for Gunther to see the address. Can you get us there without a vast sidestep?'

Gunther thought for a moment and said, 'about 10 minutes, comrade Zipper.'

'OK, drive there and stop so we can't be seen by the people living at that address if possible.'

Yes, comrade Zipper.'

Bodo let out a sigh and reluctantly took the handset and called general Pieker again

'Bodo, what is it I can do this time?'

'Jürgen, I was really thinking twice about calling you again, but there is no way to color the situation I just discovered here in Schwerin. I have evidence in my hand that not only the misappropriation of construction material but also the illegal acquisition of property has been committed by the FDS, and there are several indications that the LVO was inappropriately used to get foreign materials for private usage. After I had a somewhat strange collision with the FDS just about 35 minutes ago, it could be that he might try to destroy evidence. I am on the way to his stolen property, and I need you to send teams to his office and his home. The team coming to his home should contact me. I will be waiting for them, covered.'

'Bodo, nothing to apologize for. We all knew that there had to be a reason why the average citizen was so angry about our party and its leadership. You are doing what the ICC and our organization should have done for more than 25 years. But we had no teeth. The personal relationships of the old guard pulled those out.'

'Stay put. I'll send the order out immediately. And again, Bodo, you are doing the right job. I am satisfied that we at the CC had the guts to nominate and confirm you. Don't let the dirt you find among our leadership stop you. Clean it out with a steel broom!'

'Thanks a lot for your encouragement. I needed it. I am feeling like diving into a sewer pond. Talk to you later, but wait, did you hear anything from your office in Neubrandenburg? I had the officer in charge set up surveillance after I discovered my brother's car in Neubrandenburg on a workday.'

'No, Bodo, I did not get any information about that. Let me check what I can find out, and I will get back as soon as I have something. This is not unusual since these would be local affairs as long as it doesn't cross regional borders.

'Great, and thanks again.' Bodo placed the handset on the holder, and when he looked out the windshield, he saw that they were already entering the small sidestreet where the house of the FDS would be. The massive house was not to be overseen. It set back on the property about 150 yards. The hedgerow that should later shield the property wasn't grown enough to cover the view of a house that could easily belong to a successful entertainer or international medical specialist like the guy from whom Bodo now inherited his house. The party had no issues with having citizens rewarded with extraordinary possessions as rewards for bringing international acknowledgments for the Republik. And Bodo agreed with that approach to the success of an individuum for the benefit of the collective.

'Comrade Bodo, the SSP team is here.' Gunther woke Bodo out of his thoughts.

'Thanks, Gunther, stay tight,' Bodo left the car and met one of the officers in civil clothing halfway.

'Comrade Zipper?' the officer asked.

'Yes, that's me. You are ready to act?'

'We just got a message from the team sent to his office that he wasn't there. His secretary said he left the office a few minutes after you and said he didn't feel well and would go home.'

'Ok, looks like we are here then to act. Please go ahead. I will be right behind you. You have the arrest warrant?'

'Yes, comrade Zipper, I have it here and the copy for him too."

They walked up to the gate at the wrought-iron fence, which was not locked, and when they reached the door, Bodo was surprised that nobody came to receive them. They must have been seen walking to the house if somebody was home. He stopped one of the officers about to ring the bell and said, 'One of you stay here. The other one follows me.' They walked around the side of the house that led down towards a lake, and there was a large french door with a terrace. Staying close to the wall, they moved slowly toward that door until they had a clear view of the room. It was the home office of the FDS, and he was hectic loading paper into a carton box standing in front of him on the floor. Bodo had seen enough and, while the officer still hidden outside of the view from inside, Bodo knocked on the french glass door and, raising his voice, said, 'Secretary, you can stop it. It won't do you any good to destroy evidence.' While he was still speaking, the FDS turned his attention to Bodo, his face turned angry, and he yelled, 'You again, haven't you created enough turmoil/ I will show you who is in power!' and with these words, he picked up a handgun, which was out of view for Bodo behind a sculpture on the desk and fired two quick shots at Bodo through the closed french doors.

One shot hit Bodo in the left arm. The second went wide. Bodo had his Glock out before even the second shot left the gun of the FDS, and with a double tap to the chest and a third to the head, it was over. The FDS was dead before he hit the floor. The officer went to Bodo and asked him if he was OK, and Bodo said, no problem. Just a gazing shot. In the meantime, the other office was around the corner, and after he saw that they were both OK, he slowed down and walked over. They broke open the french door and checked the pulse of the FDS.

'It was utterly justified for comrade Zipper to use his gun after the FDS shot at him first.' Stated the officer who was with Bodo. 'I am amazed, comrade Bodo, how fast you were able to react.'

Just that moment, Gunther came running around the corner, his pistol at the low ready, and Bodo had to stop the officers from pulling their guns on him, 'that's my driver.'

'Good training at the SSP headquarters, officer. And it definitely paid off.' In the meantime, the other officer informed the office and initiated all the necessary steps for securing the crime scene and getting all the officials over.

'The officer with Bodo asked, 'comrade Zipper, are you able to wait for the protocols to be taken?'

'No, actually not. I need to go to Rostock and back to Berlin today. As far as I know, police work can take hours. Please secure all the papers; I declare herewith Top Secret and send it to my office. Here is my business card. Send the statement, and I will sign it and send it back to you and the police.

He called Gunther, and they walked out to the car. While Gunther turned around, the official colon of administration for such an event turned into the street, and Bodo was glad they were on their way out.

After about one and a half hours of fast driving, Gunther stopped the car at the front of the party office building in Rostock. 'No need to come with me, Gunther. I will only be in there for a few minutes.' Just as he had said it, Bodo realized that he had said the same sentence a couple of times that day, and it always turned out to be not the case.

Shaking his head, he walked into the building, where a friendly young secretary behind the reception desk asked him if she could help. He said, 'sure. I am here to pick up some material from the DS-ICC.'

'Oh, are you working with comrade Lenner?'

'Not really, but kind of; why are you asking?'

'Last time he was here, he said if I would like to change my environment, he may have a position for me in Berlin. And after what happened here in the morning, I am really ready to change.'

'What is your qualification?'

'I am a certified Secretary with an additional international degree from the University of Moscow.'

'That is just great. I will arrange your transfer to my new office in a few days. Here is my business card. What is your name?'

'Maria Hafler.'

'Great, Maria, just be a little more patient, and we will transfer you within the party to your new position. But now I need the box because I need to return to Berlin today.'

'Of course, comrade Zipper, I am so sorry to hold you up.' She grabbed the phone, dialed a number, and said, 'bring the box out to the reception now. Comrade Zipper is here.'

Oh, that was easy,' Bodo said., 'Many thanks, and you will hear from me soon.'

The DS-ICC arrived with the box of file folders as large and heavy as the others he had already, and Bodo thanked him. He did not want to spend more time concerning the drive he had before him. He apologized and walked out to the car. Gunther was outside waiting for him as if he was ready to run into the building if anything unusual should happen. Dropping the box into the trunk and sitting in the back passenger seat was all one action. It was already after 4:30 PM, and Bodo was deadbeat. The wound on his arm wasn't hurting much, but it was still a wound and costed energy.

'Gunther, get me home. Address is Karolinenhof.'

'Yes, comrade. On our way.'

Just when Bodo closed his eyes to sleep off the stress of the day, the phone startled him. 'Comrade Bodo.'

'Hello, Bodo, you sound deadbeat. But no wonder what you have accomplished just in one day. You need to slow down; otherwise, we must send you to recovery soon.'

'Comrade Bruno, very kind of you to call at the end of an active day. I did not plan on arresting one FCS and one FDS and killing another FDS on the same day. But thanks for the praise.'

'First, you really deserve it, Bodo, and secondly, skip the comrade. We both know we are comrades and on the same level of power. I had a lengthy call with Jürgen, and he said you got shot in Schwerin,' I was concerned that you did not go to the hospital. But the officers said it was just a gazing wound.'

'Yes, just a gazing shot. It hurts, but Gunther cleaned it well, and the bandage is holding. Not bleeding anymore, so I am fine. Did Jürgen say anything about the surveillance on my brother?'

'Actually, not. I can ask him if you want.'

'Not necessary, Bruno. I will be back tonight and tomorrow is early enough to see what came out of it.'

'Great Bodo. Stay safe, and have a safe trip home. See you soon.'

'See you soon, Bruno.'

Bodo placed the handset back on the holder, fell back into the seat, and said, 'Gunther, when the phone rings again, cap the line. Get me home. Just kidding, I will take a nap.'

WHAT IS IN PART II

See how Sarina enjoys moving into a luxurious home that she never thought she would ever see the inside of, not even talking about owning it soon

What did the surveillance team of the State Security Police discover? Were they able to follow Fritz Zipper to all of his meetings?

Could they find out what he was up to?

How many of the files Bodo collected had similar consequences as the three he just looked into driving crisscross the northern region of East Germany or, as the communists proudly named it, the German Democratic Republic?

Accompany the different comrades moving into their new job and how they are adapting to the new challenges.

Experience the research for additional officers for the new agency, which need to be accomplished officers in action, and some with the investigative skills of a bloodhound, able to stay on a trace to pull out the necessary evidence to nail the treasonous party members and others to the wall for shooting.

Experience how blind commitment to the cause of the victory of communism destroys the heart of human beings to the point that even their own blood doesn't count anymore

Learn how the AWOL soldiers of the Red Army decide not to cross the border for freedom but stay and support the Underground Resistance.

And see how the new leaders of the GDR can pull the stunt to receive billions of hard currency for a weapon control system that is unblockable, which was discovered by chance

And experience how the new leaders use deadly force to end the more annoying demonstrations after changing the chanting at their Monday Demos from "We Are The People" to "We Are One People."